THE PLAYS OF OSCAR WILDE

Alan Bird

BOOKS
10 East 53d St., New York 10022
(a division of Harper & Row Publishers. Inc.)

Barnes & Noble Books
Harper & Row, Publishers, Inc.
10 East 53rd Street
New York

ISBN 0–06–490415–6

To

Robert Liddell

First published in the U.S.A. 1977
© 1977 Alan Bird

Printed and bound in Great Britain
MCMLXXVII

Barnes & Noble Critical Studies

General Editor: Anne Smith

The Plays of Oscar Wilde

Emery Pratt

Contents

Acknowledgements

Thanks are due to the Estate of the late Hesketh Pearson for permission to quote from his works, and also to Mrs. Vyvyan Holland and Sir Rupert Hart-Davis to use extracts from *The Letters of Oscar Wilde*.

Introduction

It is often claimed that Oscar Wilde's life is more interesting than his work and that only one of his plays, *The Importance of Being Earnest*, is worthy of consideration. Both of these claims are incorrect. Intriguing as it is, Wilde's life is less important and less absorbing than his work of which his dramas are an integral and vital element. Indeed, his development as a dramatist is hardly known at all either by the reading or by the theatre-going public, although it well repays study because Wilde was a versatile dramatist whose lesser plays are valuable in their own right and because they demonstrate a remarkable progress in construction, ideas, style, and the way in which they embody his most serious views on society. An account of his theatrical achievement also sheds much light on the state of the commercial theatre in the last decades of the nineteenth century as well as providing an insight into his struggles with actors, actresses, managers, critics, and the public itself.

Oscar Wilde's life is sufficiently notorious and so amply documented as not to need retelling, least of all in this book which is concerned with his dramatic work. However, it is useful to trace in brief the course of his life prior to the writing of his first play *Vera* in 1880.

Oscar Fingal O'Flahertie Wills Wilde was born on 16 October 1854 at 21 Westland Row, Dublin. His father was a well-known eye specialist who was to be knighted for his services to medicine in 1884. Sir William seems to have had an insatiable sexual appetite so that in addition to his two sons born in wedlock he had a brood of illegitimate children of both sexes. This propensity was to cost him dear when he became involved in blackmail and scandal. He was outlived by his wife, née Jane Francesca Elgee,

7

INTRODUCTION

who died in 1896, some twenty years after him. For her part Lady Wilde was by all accounts a lady striking as much for her artistic and romantic temperament as for her general largeness of person: she wrote under the nom-de-plume of *Speranza* and gathered a literary salon of sorts around her in Dublin and, later, in London.

Lady Wilde had grounded her two sons in the classics and introduced them to English, French and Italian literature so that when Oscar went to board at the Portora Royal School, Enniskillen, he was far ahead of the other pupils in academic ability and literary culture. In 1871 he went to Trinity College, Dublin, and proved himself a brilliant scholar in the fashion of the time. He came under the influence of the Professor of Greek, the Rev. John Pentland Mahaffy, famed for his wit as well as the undoubted scholarship revealed in books which are still in use today. Three years later Wilde moved to Oxford where he entered Magdalen College which he left in 1878 after winning the Newdigate Prize for Poetry and gaining a first in Greats.

Oscar Wilde was now a great strapping fellow, over six feet in height, already a trifle over-weight, usually over-dressed, and handsome in a somewhat overblown way. Although he preferred not to air such topics in public, he was quite an able shot, fisherman and swimmer. He was remarkably healthy and reasonably lazy. Physical cowardice was never among his failings; when absolutely necessary he was able to defend himself by sheer strength. Above all he had a gift for so enriching the life around him by his wit, kindness and good spirits that he was frequently adored by the most simple of men as was to be shown during his lecture tour of America.

Early in his student life he had acquired an admiration of Disraeli whose witty and elaborate style, fustian romanticism and capacity for self-advertisement were to be reflected in his own writings and life-style. Moreover, Wilde, like Disraeli, was essentially a *parvenu*; neither was wholly accepted by the society of his day. Wilde's style was also set by his identification with Mahaffy who was as much at home in the more amusing Dublin drawing-rooms as in the lecture theatre. At Oxford two other men influenced his life—John Ruskin and Walter Pater, the one Slade Professor of Fine Art and the other Fellow of Brasenose College. From them he acquired a philosophy of aestheticism, of

8

self-cultivation and improvement, and also of the need to work for others. Apart from a few hours spent toiling on the construction of a country road near Oxford he paid little attention to this last aspect of his masters' teaching although he was by nature a generous man who would part, if pressed, with his last sovereign to someone less fortunate than himself. And, perhaps, the absolute importance which both Ruskin and Pater in their different ways attached to art really did not mean a great deal to Wilde who was fairly indifferent to painting and music and whose moral code was a valid but singularly personal one.

When, in 1878, Wilde descended on London he had little else to his credit, as he himself was to declare, than his genius, a commodity which, at that stage in his career, had little attraction for bank managers or money-lenders. Cash he certainly lacked, at any rate in comparison with the income of some of his friends and the society which he intended to enter at the first possible opportunity. His Irish ancestry and the scandals surrounding his father's life were the foremost but not the least of his handicaps. Meanwhile he shared rooms in the Strand with a fellow Oxonian, Frank Miles, who earned money by drawing portraits of the beauties of the day. He found Wilde a sympathetic companion always ready to present a bouquet, verbal or floral according to the occasion, to Lily Langtry, Helen Modjeska, Sarah Bernhardt or Ellen Terry or other of those semi-professional beauties who were profitable subjects for his pencil. In turn, Wilde earned himself a degree of useful notoriety and a foothold in a certain kind of London society.

Wilde sought avidly for fame and fortune, neither of them likely to be achieved through solid and regular employment. He could achieve his aims by a successful marriage or by writing although this last seemed near to drudgery. Almost inevitably he turned his attention to dramatic work—writing for the stage. The theatre was immensely popular throughout the whole of the nineteenth century and offered rich rewards to popular dramatists: but Wilde knew comparatively little about theatrical conditions let alone dramatic techniques. Nothing daunted he sat down to write a serious drama—and thus, as we shall see, began his career as a dramatist.

1

Vera, or the Nihilists

In the autumn of 1880, when he was twenty-five, Wilde published
his play *Vera, or the Nihilists* at his expense. *Vera* was, in effect,
his first published work. Only three copies of this edition are
known. The play was sent to the leading actresses of the day, including Ellen Terry, without any of them showing practical interest.
Eventually the English actress, Mrs. Bernard Beere agreed to play
the leading rôle and to present the play at the Adelphi Theatre on
17 December 1881, but three weeks beforehand the production
was cancelled 'considering the present state of political feeling in
England'.[1] Tsar Alexander II had been assassinated on 13 March
1881 and Wilde, shrewd and tactless at the same time, probably
saw this event as a kind of publicity which would greatly increase
Vera's chances of success. What he had forgotten was that the new
Tsarina was the sister of the popular Princess of Wales, Alexandra
of Denmark, and that both she and the Prince of Wales with whom
he was anxious to be on good terms might have taken justifiable
offence. It was sensible for the play to be withdrawn, particularly
as Wilde was said to have been dissatisfied with the cast.

On 24 December 1881 Wilde sailed for America on a lecture
tour. He took with him copies of *Vera* which Richard D'Oyly Carte,
an astute lecture agent and producer who not only presented the
comic operas of Gilbert and Sullivan but also outstanding personalities, had agreed to have printed in America in a revised edition.
A prologue was to be added and Wilde would thus secure the
American copyright against piracy. Richard D'Oyly Carte was not
exactly esteemed for his generosity so that this action needs an
explanation. In April 1881 *Patience* had been given by D'Oyly
Carte at the Opéra Comique in London and moved in the October

11

of that year to the newly built Savoy Theatre. *Patience* poked fun at the English aesthetic movement which included the so-called Fleshly Poets and the later Pre-Raphaelites of whom Rossetti was considered to be the leader. He was satirised as Bunthorne but the operatic character in no way resembled him and was generally taken to be a caricature of Wilde who, to be truthful, seems to have welcomed the publicity, falsely based though it was. When D'Oyly Carte thought of producing *Patience* in America in September 1881 either he or his agent there, Col. W. F. Morse, decided that ticket sales would be improved by the appearance of Wilde, a real live and genuine aesthete, who would appear in fancy dress (velvet knickerbockers, lace cravat, long hair, buckled shoes and all) lisp a few affected phrases and behave in so 'aesthetic' a way that the public would know what *Patience* was about. Wilde agreed to the tour largely because he needed money, because it satisfied his outsize ego, because he was curious to see a new country and because he had persuaded D'Oyly Carte to have *Vera* printed there. It can be argued that Wilde disgraced a whole generation of 'aesthetic' poets and writers by his behaviour on this tour as well as creating a widespread hostility which was to play an effective part in bringing about his own downfall and setting back the cause of the arts in Britain for a long time after his death but it cannot be denied that from the moment he stepped ashore in New York on 2 January 1882 he captivated and delighted the American public, earning the friendship of Walt Whitman, Oliver Wendell Holmes, Henry Wadsworth Longfellow, and Louisa M. Alcott, the amiable and justly famous authoress of *Little Women* and *Jo's Boys*. He not only turned the tables on the organisers of his lecture tour by becoming a great success, but showed considerable courage and an engaging ability as a lecturer on artistic and literary topics.

Throughout the tour Wilde kept up a correspondence with D'Oyly Carte on the subject of his play. As early as September 1880, when the play was first printed, he had written to the American actress and producer Clara Morris offering her the opportunity to perform it and stating that it was a drama of private passions, not of political sympathies. In an attempt to flatter American republican sympathies he wrote:

On account of its avowedly republican sentiments I have not been able to get permission to have it brought out here, but with you there is more freedom, and though democracy is the note through which the play is expressed, yet the tragedy is an entirely human one.[2]

Although it might be argued that there was a degree of insincerity in this letter it should be remembered that Wilde was an Irishman, proud of belonging to what he called the 'Hibernian school', and that he shared in part the republican, nationalist sentiments of his countrymen; his mother, whom he adored, was well-known for her fervent Irish patriotism.[3] Wilde also shared the common belief of his time and his countrymen that the floors of the American theatres, if not the streets, were paved with gold only waiting to be picked up by an astute foreigner. He hoped to receive a guarantee of two hundred pounds which would be deducted from his share of the subsequent profits (if any) and pressed the claims of Clara Morris to the name part. If she was not available—and, apparently, she was *difficult*—then Rose Coghlan would be suitable.[4] In March 1882 he wrote on the subject of the play itself:

> Dear Mr. Carte, I send you the prologue: if it is too long cut it. I have introduced Prince Paul Maraloffski in it as a simple Colonel: this will give a dramatic point to his meeting Vera among the Nihilists in the third act, where I will introduce a little speech about it. I will also give Vera a few sentences about her brother being sent to Siberia to show the connection of the prologue. This will be a matter of a few minutes only, when I get to New York.
>
> The first act, which at present stands "Tombs of the Kings at Moscow," has too operatic a title: it is to be called "99 Rue Tchernavaza, Moscow," and the conspirators are to be *modern*, and the room a bare garret, painted crimson. It is to be realistic not operatic conspiracy.   (*Letters*, 104)

A little later in the month he says that the 'only reason, to speak honestly, that the play is as good an acting play as it is, is that I took every actor's suggestion I could get', and again urges D'Oyly Carte to engage Clara Morris. Kyrle Bellew or Johnston Forbes-Robertson would do for the Czarevitch while Flockton would make an able Prince Paul.[5]

After the play had been printed in America and copyright

13

secured, Wilde sent copies to people who he thought would be interested, such as William Henderson, manager of the Standard Theatre, New York, and to the celebrated American actress Mary Anderson who wrote: 'Vera charms me; it is very mournful. I think I would like to play the part' (Letters, 130). But Wilde was obliged to sail for England without having secured firm promises from anyone either to act in or produce his play; and once Wilde had completed his lecture obligations and secured the requisite publicity for Patience it was inevitable that D'Oyly Carte would promptly and finally lose the little interest he may have had in the presentation of Vera.

Wilde continued to persevere and in March–April 1883 we find him writing to the American actress Marie Prescott who had read Vera and agreed to play the title-rôle. He told her not to be afraid of laughter in a tragedy because it does not so much destroy terror as relieve (an aspect of theatre which he may have learned from the famous essay by De Quincey on the porter's monologue in Macbeth) and in any case he was unwilling to cut any of the comic lines—and it must be admitted that there are precious few of them in this play. This wish to keep the comedy at all costs seems to show that he already had an instinctive appreciation of his true gifts as a dramatist. In July he wrote to Miss Prescott again, laying on flattery not with the proverbial trowel but with a large shovel: he had recognised in her, he said, a great artist, for not only was there 'strength, music and melody' in her voice, 'and in every pose and gesture' but as she walked the stage she showed 'the infinite grace of perfect expressiveness . . .' and lots more besides. He congratulated her on the company she had assembled and expressed himself as much pleased at the way his directions as regards scenery and costume had been carried out. The yellow satin council-chamber was sure to be an artistic success and as Miss Prescott had been unable in New York to match the pattern of vermilion silk which he had sent her he hoped to be allowed to bring over a piece large enough for her dress in the last act. About the drama itself Wilde wrote:

> As regards the play itself, I have tried in it to express within the limits of art that Titan cry of the peoples for liberty, which in the Europe of our day is threatening thrones, and making

governments unstable from Spain to Russia, and from north to southern seas. But it is a play not of politics but of passion. It deals with no theories of government, but with men and women simply; and modern Nihilistic Russia, with all the terror of its tyranny and the marvel of its martyrdoms, is merely the fiery and fervent background in front of which the persons of my dream live and love. With this feeling was the play written, and with this aim should the play be acted.

(Letters, 148–149)

Wilde said he looked forward with much interest to a second visit to America. He set sail from Liverpool on 2 August 1883 and reached New York on 11 August.

Vera opened at the Union Square Theatre on 20 August but ran for only a week. The course of the first night was interesting. At the end of the first act the play was given an ovation by the New York theatre audience whose enthusiasm died a rapid death when the heroine appeared in a flaming red dress, symbolic of her revolutionary sentiments. Hoping, perhaps, to recoup her losses Marie Prescott had the brilliant idea of taking the play on tour throughout America provided Wilde would play the part of Prince Paul. The young author's notoriety and histrionic gifts (at any rate, as evidenced off the stage) would undoubtedly have ensured a profitable run. How that might have changed the whole course of Wilde's life and career can only be a matter of conjecture, since Wilde refused the proposal.

Vera begins with a prologue set in a Russian inn. With a keen eye to local colour Wilde specifies: 'Large door opening on snowy landscape at back of stage'. Peter Sabouroff, the innkeeper, is warming his hands at a stove, not an unnatural activity in a man confronted with large open door and a snowy landscape in close proximity. He is talking to a young peasant called Michael Stroganoff, gamekeeper to Prince Maraloffski. It transpires that Peter's son Dmitri has gone to Moscow to study law and has not written home for four months. His daughter Vera then enters and in reply to a question from Michael who has previously declared his love to her says '. . . there is so much else to do in the world but love.' A metallic clinking is heard and Colonel Kotemkin enters with eight prisoners—Nihilists on their way to exile in Siberia. Vera challenges the Colonel in argument and then, after he has gone

15

THE PLAYS OF OSCAR WILDE

to eat, talks with one of the prisoners who turns out to be her brother Dmitri who has been arrested and condemned for his revolutionary activities in Moscow. He is about to tell her where exactly the revolutionaries hold their meetings there when the conversation is terminated by the return of the Colonel from an exceedingly speedy meal. As the party moves off Peter recognises his son and flings down the money which the Colonel has given him as payment for the meal. Dmitri manages to leave a note which Vera picks up and reads. It gives the meeting place of the revolutionaries as 99 Rue Tchernavaya, Moscow. Vera cries aloud:

> To strangle whatever nature is in me; neither to love nor to be loved; neither to pity nor to be pitied; neither to marry nor to be given in marriage, till the end is come.

On this note the prologue ends. Wilde could certainly claim to have mastered the art of a curtain line early in his career.

Act I is set at 99 Rue Tchernavaya, Moscow. The date is five years later. A group of masked conspirators awaits the arrival of another conspirator whom we may guess is none other than Vera herself. One of the leading conspirators is Michael, the former peasant gamekeeper who we have already met in the Prologue and who has followed Vera to Moscow. Questions are asked as to the character of the Czarevich who has been imprisoned in the palace by his father and who is said to have liberal tendencies. One of the conspirators, Alexis, a young medical student, appears to have a detailed knowledge of the geography of the imperial palace. Vera then enters. Throwing off her cloak she reveals she is wearing full ball dress, for she has ventured in to a ball at the palace and learnt there that the Czar has decided to proclaim martial law all over Russia, thus somewhat unfairly putting an end to their nihilist pranks. She exclaims:

> O God, how easy it is for a king to kill his people by the thousands, but we cannot rid ourselves of one crowned man in Europe!

While the others conveniently retire into a corner, Alexis and Vera have a conversation in which romantic, patriotic and nihilistic sentiments tread on each other's toes. Vera is leaving for

Novgorod to stir up the faint-hearted brotherhood there. Alexis is astonished at the news of the proclamation of martial law, blames it on the devilish Prince Paul Maraloffski and swears that he will plead with the Czar next day—a strange promise on the part of a medical student! Despite her oath not to fall in love, Vera finds herself attracted to Alexis with his 'bright young face, his heart aflame for liberty, his pure white soul'. But now the jealous Michael steps forward to say that he has trailed Alexis and seen him enter the palace by a private door after giving the guards a secret password: he then denounces Alexis as a spy. The other conspirators rush forward to kill him but Vera throws herself in front of the unhappy young man and says she will leave the group if so much as a finger is placed on him. At that moment there is heard the tramping of soldiers outside and a knocking at the door. The conspirators mask themselves. General Kotemkin enters with his guards. Vera explains that she and her friends are a group of strolling players travelling from Samara to Moscow where they hope to be able to amuse his Imperial Majesty the Czar. The General is neither amused nor convinced by this ingenious tale but Alexis saves the day by unmasking and revealing himself as the Czarevich. He says (as Hamlet might have done, and perhaps Wilde had him in mind) he has been spending a few hours with these players. The General announces that he is hunting for the dangerous woman Vera Sabouroff whom he saw years ago as a common waiting-girl in an inn and also at Odessa where she shot his horse from under him as he was gaining on her in a pursuit. After passing a few lecherous comments on the veiled Vera, the General departs with his soldiers. Wilde has engineered yet another startling curtain-drop:

> Exeunt General *and the soldiers.*
> Vera (*throwing off her mask*): Saved! and by you!
> Alexis (*clasping her hand*): Brothers, you trust me now?
> Exit.

It was at this point, presumably, that the New York audience gave the play an ovation: they little thought of the three further acts which lay before them and which were to prove too much for their attention and even their republican sympathies. Act II is set in the (yellow satin) Council Chamber of the Emperor's palace

17

at dusk. Present are Prince Paul Maraloffski, Prince Petrovich, Count Rouvaloff, Baron Raff and Count Petouchof. The Czarevich enters, understandably a trifle pale since he has been woken early to see some wretched nihilists hung. Prince Paul reveals himself a master of the *bon mot* if not of diplomatic intrigue. When the Czar enters he is observed to be mentally deranged and morbidly suspicious of everyone around him. The Czarevich Alexis is not himself above a rhetorical phrase and when his father is about to sign the declaration of martial law he intervenes, shouting:

> Stay! I tell you, stay! The priests have taken heaven from the people and you would take away the earth too!

He declares his nihilist sympathies and prophesies that,

> ... from the sick and labouring womb of this unhappy land some revolution, like a bloody child, may rise up and slay you ... The star of freedom is risen already, and far off I hear the mighty wave Democracy break on these cursed shores ... The people suffer long, but vengeance comes at last, vengeance with red hands and silent feet!

These are perfectly respectable sentiments for a young man passing through the customary revolutionary pains of youth but the Czar will have none of them and calls for guards to lead away his son and shoot him in the square below. The better to behold this improving spectacle he throws open the window and goes out on to the balcony. There follows a sensational development:

> *Voice (outside in the street)*: God save the people! (Czar is shot and staggers back into the room.)
> *Czarevich (breaking from the guards, and rushing over)*: Father!
> *Czar*: Murderer! Murderer! You did it! Murderer! (*Dies.*)

Act III sees an even more astonishing event. We are back again in the cellar of 99 Tchernavaya where we find a new recruit to the nihilists—Prince Paul, who has been dismissed from office by the new Czar Alexis. As he assures his fellow conspirators, had he not had the *entrée* to the very best society and the very worst conspiracies he could never have become Prime Minister of Russia. Despite his declaration that nowadays every baby seems born with a social manifesto in its mouth and that he is willing to sacrifice his own rights in respect of the nihilist manifesto that 'Nature is not a temple, but a workshop' in which they demand the right to labour, he is quickly enlisted as a member. Vera, being a girl of some commonsense, is disturbed by this turn of events. Michael enters and is acclaimed for his assassination of the previous Czar. He is now determined to assassinate the new Czar, in which aim he is seconded by Prince Paul who ventures the statement that, 'Good kings are the only dangerous enemies that modern democracy has . . .!'. Lots are drawn for the person who is to kill the young Czar. The election, as might have been expected in a drama of this kind where coincidence plays a remarkably potent rôle, falls on Vera. Prince Paul comments on all this in an aside:

> This is the ninth conspiracy I have been in in Russia. They always end in a *voyage en Siberie* for my friends and a new decoration for myself!

Vera dedicates herself to liberty—and assassination. On that stirring note the curtain descends.

Act IV is set in an antechamber of the Czar's private room. Various ministers are discussing among themselves the folly of the young Czar's liberalism. Unknown to them he enters and hears their conversation. He promptly dismisses them from office because of their illiberal sentiments and their bad jokes. Alone he apostrophises the crown as a gaudy bauble and in other terms not unknown to Shakespeare and his successors in the field of historical drama in blank verse. Thinking of Vera he lies down beside a convenient charcoal brazier and falls asleep. Vera enters draped in a black cloak. She is about to stab him with a dagger when he starts up from his sleep and seizes her hands. There follows a rapid and rapturous exchange of vows of liberty and love. Meanwhile outside the room can be heard the loud murmurs of the conspirators who have also made their way into the palace and are calling for the Czar's blood. Vera stabs herself with the dagger which by yet another coincidence turns out also to be poisoned. The Czar is determined that they shall die together and snatches the dagger from her hands to stab himself. In turn Vera grabs it from him and throws it out of the window into the wings of the stage. The conspirators shout, 'Long live the people!' Bewildered by all these events the Czar asks, a trifle naïvely, not to say unnecessarily,

'What have you done?' To which Vera replies: 'I have saved Russia!' (*Dies*.)

Tableau
Curtain

The inspiration of Wilde's version of *A Life for the Tsar* is unknown, although the subject was not without topicality. It must be remembered that Wilde had published *Vera* in 1880 and that it had certainly been written earlier. He had thus prophetically foreseen the assassination of the Tsar Alexander II by nihilists, among them Vera Figner, in March 1881. Vera Figner eluded arrest for two years, survived twenty-two years of imprisonment in Schlusselburg Fortress, witnessed three Russian revolutions and even part of the Second World War, and, universally recognised as the Grand Old Lady of Russian nihilism, wrote and published her best-selling memoirs. A few years earlier than 1880, on 24 January 1878, yet another Vera, this time Vera Zasulich, shot and wounded General Trepov, City Prefect of St. Petersburg. Amazingly enough, Vera Zasulich was acquitted at her trial and went on to launch a campaign directed at the assassination of the Tsar himself. Thus there was no lack of actual working Veras to justify Wilde's choice of name for her heroine. (For an interesting account of the Nihilists see Ronald Hingley, *Nihilists*, 1967.)

It will be remembered that Wilde gives the meeting place of the nihilist conspirators as 99 Rue Tchernavaya, Moscow. This suggests that he may have had a French source for his material but it is probable that he had been inspired by what he had read about one of the most influential novels of nineteenth-century Russia, *What is to be Done?* by Nicholas Tchernyshevsky. It has been described as the worst novel ever written and although one might have thought it would not have been necessary to look outside the British Isles to find candidates for that title, there seems considerable justification for the claim. But to young Russians of the 1860s when it first appeared it was a sacred text which did more to mould the Nihilists' beliefs and influence their actions than any other piece of writing. What is of special interest is that Tchernyshevsky created a heroine called Vera who is helped to escape from the middle-class society of St. Petersburg by a young medical student who introduces her to revolutionary ideas. It would be useful if one could show that the seeds of Wilde's drama lay in a reading by him of this novel but there is no evidence in his letters that he had ever actually read it. It was certainly not available in English translation until much later in the century although—not improbably—he may have read it in French. It is known that Wilde met Prince Peter Kropotkin (1842–1921), Russian author, geographer and anarchist, at the home of William Morris and retained such a tremendous admiration for him that he wrote in *De Profundis* that Kropotkin's life was one of the two most perfect lives he had come across in his experience. He might very well have learned of Tchernyshevsky and the Nihilists from this eminent Russian as well as from the many newspaper accounts of the more sensational nihilist activities which were printed in the *London Illustrated News* and elsewhere.

Sarah Bernhardt, the celebrated French actress,[6] was, as it is well known, adored by Wilde who contrived to meet her on her first visit to London and strew lilies in her path, an antic he was to repeat a number of times both with Sarah and Lily Langtry.[7] These two ladies and Queen Victoria were the only women, he claimed, he could have happily married at any time. It is ironic that at the very time when his *Vera* was proving such a flop in America the French actress was triumphing in a play by Sardou with a similar theme of revolutionary intrigues in Russia. In 1882 Bernhardt had agreed to open her season with Sardou's *Fédora* which she intended to take to America for fifty performances and to use on her forthcoming European tour. So successful was the play that she continued to play it in order to pay off debts; when she appeared in London in July 1883, she was obliged to present it nine times within the week. In 1898, slightly adapted and set to music by Umberto Giordano, *Fédora* was to take on another lease of theatrical life. In the case of this opera, it is the woman Fédora who in trying to secure revenge for the murder of her fiancé, Count Vladimir Andrevich, accuses the man with whom she later falls in love, Count Louis Ipanov, of being a Nihilist and implicated in a plot against the Tsar's life. When she finds that she is totally mistaken and is sending her innocent lover to his death, she swallows the poison she has always had about her concealed in a Byzantine crucifix. This is a ruthless simplification of the main line of the plot but it is by no means certain that Wilde's

21

Vera would not have made a better libretto. Sardou's play is rather more skilfully constructed but yet even sillier in plot. The questions of interest are whether Wilde knew of Sardou's play and how popular were stories and dramas involving the Nihilists. It would be equally intriguing to know whether Wilde was aware of that 'darlin' book' *Elizabeth or the Exiles of Siberia*, (from the French of Madame Cottin, 1880) so beloved of Joxer Daley in O'Casey's *Juno and the Paycock* and by countless young people in Ireland and elsewhere, since it is also concerned with revolutionary struggles against the tyrannical Tsars.

It is interesting to speculate on the reasons for the play's failure, for, after all, many worse plays have succeeded or, at the least, enjoyed longer runs. That *Vera* is the work of an unpractised hand is obvious but it does contain some highly effective moments. It has been said that the serious passages are stilted and lifeless and that the serious characters speak like no one on earth but exactly the same things might be said of the serious parts in the comedies with which he made his name a few years later. It is a mistake to write off this play, for it shows us the serious Wilde, author of 'The Soul of Man', and the humanitarian Wilde whose letters to the press on the cruel evils of the imprisonment of young children were successful in partly alleviating this vicious practice. It shows us, also, Wilde as a critic of the social system, an aspect which is less evident in his later work: in *Vera* he is clearly trying to set himself up as a dramatist of ideas, an intellectual playwright of the modern theatre. But his audiences did not want intellectual drama —some years later Shaw's *Widowers' Houses* was practically hooted off the stage—least of all drama concerned with revolutionary social themes. Nor did the actors and actresses of the period. And *Vera* isn't sufficiently an intellectual drama when compared, for instance, with the early plays of Shaw: the background of nihilism may be said to be intellectual in tendency but the actual conflicts within the play are the conventionally heroic ones of love versus duty. Wilde had insufficient experience or intensity of purpose to reconcile the background and the conflicts in a satisfactory dramatic mode, no matter how earnest his intentions. There was little sense in setting the play in Imperial Russia and showing the advent to the throne of a democratic Tsar when it was a historical fact that there was no member of the Imperial family on whom either revolutionaries or liberals could rest the slightest hope. Nor was there any strength in the character-drawing. The Czarevich Alexis is milk-and-water and totally unrealistic, and Michael's character is insufficiently worked out to be effective either as a jealous rival or as a revolutionary. Vera is, it must be admitted, an interesting study. Women of a revolutionary character were by no means a commonplace on the English stage of the period; and she seems to be the forerunner of Shaw's fiery intellectual heroines and even to anticipate his Saint Joan. What disrupts any unity of action which the play may possess, and totally destroys its seriousness is Wilde's creation of Prince Paul Maraloffski whose epigrams and witticisms are entirely, not to say devastatingly, out of place in *Vera*.

Prince Paul is certainly Wilde's mouthpiece. In fact, several of the epigrams coined for him were so good that they were employed in later plays. 'Experience—the name men give to their mistakes' was to reappear in *Lady Windermere's Fan*. If Wilde had read up on Nihilism he had also spent time on the study of the prince of wits and fantastics, Sidney Smith, several of whose witticisms he was to utilise in slightly altered form and whose personality he would exploit in future plays. Shaw, who could not but be acquainted with the text of *Vera*, seems to have taken good note of one of the Prince's remarks: 'Good kings are the only dangerous enemies that modern democracy has,' for this paradox was to form the basis of his *The Apple Cart* in which, moreover, he was careful to sugar his political pill by an admixture of sex rather more playful and brazen than anything Wilde dared to essay in the 1880s. Delightful as is Prince Paul and his cynical humour he is out of place in *Vera* and from the moment he enters and begins to throw out his epigrams the balance of the play is irretrievably lost: the Nihilist Michael, the Czarevich Alexis and Vera herself fade into insignificance. When Prince Paul is on the stage the play comes alive but the drama of a nihilistic conspiracy dies. Mary Prescott was absolutely right to suggest that a tour of the play with Wilde as Prince Paul would be a money-making success: we can be quite sure that if none of the actors on the stage knew what Prince Paul was going to say next they would at least have known that it would be something extremely funny which would have both them and the audience in fits of laughter. 'The modern Nihilistic Russia', wrote Wilde, 'with all the terror of its tyranny and the marvel of its martyrdoms, is merely the fiery and fervent background in front of which the persons of my dreams live and love'. He might more accurately have said that it was the background against which Prince Paul strutted armed against all disaster by the charm of his wit and the power of his cynicism.

Vera has received little critical attention. The New York press was generally scathing at the time of its performance there. The New York Daily Tribune referred to the unbearable heat in the theatre, a factor which did not tend to improve the play's chances of success and which must have prejudiced critics and public alike. The New York Times treated the play seriously; and also showed some respect for the author:

> . . . his chicanery has not quite destroyed our faith in him. In the midst of his foolish, green-sick business as a *poseur*, versifier, and apostle—he is certainly an apostle of things which others have made evident to us—he has shown a suggestive talent which no one cares to underrate. He has accomplished as little as possible, but we have been willing to believe that he could accomplish more.

It is interesting that the rest of the review whilst discussing the play and its ideas in a lively fashion sounds, at times, as if it were referring to one of Shaw's comedies or even a dramatic piece of the 1970s:

> These rapid fellows . . . do not act—they talk. They yell their theories of liberty. They argue and quarrel. What one asserts another is bound to repeat . . .
> (Unsigned review, New York Times, 21 August 1883, 4–5)

The New York Daily Tribune thought the play was a melodrama without the benefit of music but made several critical points which were later to be raised against Wilde's other plays, comic or serious. It discerned Wilde's ability as a dramatist whilst scoring points against his muddled conception of drama:

> A new play entitled Vera, written by Mr. Oscar Wilde, was presented last night at the Union Square Theatre . . . and was seen by an audience that completely filled the house . . . The piece

poorly rewarded the public curiosity, however, by a display of several queer scenes, picturesque at points, but mostly ugly, and by the exposition of a fanciful, foolish, highly peppered story of love, intrigue and politics, invested with the Russian accessories of fur and dark-lanterns, and overlaid with bantam gabble about freedom and the people . . .

Mr. Wilde's play of *Vera*, thus untimely launched, is clumsily constructed according to the accepted principles of modern melodrama. That is to say, its author has aimed to compose it of strong incidents, surprises and theatrical situations. Such a piece, if acted a hundred years ago, or less, would have been interspersed with songs and illustrated or emphasized with frequent bursts of instrumental music. To-day the melodious accompaniment is virtually discarded, but the same old literary fashion remains. The writer of melodrama is not constrained to square his ideas with probability, or to maintain a nice and exact observance of nature in his portraiture of the development and display of character under the stress of emotions and the pressure of circumstances. Without venturing into the realm of the ideal, he nevertheless steers as widely as he likes away from the realm of the actual.

He generally assumes, indeed, to deal with the facts of some specific phase of social life, but he does not scruple to wrest those facts to the theatrical purpose of his melodrama—making the conduct of individuals and the occurrence of events to take any course that may happen to be preferred by his fancy or enjoined by the necessities of the play. Hence it is that if we were to take our knowledge of countries and peoples and distant aspects of civilization from contemporary melodrama, we should depart away from the theatre with extraordinary ideas. But, indeed, the melodrama does not aim to teach. Its object is to surprise, dazzle, and excite. It begins and ends in sensation, and if this be attained it does not trouble itself about the means that were used to effect this result.

Mr. Wilde, as true as he can be to the traditions of the craft, which he seems carefully to have observed without having as yet conquered, has built his play upon a central idea which is incredible and preposterous, but which, nevertheless, is useful as the motive or spring of climacteric situations; and these situations he has devised freely and with occasional slight felicity. *Vera* is high-stepping, wordy, and long-winded; but it is, in substance, and after much condensation shall have formed it, a practical piece of a common-place order. . . .

(Unsigned review, *New York Daily Tribune*, 21 August 1883, 5)

What the reviews do not state directly is that the New York press seized the occasion to proclaim the blessings of freedom in the United States and the horrors of Nihilism in Russia or elsewhere. Wilde had sadly overestimated the republican and revolutionary sympathies of the American public which was more xenophobic and conservative than many a European monarchy. Brilliant red dresses worn by nihilist young ladies were no more appreciated than brilliant red flags waved by revolutionary young men. At home there was more understanding; his future wife Constance Lloyd wrote to her brother that she had read *Vera* through again and really thought it was very fine, adding,

> Oscar says he wrote it to show that an abstract idea such as liberty could have quite as much power and be made quite as fine as the passion of love (or something of the sort).

(Letters, 153)

Punch rubbed salt into the wound by commenting that the play was 'vera bad'.

It cannot be said that *Vera* has received kinder treatment in recent years: in fact, it has been almost totally ignored. Writing on the rise and fall of the well-made play (a trifle prematurely, one might have thought) John Russell Taylor says that in his aesthetic days Wilde 'dabbled in overblown verse drama with *Vera; or the Nihilists* . . .' (*The Rise and Fall of the Well-Made Play*, 1967, 89). Overblown *Vera* may be but it is definitely not written in verse. The prize for crass stupidity in this direction must go to Wilde's most notorious friend; and this extract may serve to show the invaluable aid Lord Alfred Douglas must have given him in the realms of literary criticism and appreciation.[8] When he came to write his study of Wilde in 1940 his memories of the plays were probably a trifle dim but it might have been expected that he would have spent a few hours going through them again to refresh his memory. Perhaps he had never even read them. This is what he has to say about *Vera*:

> It ought to encourage anyone who tries to write a play to read *Vera, or the Nihilists* and to remember that the man who wrote

this preposterous rubbish produced, a few years later, those four masterpieces: *Lady Windermere's Fan, A Woman of No Importance, The Ideal Husband* and *The Importance of Being Earnest.* The play *Vera* was produced in New York, where it was a complete failure, and it was announced as to be produced at the Adelphi Theatre in London, but it was mercifully withdrawn and was never presented . . .

Mr. Boris Brasol, whose book on Wilde I have already quoted, is a Russian and had an official post under the Imperial Russian Government from 1910 to 1916. He also served as a lieutenant in the Imperial Russian Guard. So he is particularly well qualified to deal with the absurdities of *Vera, or the Nihilists*, which is supposed to represent the period about 1880. He does so in a very amusing way. One example will suffice. Wilde makes the Czar scolding his officers say, 'I banish you for your bad jokes. *Bon voyage, Messieurs!* If you value your lives you will catch the first train to Paris.'

In 1800, of course, as Mr. Brasol points out, there were no trains to catch in Russia or anywhere else!

(Oscar Wilde, *A Summing-Up*, 1940, 86–87)

Mary Prescott paid Wilde one thousand dollars for *Vera*, a fairly large sum which he proceeded to spend in Paris on entertaining, meeting literary men and generally furthering his career. The sting of his play's failure must, nevertheless, have lasted a considerable time and temporarily frustrated his ambitions for a career as a dramatist using serious themes from contemporary political or social life. It may have been that he began to see his true vocation lay in comedy—as his portrait of Prince Paul seemed to indicate—but the importance of *Vera* as an attempt at drama of a serious, political and topical kind should, despite its ignominious failure on the New York stage, never be discounted in the history of Wilde's career as a dramatist. He had yet to find a way of reconciling the strengths of the commercial theatre at the end of the Victorian age, the limits of his audience's sympathies and his own highly ironic and almost irresponsible wit; to this end *Vera* afforded him a highly valuable and not altogether unprofitable lesson.

27

NOTES

1. Hesketh Pearson, *The Life of Oscar Wilde* (1946), 54 Hereafter referred to in text as *Pearson*.
2. *The Letters of Oscar Wilde*, ed. Rupert Hart-Davis (1962), 130. Hereafter referred to in text as *Letters*.
3. It says something for Wilde's innate Irish patriotism as well as his shrewdness in the choice of topics for lectures that in San Francisco, a city full of Irish immigrants, he spoke on 'The Irish Poets of '48'.
4. Rose Coghlan (1851–1932): English actress who worked mostly in America where she was for many years leading lady at Wallack's Theatre in New York. She produced *A Woman of No Importance* there in 1893.
5. Kyrle Bellew (1855–1911): English actor; Johnston Forbes-Robertson (1853–1937): English actor and manager; Charles P. Flockton (1828–1904): English actor who made his career in America.
6. Bernhardt, as notorious for her showmanship as she was famous for her acting, first visited London in 1879.
7. Emily Charlotte Le Breton (1852–1929): became a leading figure in London society, a close friend of the Prince of Wales, and, for a time, an actress-manager.
8. Lord Alfred Bruce Douglas (1870–1945) was the third son of the eighth Marquess of Queensberry.

2

The Duchess of Padua

In September 1882 Wilde began writing to Mary Anderson about a play which he wished to write for her using terms which might very well have frightened off an actress with any feeling for economy of language:

> I cannot write the scenario till I see you and talk to you. All good plays are a combination of the dreams of a poet and that practical knowledge of the actor which gives concentration to action, which intensifies situation, and for poetic effect, which is description, substitutes dramatic effect, which is Life. I have much to talk to you about, having thought much since I saw you of what you could do in art and for art. I want you to rank with the great actresses of the earth. I desire your triumph to be for all time and not for the day merely, and having in you a faith which is as flawless as it is fervent I doubt not for a moment that I can and will write for you a play which, created for you, and inspired by you, shall give you the glory of a Rachel, and may yield me the fame of a Hugo. The dream of the sculptor is cold and silent in the marble, the painter's vision immobile on the canvas. I want to see my work return again to life, my lines gain new splendour from your passion, new music from your lips . . .
>
> (*Letters*, 125)

Throughout September he kept writing to the actress, asking her for a decision as to whether or not he was to write a play which she would undertake to produce. He claimed that the American actor-manager Lawrence Barrett had made him a large offer. This does not sound at all like Barrett who was a remarkably shrewd business man; and on whom the names of Victor Hugo and the fame of the actress Rachel would have been wasted. Wilde did not think the figure of ten thousand dollars which

29

was the estimation of the cost of the settings was at all excessive as nothing but the best would do for the play and its leading actress, Mary Anderson herself; and because the properties, dresses, etc., would all be available for the London production. A short time afterwards, in early October, she seems to have capitulated to Wilde's importunities and to have agreed to employ Steele Mackaye as designer, to have thought of taking Booth's Theatre, and to have suggested that business negotiations should be conducted with her stepfather and manager Hamilton Griffin. Jubilant, Wilde proclaimed, 'Written by me, acted by you, and set by Steele Mackaye, this tragedy will take the world by storm' (*Letters*, 132). His terms for the play were simple: one thousand dollars down: four thousand dollars on the acceptance of the manuscript and a royalty of twenty-five dollars per performance in the big towns, and ten in the smaller ones.

By the end of the year it must have seemed to Wilde that a great success lay immediately before him. He was even prepared to modify his terms a little, as he wrote to Hamilton Griffin:

> Dear Sir, As I informed you by telegraph I accept your terms for writing a play for Miss Anderson. Will you have an agreement drawn up with the agreed-on terms: $1000 down: $4000 when it is finished: the play to be ready by March 31st and played a year from now.
>
> On the question of dresses and mounting we are agreed: in that respect I always found your views coinciding with mine.
>
> In surrendering the customary author's royalty I have been actuated by a wish not to allow a money matter to stand in the way of an artistic success.
>
> Will you give Miss Anderson my compliments and assure her from me that I count it a pleasure to write for one whose capabilities as an artist are so great. I am convinced that for both of us a great triumph is in waiting.
>
> (*Letters*, 132)

Hamilton Griffin, a sensible and experienced man of the theatre, was not so confident of the play's success that he would agree to pay the four thousand dollars that Wilde requested but expressed himself as willing to hand over one thousand dollars the moment he received a signed contract. This was effected with alacrity. Wilde left America on 27 December 1882, on the conclusion of his American lecture tour, spent a few weeks in London, and then went to Paris for three months, presumably writing the play for Mary Anderson. It appears to have been finished on 15 March 1883 when the play, entitled *The Duchess of Padua*, was sent off to America.

On 23 March Wilde sat down and wrote a lengthy and enthusiastic letter to the American actress in which he tried to explain what he had aimed at in his verse and what effects he thought the production could achieve in the theatre. Reference will be made later to this important letter. The reply was briefer and more pointed than he could ever have imagined: it came in the form of a telegram turning the play down. Robert Ross was present when Wilde opened it and read the disappointing news. He did not show the slightest sign of chagrin or annoyance but merely tore a tiny strip off the blue form, rolled it into a pellet, and put it into his mouth. He then passed the cable over to him and said, 'Robert, this is very tedious.' He never referred again to his disappointment. But with a feminine weakness for the last unwelcome word, Mary Anderson wrote, 'The play in its present form, I fear, would no more please the public of today than would *Venice Preserved* or *Lucretia Borgia*' (*Letters*, 142).

Wilde presumably tried to interest other theatre people in his play but there were no other developments for eight years. Then, in 1891, the play was finally given a stage production by Lawrence Barrett. He had taken over the script from Mary Anderson but had decided that since the original title was associated with failure it would be wiser to change it: *The Duchess of Padua* became *Guido Ferranti*. With unusual modesty of manner Wilde wrote to George Alexander on 2 February 1891:

> You will be interested to hear that the *Duchess of Padua* was produced in New York last Wednesday, under the title of *Guido Ferranti*, by Lawrence Barrett. The name of the author was kept a dead secret, and indeed not revealed till yesterday when at Barrett's request I acknowledged the authorship by cable. Barrett wires to me that it was a huge success, and that he is going to run it for his season. He seems to be in great delight over it.
> (*Letters*, 282)

Barrett's astuteness had clearly deserted him: his great delight ended when the play ended its run on 14 February after some-twenty-one performances. Nevertheless a run from 26 January to 14 February must have been a source of satisfaction to Wilde after the dismal failure of *Vera* nine years previously and Mary Anderson's rejection in 1883.

The plot is complicated. We find ourselves in the market square of Padua in the early sixteenth century: it is noon and the bells of the Cathedral of Santa Croce are summoning the citizens to prayer. There enter two young men, Guido Ferranti and his friend Ascanio Cristofano, both from Perugia. Guido has received a mysterious letter calling him to Padua where he will meet a man wearing a violet cloak with a silver falcon embroidered on the shoulder. From this man he will learn the secret of his birth. Ascanio, 'as hungry as a widow is for a husband, as tired as a young maid is of good advice, and as dry as a monk's sermon' is impatient to find a tavern where he might ease his hunger. He is sent on his way by an old man—dressed as detailed in the letter—who reveals himself as Count Moranzone, an embittered nobleman, who tells Guido that his father was once the Duke of Padua but was betrayed into the fatal hands of Malatesta, Lord of Rimini. This was brought about by the treachery of a man who has since been rewarded with high office and power. Who this man is Moranzone indicates by kneeling to him—the Duke of Padua, who has just approached them. Moranzone cunningly introduces Guido to the Duke who thinks that something about the young man is familiar to him and who also offers some advice (in the blank verse into which the play has moved with the advent of Moranzone):

> Be not honest: eccentricity
> Is not a thing should ever be encouraged,
> Although, in this dull stupid age of ours,
> The most eccentric thing a man can do
> Is to have brains, then the mob mocks at him;
> And for the mob, despise it as I do,
> I hold its bubble praise and windy favours
> In such account, that popularity
> Is the one insult I have never suffered.

If this speech sounds not a little like the utterance of a poetic Lady Bracknell or Prince Paul Maraloffski, Guido's speech of revenge (Moranzone has commanded him to work his way into the Duke's confidence and eventually to assassinate him with his father's dagger) is like that of a latter-day Hamlet:

> ... from this hour, till my dear father's murder
> In blood I have revenged, I do forswear
> The noble ties of honourable friendship,
> The noble joys of dear companionship,
> Affection's bonds, and loyal gratitude,
> Ay, more, from this same hour I do forswear
> All love of women, and the barren thing
> Which men call beauty ...

Which is the signal, ironically, for the organ to peal and for four pages in scarlet to come down the cathedral steps bearing a canopy under which there walks a richly clad and very beautiful woman. Her eyes meet those of Guido who cries in wonder, 'Oh! who is that?'—to which the answer comes, 'The Duchess of Padua'.

After this effective act crowded with incident, the second act is much less absorbing. Its purpose is to demonstrate the badness of the Duke, the goodness of his Duchess and the dilemma of Guido who is torn between love and duty. The scene is set in the Duke's palace. Outside two thousand people are clamouring for bread, more food and water, and less taxation. The Duke orders his soldiers to fire on them but the Duchess, Beatrice, countermands this order. She pleads the cause of the citizens:

> *Duchess*: They say the bread, the very bread they eat,
> Is made of sorry chaff.
> *First Citizen*: Ay! so it is,
> Nothing but chaff.
> *Duke*: And very good food too,
> I give it to my horses.
> *Duchess*: They say the water,
> Set in the public cisterns for their use,
> Has, through the breaking of the aqueducts,
> To stagnant pools and muddy puddles turned.
> *Duke*: They should drink wine; water is quite unwholesome.
> *Second Citizen*: Alack, Your Grace, the taxes which the customs
> Take at the city gate are grown so high
> We cannot buy wine.

Duke: Then you should bless the taxes
Which make you temperate.

This is casuistry *à la Marie Antoinette* rather than downright wickedness. When the Duke goes out Guido enters and confesses to the Duchess that he loves her. Just at this moment Moranzone is seen and a short time afterwards a servant enters with a package which the Duchess opens to reveal a dagger—Moranzone's signal that the time for revenge has come. Guido is forced to tell her that an unsurmountable barrier has come between them. He leaves her. After Moranzone has appeared again and told her there is no hope of Guido being able to return her love she resolves to kill herself:

Duchess: 'Tis true men hate thee, Death, and yet I think
Thou wilt be kinder to me than my lover,
And so despatch the messenger at once,
Hurry the lazy steeds of lingering day,
And let the night, thy sister, come instead,
And drape the world in mourning; let the owl
Who is thy minister, scream from his tower
And wake the toad with hooting, and the bat,
That is the slave of dim Persephone,
Wheel through the sombre air on wandering wing!
Tear up the shrieking mandrake from the earth
And bid them make us music and tell the mole
To dig deep down thy cold and narrow bed,
For I shall lie within thine arms tonight.

The night to which the Duchess refers in this speech (which owes as much to the aesthetic 'decadent' poetry of the end of the century as to Shakespeare and his contemporaries) forms the third act, an act even more crowded with incident. It is stormy. Guido enters the palace through a window, having climbed up by means of a rope ladder. At the foot of the staircase leading to the Duke's chamber he finds Moranzone who has apparently entered by some more orthodox and easier means. Guido has changed his mind about murdering the Duke but intends instead to lay the dagger together with a piece of paper on his breast as he sleeps—and, thus, when he awakes he will know who has spared his life. Moranzone is extremely annoyed at this turn of events. Almost at once, however, a groan is heard from the Duke's bedchamber. The Duchess comes down the stairs. She has changed her mind about

killing herself and after realising that the Duke is the unsurmountable barrier of which Guido has spoken has stabbed him to death.
Guido is horrified. He orders her away. No sooner has she gone
than he changes his mind and calls her back. It is too late. Beatrice
is heard crying to the guards, 'This way went he, the man who slew
my lord.' Still holding in his hand the blood-stained dagger with
which the Duchess killed her husband, Guido is taken for guilty
and arrested by the soldiers.

The fourth act is basically a confrontation between Guido and
the Duchess. The scene is the Court of Justice and the time the
following day. Guido is on trial for the murder of the Duke. Moranzone (who had left the palace early the previous evening and does
not, therefore, know of the Duchess's actions) suspects that his
protégé has been falsely accused. Time and time again the Duchess
insists that Guido has no right to speak in his own defence; and
time and time again she is over-ruled by the judges whose suspic-
ions seem to have been awakened by Moranzone. Eventually the
Lord Justice takes up a sand-glass and tells Guido he may speak
until the sand has run through. The resulting speech and subsequent turn of events might have been unexpected in real life but
not in this kind of pseudo-Elizabethan drama:

> Guido: I smote the treacherous villain to the heart
>   With this same dagger, which by chance I found
>   Within the chamber.
> Duchess: Oh!
> Guido: I killed the Duke.
>   Now, my Lord Justice, if I may crave a boon,
>   Suffer me not to see another sun
>   Light up the misery of this loathsome world.
> Lord Justice: Thy boon is granted, thou shalt die to-night.
>   Lead him away: Come, Madam.
>
> Guido is led off: as he goes the Duchess stretches out her arms
> and rushes down the stage.
>
> Duchess: Guido! Guido! (Faints)

After that splendidly dramatic ending, Wilde could hardly expect
to open his fifth act in a similarly exciting fashion: like many a
dramatist before him he restricts the action to a very limited area,

to the confines of a prison cell. Guido sleeps while his guards discuss his fate. The Duchess has been making vain attempts to secure a pardon for him. In any case it is unlikely that he will die on the block—he will be given the choice of drinking the goblet of poison which presently stands on the table. A masked woman is admitted. She shows her ring—the Duchess's ring—to the soldiers who leave the cell. Looking on the sleeping Guido she ruminates on her actions in the courtroom:

> *Duchess*: I have been guilty, therefore I must die . . .
>   . . . I did not know him.
> I thought he meant to sell me to the judge;
> That is not strange; we women never know
> Our lovers till they leave us.

The execution bell is heard tolling. The Duchess drinks the goblet of poison. Guido wakes. She tells him he must escape, wearing her mask and cloak, and using her signet ring to get past the guards:

> *Duchess*: You shall not die for me, you shall not, Guido,
> I am a guilty woman.
> *Guido*: Guilty?—let those
> Who know not what a thing temptation is,
> Let those who have not walked as we have done,
> In the red fire of passion, those whose lives
> Are dull and colourless, in a word let those,
> If any such there be, who have not loved,
> Cast stones against you. As for me—
> *Duchess*: Alas!
> *Guido*: You are my lady, and you are my love!
> O hair of gold, O crimson lips, O face
> Made for the luring and the love of man!
> Incarnate image of pure loveliness!
> Worshipping thee I do forget the past!
> Worshipping thee my soul comes close to thine,
> Worshipping thee I seem to be a god,
> And though they give my body to the block,
> Yet is my love eternal!

He goes to drink the poison but finds the goblet drained dry. The chanting of monks is heard. Beatrice is gripped by the pains of death. Guido clasps her to him: and the rest is silence:

[*Stage Direction*:] They kiss each other now for the first time in this Act, when suddenly the Duchess leaps up in the dreadful spasm of death, tears in agony at her dress, and finally, with face twisted and distorted with pain, falls back dead in a chair. Guido, seizing her dagger from her belt, kills himself; and, as he falls across her knees, clutches at the cloak which is on the back of the chair. There is a little pause. Then down the passage comes the tramp of soldiers; the door is opened, and the Lord Justice, the Headsman, and the Guard enter and see this figure shrouded in black, and Guido lying dead across her. The Lord Justice rushes forward and drags the cloak off the Duchess, whose face is now the marble image of peace, the sign of God's forgiveness.

This plot is not lacking in the irony, peripeteia, and anagnorisis called for by Aristotle as essential ingredients of poetic tragedy and which the Elizabethan dramatists used to excess. In fact, it cannot be said that the plot is any more unnatural than that of the average Jacobean tragedy which is surely the model Wilde had in mind rather than any particular play of Shakespeare. Nor does it contain anything quite as bewildering as Vera's sudden (and fatal) conversion to Tsardom, belated as it was, in his first drama. Its initial weakness is its length: five acts take a lot of sitting-through today and did so even for the late Victorians whose appetite for a long night's entertainment was quite voracious. The play needed two things for success—and both were lacking for the New York production. It needed the attention of a play doctor such as Scribe who would have concentrated the action, probably in fewer words, and who would have made Moranzone more of a protagonist. But, more urgently, it needed the services of a great and showy tragic actress such as Bernhardt or Duse who would have made it a vehicle for their genius, dying amidst clouds of tears. Neither Miss Prescott nor Miss Anderson was a match for Bernhardt whose influence seems to hover over Wilde's early plays.

As in the majority of blank verse dramas of a vaguely historical kind there are examples of unconscious humour although it has to be admitted that these are more apparent in the printed text than they might possibly have been in performance. One such instance occurs at the beginning of Act III when we find ourselves in a large corridor in the Ducal Palace:

*. . . the hall is lit by an iron cresset filled with burning tow:
thunder and lightning outside: the time is night.*

Enter Guido through the window.

Guido: The wind is rising: how my ladder shook!
I thought that every gust would break the cords!

Looks out at the city.

Christ! What a night . . .

Wilde could not hope to escape the influence of the Elizabethan
and Jacobean dramatists nor the memories of his own study and
reading (and it should be remembered that Wilde's study at university had been largely in the area of classical literature, language,
and philosophy, which makes his knowledge of English drama the
more remarkable) so it is inevitable that time and time again we
should be reminded of such diverse plays as *Julius Caesar, Hamlet,
Antony and Cleopatra* and *The Duchess of Malfi.* Since the early
dramatists kept commonplace books in which they jotted down
for use in their own plays such snippets of verse or poetic or unusual images as appealed to them in the work of other writers
Wilde can hardly be blamed for borrowing or adapting from earlier
writers. In Act II which is set in the Ducal Palace a number of
'meanly dressed Citizens' address their complaints to the Duke who
refuses to make reforms and promises them instead a sermon upon
the Beauty of Obedience. The citizens 'murmur':

> *First Citizen*: I'faith, that will not fill our stomachs!
> *Second Citizen*: A sermon is but a sorry sauce, when
>   You have nothing to eat with it.

Wilde finds the style all too easy and continues:

> *Citizens applaud and go out.*
> (*Going out*): Why, God save the Duchess again!
> *Duke* (*calling him back*): Come hither, fellow! What is your
>   name?
> *First Citizen*: Dominick, sir.
> *Duke*: A good name! Why were you called Dominick?
> *First Citizen* (*scratching his head*): Marry, because I was born on
>   Saint George's day.

> *Duke*: A good reason! here is a ducat for you!
> Will you not cry for me God save the Duke?
> *First Citizen (feebly)*: God save the Duke.
> *Duke*: Nay! louder, fellow, louder.
> *First Citizen (a little louder)*: God save the Duke!
> *Duke*: More lustily, fellow, put more heart in it!
> Here is another ducat for you.
> *First Citizen (enthusiastically)*: God save the Duke!
> *Duke (mockingly)*: Why, gentlemen, this simple fellow's love
> Touches me much. (*To the Citizen, harshly.*) Go!

The Duchess of Padua suffers from a major defect which was also observable in *Vera*: too many characters are too witty by far. In *Vera*, it is true, there are some unbearably stuffy characters but Prince Paul has enough epigrams to make the fortune of any other play. In *The Duchess of Padua* almost everyone (except, unfortunately, the Duchess and Guido) is amusing verbally. At the very beginning of the play we meet Ascanio, a youth from Perugia to whom Guido is deeply attached, who says:

> Now by my life, Guido, I will go no farther; for if I walk another step I will have no life to swear by.

From this rather pedestrian humour we move to the keen wit of the wicked Duke of Padua who is, linguistically speaking, a blood-brother of Prince Paul Maraloffski, although his style is hampered by the necessity of expressing himself in extremely blank verse:

> Why, every man among them has his price,
> Although, to do them justice, some of them
> Are quite expensive.
>   The Cardinal!
> Men follow my creed, and they gabble his.
> I do not think much of the Cardinal;
> Although he is a holy churchman, and
> I quite admit his dulness.

At times, Lady Bracknell herself appears to be peeping over his shoulder:

> . . . eccentricity
> Is not a thing should ever be encouraged,
> Although, in this dull stupid age of ours,
> The most eccentric thing a man can do
> Is to have brains . . .

Even the bitter Count Moranzone can coin an epigram:

> Oh, I have done the tricks!
> I know the partings and the chamberings;
> We are all animals at best, and love
> Is merely passion with a holy name.

It would be unfair to the play to suggest that it is without moments of lyrical beauty or a poetic charm which owe more to Wilde's contemporaries among the aesthetic poets than to the Elizabethans. Guido has an outburst in favour of love that foreshadows some of his speeches from the dock during his trial and passages in *De Profundis*:

> Love is the sacrament of life; it sets
> Virtue where virtue was not; cleanses men
> Of all the vile pollutions of this world;
> It is the fire which purges gold from dross,
> It is the fan which winnows wheat from chaff,
> It is the spring which in some wintry soil
> Makes innocence to blossom like a rose . . .

Wilde said of the poet and writer, William Watson, that he hadn't enough spirit to boil a tea-kettle: *The Duchess of Padua* shows that Wilde had more than enough. When he confided to a friend, 'Between them Hugo and Shakespeare have exhausted every subject. Originality is no longer possible, even in sins. So there are no real emotions left, only extraordinary adjectives,' he was less than just to himself. It is true that English drama has been blighted through the centuries by an odd but understandable equation; the dramas of the Elizabethans and Jacobeans, the miraculous outpourings of Shakespeare and his contemporaries, were written in verse—as was the drama of the ancient Greeks—and therefore any drama worthy of the name must be written in verse; and not rhyming but blank verse. Hence the endless list of wretched verse dramas from Wordsworth, Keats, Shelley, Tennyson, Browning, Swinburne, and T. S. Eliot, not to mention the hosts of lesser writers who have essayed such works. Wilde wished to be included in this lamentable tradition; and like poets who were greater than himself wasted time and energy on the production of verse dramas such as *The Duchess of Padua* which were doomed from the moment of their conception. This is not to deny that there are moments of charm and occasional beauty in his play, even of drama and pathos, but the work is best seen as a late flower in the aesthetic tradition rather than as a Shakespearian drama born out of its time. It has little relationship with Victor Hugo's rhetorical dramas, but more with those of Swinburne. Read as a chamber drama, the play does not fail to please; and it could still be effective on the stage as a brilliantly dressed and decorated pageant.

The failure of the play on the stage at the time of its first production can also be partly attributed to a lack of definition as to who exactly is the leading character—this may have been a reason for Mary Anderson's rejection of it. To call it *Guido Ferranti* is as exact as to call it *The Duchess of Padua*, as Lawrence Barrett realised, for both characters are of equal importance in the play. Henry Irving was also sensible to refuse it because the two older parts, those of the Duke and Moranzone, which offer scope for a display of acting technique and which would have suited his mordant style, are not on the stage long enough to make a lasting impact: the Duke is killed off in Act III (like Lady Macbeth his Duchess wonders at the amount of blood in him:

> I did not think he would have bled so much
> But I can wash my hands in water after . . .)

and Moranzone does not appear in the last prison scene. In the hands of a fiery actress and an ardent juvenile lead the play might very well have had a good run in the theatre: it needed an actress of the calibre of Mrs. Patrick Campbell who was yet to make her name. It has been said that Wilde had Sarah Bernhardt in mind for the Duchess if the play were produced in Europe and it is certain that with her tremendous impetuous energy and pale, wraith-like beauty she would have made a memorable impact, particularly if she could have persuaded Wilde to have written in sufficient text to prolong her death-agonies by another quarter of an hour.

The Duchess of Padua, like *Vera*, has been ignored by most writers on Wilde. He himself wrote a long letter on the play to Mary Anderson which represents a major commentary: it is dated 23 March 1883:

> My dear Miss Anderson, The play was duly forwarded some days ago: I hope it arrived safe: I have no hesitation in saying

that it is the master-piece of all my literary work, the *chef-d'oeuvre* of my youth.

As regards the characters, the Duke is a type of the Renaissance noble: I felt that to have made him merely a common and vulgar villain would have been "banal:" he is a cynic, and a philosopher: he has no heart, and his vileness comes from his intellect: it is a very strong acting part as you see, and must be given to an experienced actor. To write a comedy one requires comedy merely, but to write a tragedy, tragedy is not sufficient: the strain of emotion on the audience must be lightened: they will not weep if you have not made them laugh: so I proceeded in the following fashion.

At the beginning of the play I desired merely to place the audience in full possession of the facts, of the foundation of the play: comedy would have been disturbing, so with the exception of Ascanio's few prose speeches there is none: the action begins with the entrance of the Duke, whose comedy is bitter but comedy still, and the culmination of the act is the entrance of the Duchess: I have ended the act with the words

"The Duchess of Padua"

which strike the keynote of the play, and make a very novel and striking effect.

The comedy of Act II is the Duke's comedy, which is bitter, the citizens', which is grotesque, and the Duchess's comedy which is the comedy of Viola, and Rosalind; the comedy in which joy smiles through a mask of beauty.

Act III. Here there is no need of comedy: the act is short, quick, terrible: what we want is to impress the audience clearly with the two great speculations and problems of the play, the relations of Sin and Love: they must see that both Guido and the Duchess have rights on their side: Guido is cruel, and the Duchess has done wrong: but they represent great principles of Life and Love.

The Duchess's   *Sure it is the guilty*
Who being very wretched need love most:

Guido's   *There is no love where there is any sin:*

and the great speech of the Duchess that follows give to the audience exactly what one wants to produce: *intense emotions*

with a background of intellectual speculation. Which is right?
That is what they will ask.

The comedy of Act IV is elaborate, and necessary to relieve the
audience: you must not think it too long: believe me it is vitally
necessary to make our audience merry after the horror in the
corridor. I have selected, as you see, the style of comedy which
never fails to raise laughter: the unconscious comedy of stupidity,
missing the meaning of words, yet in all its solemn ignorance
stumbling now and then on a real bit of truth.

Act V. The comedy of the soldiers: this relieves the audience
from the strain of the trial: and is a bit of realism not I think
put before into a dungeon scene.

Well, there is my comedy: and I hope that you have laughed
over it as you read it: for myself, I am devoted to the *"second
citizen"* who seems to me an unconscious humorist of the highest
order; he should get a great deal of fun out of his part.

To proceed with the characters:

Moranzone. He is the incarnate image of vengeance: the bird of
evil omen: the black spectre of the past moving like Destiny
through the scene.

Guido. Impulsive, ready to take oaths, to forget the past, to
realise the moment only: full of noble ideas, but "Fortune's
fool."[1]

As for the *Cardinal*, he is the polished pompous churchman of
the time, and the *Lord Justice* the impassive image of justice,
the rock against which the passion of the Duchess breaks like
foam.

Lastly, *the Duchess.*

Her first effect is that of pure beauty merely: she passes across
the stage and says nothing: but it is not enough to make her
stir the artistic sensibility of the audience, so in Act II she appears
as the image of pity, and mercy: she comes with the poor about
her: she stirs the sympathy of the gallery and pit. I do not know
how it is in New York, but in London, where the misery is terrible
among the poor, and where the sympathy for them is growing
every day, such speeches as the one about the children dying in
the lanes, or the people sleeping under the arches of the bridges,
cannot fail to bring down the house: they will not expect to find
in an Italian tragedy modern life: but *the essence of art is to produce the modern idea under an antique form.*

She is insulted by the Duke, left alone on the stage, when love
comes into her life: she will not tell all at once, and like a girl

43

plays in delicate comedy for a time. Then comes the passionate love-scene, the face at the window, the desertion of her lover, and her resolve to die. The act is long, but then she passes through so many emotions, and the act is so full of incident, that I don't think it is too long. The second entrance of the Duke, and the second appearance of Moranzone, are I think quite necessary to interrupt her soliloquy, which else might be to the actress, as well as to the audience, somewhat wearing.

Now to the third act: I remember what you talked to me about it: I think I have produced exactly what you desire.

She has left the audience under the impression that she would kill herself: she commits a murder under a momentary impulse, and a mis-understanding of her lover's words. Now murder is murder, a dreadful thing: we must not explain it away: it must produce a thrill of horror when she says *"I have just killed him:"* it becomes the bloody background of the play, and we must not dim its scarlet: but this horror is changed to pity: the passionate cry of *"I did it all for you:"* the remorse shown in such lines as:

> "Will we not sit beneath our vines and laugh?
> No, no, we will not laugh, but when we weep
> Well, we will weep together: "

Guido's sternness, which is right, but unsympathetic (and in judging of a character it is *not by abstract morals but by living sympathy that an audience is affected*), all this turns the tide towards the Duchess: and chiefly have I tried to make her not merely an individual woman, but in some way the incarnation of the lives of all women: *she is universal, and her cue is "we women" always*: this note is first struck in Act II in her first soliloquy: in Act III it is of course stronger:

> "the love of men
> Turns women into martyrs; for its sake
> We do and suffer anything."

or

> "O God, how little pity
> We women get in this untimely world"
> (and the following lines)

or

> "I see when men love women
> They give them but a little of their lives,
> But women when they love give everything."

or

> "Women grow mad when they are treated thus"
> (and the lines following)

and chiefly the passage on the relations of sin and love beginning:

> "There is many a woman here in Padua,
> Some workman's wife or ruder artisans . . ."
> (and ending with the words)
> *"That is how women love."*

Well, there is a speech which will wake such pity and such enthusiasm that when her voice is heard saying

> "This way went he, the man who slew my lord"

every woman will say to herself "I would have done likewise." In London (where the misery among the wives of our artisans has required special legislation, so dreadful is it) this speech will produce an extraordinary effect. (I should like it printed at length on some advertisements substituting for *"here in Padua"* the words *"in this city here"* which indeed if you like you might speak.)

The keynote of Act IV is her saying to Guido:

> "I am what thou hast made me."

In a play the characters should create each other: no character must be ready made: the piteous cry of

> "He has changed my heart into a heart of stone"

is the expression of this great truth of dramatic art: *but as the murder had to produce its horror, so revenge must create its terror*: the sympathy of the audience is a little suspended: but why? Well, for this reason, that in Act V when she drinks the

45

poison, when she begs her lover to escape, when with wild words of self-condemnation she thrusts her lover's lips away, when the exclamation reiterated in many forms of

"I am not worthy, Guido, I am not worthy"

shows the depth of her remorse, then the sympathy of the audience returns in a great wave. An audience longs to be first out of sympathy, and ultimately in sympathy, with a character they have loved; but *this sympathy must not be merely emotional, it must have its intellectual basis*, above all it must be summed up for them briefly in the form of thought: audiences are well meaning but very stupid: they must have things told them clearly: they are nice children who need to have their vague emotions crystallised and expressed for them. They feel pity for Othello, but how incomplete the effect of that last dreadful scene would be if Othello did not say:

> *"speak of me as I am ...*
> *then you must speak*
> *Of one that loved not wisely but too well"*

and the rest of the lines. He intellectually gives them the intellectual basis for their sympathy: it seems to me that in all Shakespeare's greatest plays he gives, in the last act, lines which the audience can quote to one another as they pass out, glad, very glad, to find the shield of intellect held over the newborn babe of pity.

This intellectual idea is the *health* of art, as the emotional idea is the *heart* of art: such a play for instance as *La Dame aux Camélias* is unhealthy: *Why?* Not because sympathy is asked for a fallen woman, but because it is only played on one string, an emotional string merely: so that in the last act the sympathy of the audience naturally excited for a woman who is dying young (and has a dreadful cough!) has no real intellectual basis: it would have had if Shakespeare, not Dumas, had written it.

Well, in this play of *The Duchess of Padua* and in the last act Guido *sums up intellectually for the audience their emotional sympathy*. Emotion lives in terror of ridicule, and the imputation of weakness, and is never happy unless it has got hold of its big brother Intellect by the hand. The Duchess in Act III defended her position: that was right: in Act IV it would be horrible: so the places are changed: Guido defends her at that bar of judgment before which she passionately cries "I am guilty:" and to cry that one is guilty to God and man is to get the pardon of the one and the pity of the other.

Guido's speech:

> "Let those who have not loved
> Cast stones against thee"

down to:

> "My soul was murderous, but my hand refused;
> Your hand wrought murder, but your soul was pure"

and ending with the lines

> "let him
> Who has no mercy for your stricken head,
> Lack mercy up in heaven:"

this speech gives the audience the intellectual basis they want: emotion is momentary, ceases with the fall of the curtain, and cannot be remembered, or if remembered is thought a weakness, but intellect is eternal.

You remember what Hamlet says in the moment of his death:

> *"Horatio, I am dead;*
> *Thou livs't: report me and my cause aright*
> *To the unsatisfied."*

and so we have Horatio's noble speech to Fortinbras.

Well, this is what Guido does: he reports the Duchess and her cause aright to the unsatisfied: but not with the cold intellect of a philosopher, or the chilling plausibility of a pleader, but as a passionate lover: in the same way as Horatio speaks with the chivalry of a loving friend: but this again is not enough: the Duchess is to die: her death must be emphasised: its horror must intensify that sympathy which emotion has created, and which intellect has made invulnerable:

"Are there no rivers left in Italy to quench this fire within me?"

47

She suffers pain, that is enough to make those eyes weep that held back their tears before. But it is not merely from life that Death takes her but from love:

> "This is a wedding feast,
> You are out of place, sir,"

she cries to Death himself: but she must not die with wandering mind, and diseased vision, and physical pain stifling her utterance. That would be too material, too physical an ending for a work of spiritual art: so a calm comes after the crisis, a little peace after the whirlwind, a little quiet before the eternal silence.

Do you think that love can cleanse my hands, and heal my wounds? she says. You have not sinned at all, says Guido. No, she answers, I have sinned, and yet:

> "Perchance my sin will be forgiven me,
> I have loved much."

Well, this is what I have meant by *The Duchess of Padua*. There are of course many points in the play I would like to write about more fully: Guido's soliloquy for instance at the close of Act III: why is this necessary? It is necessary I think for this reason: suspense is immensely important for the audience: Macbeth must hesitate at the door of Duncan's room, and Hamlet behind the praying King, and Romeo before Juliet's body. "What is going to happen?" is the question which every good situation makes the audience ask themselves. For suspense, time is necessary: it must not seem as if the guards were posted outside the door: the Duchess has to alarm the house, and when the house is up and the torches seen, and the feet of the soldiers heard, the audience must not know what is happening. "Pray God they have not seized her," says Guido: "You can escape," he cries to her: and the audience must fear with him that she has been taken. Then comes the great effect. But it must be preceded by suspense (as earlier in the act the Duchess does not say the moment she sees Guido "I have killed the Duke": *suspense is the essence of situation, and surprise its climax.* Besides, and this point is equally necessary, the pity of the audience is aroused for the Duchess though she has done murder, but as long as Guido, cold, relentless, obdurate, rejects her, their pity is a little checked, but when he himself cries:

"And yet she loved me:
And for my sake has done this thing:
I have been cruel,"

then they feel as if a barrier had been taken from the path where
the steps of pity had before been checked: besides, his conduct
in the court would appear paradoxical if he did not cry in the
third act:

"Beatrice I love you: come out."

and art should always surprise, but never be paradoxical.

Lastly, it produces on the audience the most tragical effect in
the world: the effect of his speaking *too late*: the effect of Juliet
waking *too* late: "if Guido had only spoken sooner:" "if Juliet
had only sooner wakened:" "too late now" are in art and life
the most tragical words.

I have written at length which perhaps has been wearisome
to you. I wanted to show you how scientifically I have thought
out this matter in all details. I did it for two reasons: first, I was
creating a work of art: secondly, I was creating it for a true
artist.

As regards the scenery and the costumes I have already made
drawings of both: I have indicated the scenery before each act
briefly. I think you will be able to realise from the short scenarios
what I desire. In the last act, the dungeon, about which I remember your talking to me, I have, I think, got rid of the depress-
ing gloom of most such scenes: first by the gambling soldiers
which will give a sort of "Salvator Rosa" effect: secondly by the
invention of the two gratings which open into the corridor. One of
these gratings is small, the other large (almost a sort of gate),
so that when the procession enters of the Lord Justice in his
scarlet, and the headsman with his axe, as they pass through the
corridor, first, at the first grating, their heads and shoulders are
alone seen, then at the second grating they are full three-quarter
lengths: this will be new and effective: and the Duchess taking
the torch from the wall to look at Guido asleep is a good piece
of business. I remember now that in Act III I said a "crimson
velvet curtain over the door at top of staircase," an error I
forgot to rectify from my designs: the curtain is of vermilion
silk: for three reasons. First, it catches the light better in a dark
scene: secondly it is difficult to get such a good colour in velvet

49

as one can get in silk: thirdly, as the torches cannot be seen at the window, or at the sides, the curtain must be transparent as the light shining through it will be most effective: it will suddenly become a door of crimson fire! Some other points I will write to you about, but as it takes some time to prepare designs for costumier and scene-painter I will ask you to telegraph to me your decision about the play. As I may have changed my rooms in Paris would you kindly telegraph to me at Lady Wilde's London address which is 116 Park Street, Grosvenor Square, London.

This letter has become a Titan: it should have been written in the mammoth age: but there is so much to say on a play: and all art must be capable of scientific analysis, if it is not merely prettiness.

Will you present my compliments to Mr and Mrs Griffin: and believe me that writing this play for you has been a task of pleasure, and a labour of love. I remain, dear Miss Anderson, most truly yours Oscar Wilde
Post-Scriptum.

I have not forgotten your bell, Act V. We will have the most musical bell in the world.

(*Letters*, 135–142)

Wilde's total absorption in his play, in its writing and construction, in its production, even in its scenic and costume design, show how false are the charges often brought against him of indifference to his work and a frivolous lack of concern with his dramas. We shall see how increasingly he writes and rewrites and revises his work. Already he is concerned with the play as a total work of art involving lighting, scenic and costume design, and performance.

At the time of the play's performance under the title *Guido Ferranti* in 1891 the New York reviewers were more astute in their treatment than they had been with *Vera*. The *New York Times* described it as a 'sombre romantic play' and remarked without malice that there were lots of reminiscent lines but also passages 'full of the fire of eloquence'. The *New York Daily Tribune* of 21 January paid an intelligent and perceptive tribute:

> In the Broadway Theatre last night, in the presence of a numerous, eagerly attentive, and often kindly responsive audience, Lawrence Barrett . . . produced another new piece, under the name of *Guido Ferranti*. The performance was followed with deep

interest and at certain telling points was rewarded with earnest applause . . . The new play is deftly constructed in five short acts, and is written in a strain of blank verse that is always melodious, often eloquent, and sometimes freighted with fanciful figures of rare beauty. It is less a tragedy, however, than a melodrama—by which is meant a drama of situation. To this ingredient everything is moulded and sacrificed. The inevitable consequence ensues. The radical defect of the work is insincerity. No one in it is natural.

The authorship of *Guido Ferranti* has not been disclosed. There need not have been any hesitation about it—for he is a practised writer and a good one. We recognise in this work a play that we had the pleasure of reading several years ago in manuscript. It was then called *The Duchess of Padua*. The author of it is Oscar Wilde.

(Unsigned review, *New York Daily Tribune*, 27 January 1891, 6)

The time had not yet come when Wilde would welcome a criticism of his work as insincere or think it the highest praise to be told that no one in his play was natural. Such an intelligent review as this cannot have tempered his sense of failure. The critic's statement that he had read the play in manuscript some years previously is tantalising because there is so little documentation of the changes Wilde made in his script, partly, of course, because the work was not produced in England and consequently there was little need here for acting versions. Wilde had *The Duchess of Padua* printed at his own expense in 1883, probably to ensure the copyright, and of this edition only five copies are known to survive. But when he wrote to Henry Irving[2] offering him the play he said he could ask to have the acting version in the possession of Barrett (and lasting for three hours) sent if necessary although it seemed that Irving had been sent a printed (and longer) copy already.

Some ten years later, the play not being available to the reading public, Wilde raised the question of its being printed by John Lane, believing that the Mathews–Lane partnership was under an obligation to publish it together with his other collected work. Nothing happened and when the question of having an uniform edition of his plays printed came up in 1898, when he was already a sick and weary man in exile, he was less than enthusiastic about *The Duchess of Padua*, claiming that it was the only one of his works that was unfit for re-issue although, as he admitted, there were some good lines in it. It eventually came out in the Collected Edition of 1908, dedicated to Adela Schuster by Robert Ross, Wilde's literary executor, who wrote:

> A few months before his death Mr. Oscar Wilde expressed to me a regret that he had never dedicated any of his works to one from whom he had received such infinite kindness and to whom he was under obligations no flattering dedication could repay. With not very great sincerity, because I knew he was a dying man, I suggested he might still write a play or book which you would accept. He answered with truth, 'There is nothing but *The Duchess of Padua* and it is unworthy of her and unworthy of me'.
>
> *(Letters, 757)*

Wilde need not have been ashamed: plays less well-written and less well-constructed have had their periods of success on the stage. It has not attracted any critical attention in recent times.

Nor has *The Duchess of Padua* been revived. In Lawrence Barrett's production the part of the Duchess was played by Minna K. Gale who included it in a tour she began in August 1891 retaining the original title. Wilde received a trifling recompense— forty pounds for eight performances. There do not appear to have been any more performances in his lifetime; and it was not produced again until 1904 and 1906 in Germany in a translation by Max Meyerfeld. It was also given a single performance at St. James's Theatre on 18 March 1907 in order to establish the copyright here.

The failure of *The Duchess of Padua* is not to be lamented although the history of its stage presentation is singularly melancholy. It forced Wilde to stretch himself in style, characterisation and dramatic plotting and to exert himself sufficiently to complete this lengthy five-act play. He was a born dramatist; but even so gifted a writer needs to train himself in his craft and to gain practical experience in the theatre. Any ambitions he had entertained as a writer of blank verse were now put behind him and he went slowly but surely forward to discover and exploit his powers as a writer of social comedies. In both *Vera* and *The*

Duchess of Padua there is evidence of a strong radical tendency which manifests itself in sympathy with the persecuted and oppressed; and it will be remembered that he emphasises this social concern in his lengthy letter to Mary Anderson. Superficially it appears to die away in Wilde's work. To believe this, however, is to do a disservice to Wilde's basic humanitarianism, for the social comedies, whether they deal with the plight of a wronged woman or a social outcast or an ill-begotten fortune, are concerned with the fabric of life about which Wilde is frankly critical. What he had yet to find was a way of reconciling his innate sense of social criticism with the theatrical needs of the late Victorian theatre, and, even more important, he had to learn to control and discipline his characterisation so that The Wicked Man (or Woman) through whom he expresses his radical or anarchic sympathies has to be integrated within the totality of the play and not threaten it as do Prince Paul Maraloffski or the Duke of Padua. Through them—unwittingly—Wilde mocks and ridicules the dramatic (and social) structure he has himself erected and in which he wishes his audience to believe. And, also, instead of looking back with nostalgia at the colour and richness of Renaissance life he began to look about him and see an equally vivid drama in his own age. *The Duchess of Padua*, then, is an honourable and worthy step in Wilde's evolution as a dramatist and in his path to greatness as the writer of the finest social comedies of the nineteenth century.

NOTES

1. Wilde did not himself forget the past so readily: he puts into Guido's mouth two lines from his sonnet to Ellen Terry as Queen Henrietta Maria.

   O Hair of Gold! O Crimson Lips! O Face
   Made for the luring and the love of man!

2. John Henry Brodribb, stage name Henry Irving (1838–1905): the greatest actor-manager of the Victorian age.

3

Salome

Wilde did not find the path to success in the theatre very easy,
as has become evident in the two preceding chapters. After the
failure of Mary Anderson to produce *The Duchess of Padua* in
1883 it was almost ten years before he once again began seriously
to consider writing another play. He had failed to conquer the
New World: the play he now wrote was intended to make his
name as a writer and dramatist of European importance: and it
was probably the only play he wrote in absolute seriousness:
Salome. Paradoxically, *Salome* written in French for a French
actress was to make Wilde's name in Germany in a German translation and to form the libretto of an opera which is sung all over
the world. Wilde had yet to learn the folly of writing for a particular actress whose whims and caprices could never be relied upon
however distinguished the play submitted to her.

The history of Wilde's *Salome* is long and complicated. By the
late 1890s Wilde had transferred his allegiance from the English
aesthetic school to the French decadents, one of whose heroines was
the legendary princess of Jerusalem, Salome, a monster at once
beautiful and vicious and yet strangely innocent in her wilful cruelty.
The sources behind Wilde's drama will be considered later: the
various accounts as to how and when it was written are in themselves contradictory and confusing.

Hesketh Pearson says that when in 1891 Wilde was staying
in Paris he discussed the legend of Salome with some French
writers of his acquaintance and became so excited by its dramatic
possibilities that on his return to his lodgings at 29 Boulevard
des Capucines he took up a blank notebook which happened to be
lying on the table and began his play. 'If the blank book had not
been there on the table I should never have dreamed of doing

it. I should not have sent out to buy one,' Wilde is said to have stated later. Pearson also tells us that the playwright 'wrote with his usual speed and concentration, probably in English . . . and suddenly became aware that it was between ten and eleven at night' (Pearson, 226). He went out to a nearby restaurant and asked the leader of the orchestra to play some music in harmony with his thoughts—which were connected with 'a woman dancing with her bare feet in the blood of a man she has craved for and slain'. Such music—naturally—would be a commonplace in the repertoire of the average café orchestra; accordingly the music was played and the conversation in the restaurant ceased and the listeners 'looked at each other with blanched faces' (Vincent O'Sullivan, *Aspects of Wilde*, 1936, 33). It must have been a memorable experience to have heard this anticipation of Richard Strauss's operatic masterpiece! In his account of the play's genesis Pearson continues: 'We do not know for certain whether the first draft was written in English or French, but we may suspect the former, because of the obvious influence of the Song of Solomon on some of the longer passages and because in the first flush of inspiration he would naturally write in English.' Mentioning a breakfast in London at a later date when Wilfrid Blunt, George Curzon, Willie Peel and Oscar Wilde were present and during which Wilde revealed he had begun a play in French to be acted at the Comédie Française, Pearson further argues, 'This suggests that Wilde was then at work turning his play laboriously into French' (Pearson, 226).

One always hesitates to contradict Pearson who had the great advantage of knowing at first hand many of the theatrical personalities of the time, but he falls into the error of believing everything Wilde said in connection with *Salome*, a mistake that he rarely makes elsewhere. It may be, too, that Pearson had a limited knowledge of French in which case he can never have looked at the original French version of *Salome* with a critical eye. Whatever the case, Pearson appears to have been mistaken in both his surmises. That Wilde wrote his play originally in French seems to be proved by his letters and manuscripts. There was little need to turn his play laboriously from English into French for performance at the Comédie Française, in any case an unlikely *lieu* for this extraordinary drama, since the style is of a kind owing more to the phrase book and schoolboy grammatical exercises than to poetic inspiration of a feverish nature.[1] As for the fortunate coincidence of having a notebook lying about in his lodgings, it would have been extraordinary for an experienced writer and journalist as Wilde was then not to have always had one by him.

We shall try to make a prosaic summary of the events leading up to the writing of this play. Originally Wilde seems to have conceived the idea of writing in French some work or other of basically dramatic form, perhaps more akin to a 'prose poem' or 'dialogue', *genres* which have always found more favour in France than England. From this vague idea he may have moved to the more ambitious project of writing a play. Wilfrid Blunt recorded on 27 October 1891 that Wilde had told some friends that he had begun a play in French to be acted at the Comédie Française. Thus, he had a favourable opportunity for carrying out his literary plan when from early November he stayed in Paris at 29 Boulevard des Capucines. In this central and fashionable area of Paris, surrounded by theatres, bookshops and restaurants, Wilde was perfectly at ease. He was also within walking distance of the Comédie Française should he have wished to enter into serious negotiations about the performance of his play although he was probably much more at home in the theatres of the boulevards where he may have found the inspiration for some of his social dramas as well as the technique and *ambience* which were even more important requirements. During this period he could have called at a stationer's on the boulevard and bought several notebooks in which to write down literary notes and sketches. There are, in fact, three drafts of *Salome*, all in his handwriting and all written in French. There is not even a draft in English. This seems clearly to indicate that from the first Wilde intended to write a work in French and that he began serious work on it during November 1891.

What appears to be the first draft (MS. Bodmer Library, Cologny, Geneva) is not dated, but is written in a half-leather notebook bearing the ticket of a stationer's shop on the Boulevard des Capucines. A similarly ticketed notebook dated 'Paris, November '91' (now in the MS. collection of Texas University) may be a second draft. Yet another copy (MS. collection, Rosenbach Museum, Philadelphia) was submitted to the poet and writer Pierre Loüys[2] and contains his interlinear corrections and suggested improvements. Wilde seems also to have submitted a draft to Stuart Merrill who found that his suggestions were not received with any enthusiasm and therefore advised that the play should be submitted elsewhere, possibly to the symbolist poet Adolphe Retté who did, in fact, make some amendments, notably abbreviating the long catalogue of semi-precious stones and jewels which issues from the mouth of Herod.[3] It is likely that Wilde submitted his play to the scrutiny of several of his friends in search of their admiration but without particularly welcoming their criticisms (see *Letters*, 305–306, for valuable notes on this period).

In December 1891, as already mentioned, Wilde sent a rough copy to Pierre Loüys with an accompanying letter in which he said that his drama was still not finished nor even corrected but that it would give some idea of the subject and of the dramatic movement (*Letters*, 305–306). Although there were gaps, the idea of the play was clear enough. This version which has been compared with the published copy of the play by Professor Clyde de L. Ryals of the University of Pennsylvania seems to have been the text adopted by Wilde for publication (*Notes and Queries*, February 1959). It certainly does not appear that Wilde ever wrote an initial version in English and from the first he was doubtless intent on showing his brilliance in writing a play in French thus paying a tribute to French culture which he adored so inordinately and not only demonstrating his true cosmopolitanism but also revealing to his countrymen that they had a writer of international stature in their midst. And since Wilde wrote French as he spoke it—that is, charmingly, but simply and somewhat in the manner of the phrasebook—there is no need to suppose that the task of writing it down was much more laborious than the customary trials of creative writing. In fact, the repetitive style makes a virtue of Wilde's limited command of French grammatical structure.[4] The claim that he would not have begun on the play had there not been a notebook handy is seen as pure nonsense in the light of the three versions each copied out in his own hand.

At first it seems Wilde did not take his play too seriously—at any rate in public, although his later reactions show that he was, in fact, deeply concerned about its success. But after the inglorious failures of *Vera* and *The Duchess of Padua* he did not expect too much from either the public or the actress-managers, nor was he going to make a fool of himself again by proclaiming that a tremendous triumph lay at hand. He would parody lines from the play among his friends, intoning with amusement, 'Who are these wild beasts howling? They are the Jews discussing their religion', and mocking the phrase, 'And I will give you a flower, Narraboth, a little green flower', although Charles Ricketts protested that the latter line was not really funny since there actually were some flowers that were green. (Afterwards Wilde was to claim that he had created green carnations!) In the early days of *Salome*, unsure of the play's prospects, uncertain of its quality and not wishing to meet the disappointments he had suffered in relation to his earlier plays, he was not above poking fun at himself. As time went on, however, his basic earnestness began to emerge. He set about trying to arrange a production with an independent management and may have intended to offer it to Paul Fort's *Théâtre d'Art*, founded in 1890, which specialised in poetic plays. But despite his previous frustrating experiences he continued to believe that his play stood a greater chance of success if he could persuade one of the leading actresses and managers of the day to take it into her repertoire. His choice, logically in view of the play's association with France and its being written in French, fell on the actress he admired beyond all measure, Sarah Bernhardt, and influenced as much by the spell of her golden voice as by the costume dramas in which she excelled he tried to interest her in a production. In this he was not particularly original since other writers had already visualised her as the Princess Salome: in 1889 Jean Lorrain[5] had written

> Sarah is there, standing before me, with her delicate and irritating profile, her eyes as glittering and cold as precious stones. To see her thus undulating and dying under the glint of her metal belt, I dream that she is as much of the family of the old King David as of the young archangel with a woman's face. Yes, she is surely the daughter of Gustave Moreau, the enigmatic Sarah, sister of the Muses, who carried decapitated chiefs, of Orpheus and of those Salomes, willowy and bloody, the Salome of the famous water-colour, the Salome of the Apparition, whose triumphant and coruscating costume she wore even in Theodora . . .
>
> (Quoted in Philippe Jullian, *Oscar Wilde*, 1969, 252)

Sarah, whose Jewishness would undoubtedly have contributed to the general effect and who had been described often enough as a daughter of the ghetto—which she was not—seemed interested. Eventually she expressed a firm desire to play the title rôle, evidently aware of the artistic currents of the day and always athirst for publicity of any kind; and made several useful comments: "Mais c'est héraldique; on dirait une fresque,' and 'Le mot doit tomber comme une perle sur un disque de cristal; pas de mouvements rapides, des gestes stylises,' which seem to suggest she had an imaginative understanding of Wilde's intentions (see Joanna Richardson, *Sarah Bernhardt* 1951, 121). One wonders whether Wilde actually read *Salome* to her (or presented her with a copy), when she made her comments, how she came to agree to present it, and when she definitely proposed a production in London. However, since the *sobriquet* of Sarah Barnum was not awarded without cause it may have been that in the casual manner which she adopted for lesser mortals and events of little importance to her she toyed with the thought that the presentation of a short play by a noted writer would enhance the prestige of her London season without costing too much or involving much energy. It was usual at the time to open the evening with a one-act play of some kind. Hesketh Pearson and other writers on Wilde state that Bernhardt had determined to produce the play in London and took the Palace Theatre for that purpose.[6] Since she was engaged on a world tour from 23 January until May 1892 it is difficult to credit any of the information relating to her intentions with regard to the play: she can have had very little time to spare for preparation.

At the end of May 1892, on her return from the exhausting world tour, Bernhardt opened a London season that was scheduled to last almost two months. It must be presumed that she had signalled her intention of including the play in her repertoire, presenting it towards the end of the season as a compliment to her London audiences and to Wilde in particular. There is evidence as to the nature of the preparations that were made. Naturally, Bernhardt, then nearing fifty and no longer quite so undulating as in former days, cast herself as Salome, arranged for Albert Darmont to play Herod, and ordered some costumes to be designed by Graham Robertson—the rest were to be supplied from the wardrobe basket.[7] The artist saw the possibilities at once—'every costume of some shade of yellow . . . from clearest lemon to deep orange, with here and there just a hint of black . . . and all upon a pale ivory terrace against a great empty sky of deepest violet'. Wilde agreed: 'A violet sky . . . yes . . . I never thought of that. Certainly a violet sky . . . and then, in place of an orchestra, braziers of perfume. Think: the scented clouds rising and partly veiling the stage from time to time . . . a new perfume for each emotion' (Graham Robertson, *Time Was*, 1931, 126). When this particular enthusiasm had faded—the results would have been wonderfully psychedelic—Wilde consulted yet another decorative artist, Charles Ricketts, who suggested a black floor upon which Salome's feet could move like white doves.[8] The sky was to be a rich turquoise blue down which were to hang gilded strips of Japanese matting which would suggest an aerial tent high above the terraces. Herod and Herodias were to be in blood-red. Ricketts wanted a Salome in gold or silver, while Wilde wanted her to be dressed in green like a poisonous lizard. After all this, it comes as something of an anti-climax to learn from Ricketts that Wilde actually wanted as realistic a setting as possible. In any case it seems extremely unlikely that Bernhardt had the slightest intention of wasting a single franc on this novelty. Having spent a fortune on the costumes for one of her exotic productions *Cléopâtre*, she intended to dig them out of her theatrical wardrobe. 'We must contrive it all somehow out of the "Cléopâtre" costumes,' said Sarah, presuming that by arranging and altering and cutting she could obtain quite a good effect, adding that some day she hoped to produce the play 'properly'. On one effect she was insistent: Salome's hair was to be powdered blue! She would adorn herself with the cope she wore in *Théodora*—it would remind the audience, she thought, of the priestly rôle of a Princess of Judea. There is no hint as to what she was going to wear in the dance of the seven veils but it is clear that she was not willing to let this aspect of the part daunt her: 'By the by', said Graham Robertson to her reflectively, 'the dance . . .' 'What about it?' she asked. 'I suppose you will get a *figurante* to go through it, won't you?—veiled, of course, and with your blue hair . . .' Sarah was outraged at the idea: 'I'm going to dance myself' (*op. cit.*, 127). Since she envisaged the play as static, fresco-like, one supposes that any movement, even that of the mature actress, would make some effect. Actually, her comment that the play was a fresco was shrewd and seems to indicate she had studied the play with a view to its most effective presentation: an almost unsurmountable difficulty is that since Jokanaan, a central character, has to stand stock still in the centre of the stage, the other characters, principally Salome, are obliged to speak to him sideways or turn their backs to the audience, a difficulty which is largely averted by staging it as a kind of fresco.

But the audience's powers of credibility were not put to the test, for towards the end of June the Lord Chamberlain, acting on an ancient law that had been passed to suppress Catholic mystery plays, stepped in to ban the play on the grounds that it contained biblical characters. Allegedly, Bernhardt was furious with the Censor and with Wilde although she appears to have quickly recovered from her initial disappointment and, possibly, to have rejoiced in the publicity. At any rate, a reporter from *The Illustrated London News* visiting Alpha House, a villa in St. John's Wood which she had rented for the season, found Bernhardt finishing a game of croquet (in a drenching shower of rain) and stayed to view her collection of live snakes ornamented with jewelled rings and chains—but records nothing of her views on the ban (4 June 1892). The fiasco which had cost her nothing enabled her to claim that she was a serious advocate of modern drama. On the other hand, she may have come to regard Wilde as a buffoon not to be taken seriously.

Wilde was outraged. This was his third failure in the theatre although his *Lady Windermere's Fan* had begun a long run on 20 February and been hailed as one of the finest comedies of the century. But initially at any rate he regarded this social comedy as a means of making money whereas *Salome* was to have been the means of establishing himself as an European man of letters: if he had originally looked upon it as a *jeu d'esprit* he had eventually come to see in it a way of making his fame and, possibly, his fortune. The fact that Bernhardt, then recognised as the greatest actress in the world, had agreed to include it in her season, had enormously increased the play's chances of lasting success. Now he felt cheated of his proper fame and had been made to look a fool in the eyes of the world and of Bernhardt who had been ignorant of the possibility of banning by the censorship. Throughout his career he was careless about submitting his plays to the censorship, frequently leaving this necessary procedure to an inconveniently late date; but even at this early stage in his career he had had enough experience to know that he should first have applied at the Lord Chamberlain's office for a licence to perform the play and that there was a law against the representation of biblical characters in the theatre, an old law, it was true, but still in effective operation. He gave interviews to such journals as the *Gaulois*, the *Echo de Paris*, and the *Pall-Mall Gazette*, and took his indignation to a dinner at the Authors' Club where he earned himself no sympathy. The author Eden Phillpots[9] who was present said:

> He was full of indignation and unbosomed his troubles at great length, then turned his back on the assembly and departed. It was an example of pure wounded egotism, without any thought of anything but his personal grievance. A plump, pale, heavy-jowled man in evening dress with violets in his buttonhole, and only one smarting thought in his mind. On his departure amusement rather than sympathy appeared to be indicated by those who had heard him. Had he adopted a different line of approach, his very genuine grievance with an idiotic approach to art would have found everybody on his side, of course. But those who pity themselves so much are apt to lose the sympathy of their neighbours.

> (Pearson, 228)

Wilde wrote angrily to his friends, among them William Rothenstein,[10] protesting that the Lord Chamberlain had forbidden the performance of *Salome* while allowing the stage to be used,

> . . . for the purpose of the caricaturing of the personalities of artists, and at the same time when he prohibited *Salome*, he licensed a burlesque of *Lady Windermere's Fan* in which an actor dressed up like me and imitated my voice and manner! ! !

> (*Letters*, 316)

He was less than honest about this matter of his impersonation on the stage: like Bernhardt he had his fair share of Barnum showmanship and love of publicity. It is true that a musical travesty in which Wilde was impersonated had taken the stage at the

Comedy Theatre on 19 May 1892, a considerable time before the banning of *Salome*. The authors Brookfield and Glover satirised Wilde in their sketch *The Poet and the Puppets*—but not without his permission. Charles Hawtrey, who as The Poet caricatured Wilde, had lines which included verses such as these:

> They may bubble with jest at the way that I'm dressed
> They may scoff at the length of my hair,
> They may say that I'm vain, overbearing, inane,
> And object to the flowers that I wear.
> They may laugh till they're ill, but the fact remains still,
> A fact I've often proclaimed since a child,
> That it's taken, my dears, nearly two thousand years
> To make Oscar O'Flaherty—Wilde."

What Wilde did not disclose to his correspondents was that when he heard of this intended burlesque he wrote to the Lord Chamberlain and insisted that Brookfield and Glover should read the script to him. This they did and 'while cigars burned, the poet puffed, and punctuated each page as it was read to him with such phrases as: ' "Delightful!" "Charming, my old friends!" "It's exquisite!" etc., etc.' (James H. Glover, *Jimmy Glover His Book*, 1911, 20). At Wilde's insistence, however, the last line of the verses quoted above was changed to:

> To make Neighbour O'Flaherty's child.

Wilde had no just cause for complaint: when he was lampooned on the London stage it was with his full connivance (see Rupert Croft-Cooke, *The Unrecorded Life of Oscar Wilde*, 1972, 17–21). He was also caricatured in other entertainments, such as *Where's the Cat?*, *The Colonel*, and *The Charlatan* presented by Herbert Beerbohm Tree.[12] But Wilde had not seen fit to object to this jesting, and he and Beerbohm Tree remained the best of friends. It was only after the banning of *Salome* that his customary good nature failed him, for his pride was hurt severely by the fact that he had suffered at the hands of Edward F. Smyth Pigott, the Censor of the day, whom Bernard Shaw described as 'a walking compendium of vulgar insular prejudice'.[13] There is some evidence that Wilde had cause for righteous anger because the public tended to assume that *Salome* had been proscribed on grounds of indecency and a black shadow was cast over his reputation: his re-action, nevertheless, was a trifle humourless.

William Archer, the only critic and writer brave enough to write to the press and protest about the ban on performances of *Salome*, was also indignant about the burlesque of Wilde.[14] In a letter which appeared in the *Pall Mall Gazette* on 1 July 1892 he de-clared:

> A serious work of art, accepted, studied, and rehearsed by the greatest actress of our time, is peremptorily suppressed, at the very moment when the personality of its author is being held up to ridicule, night after night, on the public stage, with the full sanction and approval of statutory Infallibility.
>
> (*Letters*, 317)

'statutory Infallibility' is a reference to censorship in the theatre, a function of the Lord Chamberlain's office, of which Archer was a constant opponent. His words of support were of no avail: Wilde was determined not to be consoled.

Wilde now went out of his way to make himself appear even more silly by announcing that he intended to renounce his British citizenship and become a Frenchman. In the interview granted to *Le Gaulois* he stated:

> My resolution is deliberately taken. Since it is impossible to have a work of art performed in England, I shall transfer myself to another fatherland, of which I have long been enamoured . . . Here people are essentially anti-artistic and narrow-minded . . . Of course I do not deny that Englishmen possess certain practical qualities; but, as I am an artist, these qualities are not those which I admire. Moreover, I am not at present an Englishman. I am an Irishman which is by no means the same thing. No doubt I have English friends to whom I am deeply attached; but as to the English, I do not love them. There is a great deal of hypocrisy in England which you in France very justly find fault with. The typical Briton is Tartuffe seated in his shop behind the counter. There are numerous exceptions, but they only prove the rule.
>
> (Pearson, 228–229)

These words—Wilde was to find that hypocrisy was not a confined to Albion's shores and that Tartuffe was rightly a creation of

French culture—delighted *Punch* which was gleeful at finding another subject for a cartoon; and the poetaster William Watson wrote some would-be satirical verses entitled 'Lines to our new Censor', which began:

> And wilt thou, Oscar, from us flee,
> > And must we, henceforth, wholly sever?
> Shall thy laborious *jeux-d'esprit*
> > Sadden our lives no more for ever?
>
> > > ('Lines to our new Censor', *Spectator*, 9 July 1892,
> > > reprinted in *Lachrymae Musarum*, 1892)

On which Wilde commented that there was not enough spirit in William Watson's poetry to boil a tea-kettle. Eventually he relented on his decision to become a Frenchman and recognising that his considerable financial income came from those 'essentially anti-artistic and narrow-minded' Englishmen who were flocking to his new play decided to stay here. England was damned, as a land which 'is Caliban for nine months of the year, and Tartuffe for the other three'. So he remained here but, as his son Vyvyan Holland commented, 'As matters turned out, it is a pity that he did not carry out his threat' (Introduction to *Complete Works of Oscar Wilde*, new edn. 1966, 12).

Wilde never saw a production of *Salome* although it was once produced during his lifetime. At Reading, in prison, he was delighted to learn of a production of the play on 11 February 1896 by Lugné-Poe at the Théâtre de l'Oeuvre in Paris, where his friend Stuart Merrill was manager.[15] It was moderately reviewed and despite the fact, as J. T. Grein remarked, that 'the performance was not such as to gladden the author or add to his fame,' Wilde believed that it turned the scales in his favour as far as his treatment in prison was concerned. He felt himself eternally indebted to Paris for producing the play at that dreadful period in his life. Unfortunately, there seems to have been little financial reward for him. There is a contrast here with the attitude of Bernhardt: while in H.M. Prison, Holloway, awaiting trial and desperate for money to fight his case, Wilde wrote to his friend Sherard asking if the rights of *Salome* could be offered to her (she had said she would produce it at her theatre of the Porte St. Martin) for three or four hundred pounds. This sum would have served to avert his bankruptcy. The great actress received Sherard on Wilde's behalf, wept at the author's plight and said that although she could not afford to buy *Salome* she would send Wilde some money. She made a series of appointments with Sherard, none of which she kept, and never sent a franc to Wilde. As it happens, the play was to make a fortune from performances on the Continent, so that in her ungracious and deceitful attitude to Wilde in his dark hour Bernhardt showed neither courtesy nor friendship and, least of all, the rudiments of financial sense. Grein said that 'if Sarah Bernhardt had shown more courage, she might, by the presentation of *Salome*, have paved the way towards a rehabilitation of the author. But after the scandal the actress was ashamed to be associated with the fallen star' (*Sunday Special* 9 and 16 December 1900; reprinted in *Dramatic Criticism*, 1902–03, iii, 79–83).

After his release from prison where he had been sentenced to hard labour, Wilde searched for people to produce the play, even entrusting a copy to the somewhat mature Italian actress Eleanora Duse—an unlikely candidate, one would have thought, for the rôle of the eighteen-year old princess of Judea.[16] In 1901, a year after his death, it was produced in Berlin with great success; and after a celebrated presentation by Max Reinhardt at the Kleines Theatre it had, at one time, more performances in Germany than any other play by a British dramatist, not excepting Shakespeare. Had Wilde lived only a few years longer he would have found his faith in the play vindicated both by the flow of royalties from foreign productions and the esteem it enjoyed in the European theatre, which it has never entirely lost.

In the English-speaking world, however, the play has had a turbulent history. It was first produced in London on 10 May 1905, mainly to secure the copyright, in a private performance at the Bijou Theatre, Bayswater, by the New Stage Club. The production attracted some attention because of the fine performance of Robert Farquharson as Herod. The dramatic critics, with the naïve ignorance too common to the tribe, spoke of the play as having been 'dragged from obscurity', although a little checking would have revealed its immense popularity on the Continent. In November of the same year it was performed by the Progressive Stage Society of New York with no success. Given a professional performance at the Astor Theatre, New York, in November 1906, it was dismissed by the *New York Tribune* reviewer as 'decadent stuff, and unworthy of notice'. When the play was privately produced for a second time in England by the Literary Theatre Society in 1906 the newspaper critics were as condemnatory as ever. Public approval could hardly be forthcoming when public performances were still forbidden by the Censor who did not relent about the decision to ban *Salome* even after Wilde's death nor, indeed, for decades later, although it is only fair to admit that in New York where there was no censorship it did no better.

Worse was to come. In 1918, J. T. Grein planned another private performance of the play, this time in aid of war charities. The part of Salome was to be taken by Maud Allan, a famous dancer of the period. These tidings came to the notice of Noel Pemberton Billing, an M.P. and sometime journalist, who claimed to have discovered a secret dossier compiled by the Germans of forty-seven thousand prominent men and women whose moral, sexual and financial weaknesses exposed them to the blackmailing pressures of German secret agents. Pemberton Billing wrote a paragraph in his newsletter *The Vigilante* in which he linked the proposed performance with his notorious list implying that only potential traitors would want to see this decadent play by Wilde. Grein sued for libel and lost. He was crippled financially, dismissed by the Ministry of Information, and his resignation as drama critic of the *Sunday Times* promptly accepted. Thus a man who had striven for the best in British drama and who had generously given time, energy and the little money he possessed to this cause, was victimised and penalised in the name of patriotism. Pemberton Billing was acquitted: Grein lost: and *Salome* was condemned once more—but now it was not only immoral but also unpatriotic.

The trials and tribulations of the play were not yet at an end. In 1927 the Cambridge Festival Theatre, a progressive and adventurous group, applied for a licence to give a public performance of *Salome* only to receive the inevitable reply that it had been and was still banned. Terence Gray, the founder and director, went ahead with a special, free performance which was well received so that Peter Godfrey decided to stage it at his London Gate Theatre in 1929. The public response was so enthusiastic that the Censor was forced to yield or face general ridicule. So it was that in 1931

Wilde's *Salome* received its first public performance in Britain at the Lyceum, Henry Irving's old theatre, an ironic coincidence which must have occasioned the ghost of Oscar considerable amusement.[17] There were, as we shall see, other reasons for laughter.

Like almost everything else connected with *Salome* there are problems about the actual text used in performance. It will be remembered that the play had been written in French which was generally unsuitable for ordinary public performance here. Wilde seems to have allowed his young friends the opportunity to translate his play but with no serious intention of accepting their versions: he was, after all, the greatest living master of the English language. It appears that he agreed for Aubrey Beardsley to make a version—which he did not accept—and also Alfred Douglas.[18] Hesketh Pearson supplies a narrative:

> . . . when Aubrey Beardsley, who claimed he could make an ideal translation, begged to be allowed to do so, Wilde gave way. But he thoroughly disliked Beardsley's version and said he would rather use the one by Douglas, who thereupon gave him permission to make what alterations he pleased, but added that his own name as translator had better not appear if the text was not his. Wilde made some alterations, and dedicated the play in its English form to Douglas, whose name appears as translator, though he never considered the published version as his work
>
> (Pearson, 226)

It is true that while the French version is dedicated to Pierre Loüys, the English one bears the legend: 'To my friend Lord Alfred Bruce Douglas, the translator of my play'. Despite this dedication, Douglas's name does not appear on the title page as translator. In fact, in the long letter which Wilde wrote to Douglas in 1897 during the misery of his days in Reading Gaol, and which is known as *De Profundis* he claimed that Douglas's version had been entirely unsatisfactory, and that he had had to translate the play himself:

> . . . in September (1893), new scenes occurred, the occasion of them being my pointing out the schoolboy faults of your attempted translation of *Salome*. You must by this time be a fair enough French scholar to know that the translation was as unworthy of

68

you, as an ordinary Oxonian, as it was of the work which it sought to render.

(Letters, 432)

It is really hard to see why Wilde could not have made his own translation (or version) of *Salome* from the first and saved literary scholarship a degree of puzzlement. It seems as if the version which has come down to us must be accepted as the work of Wilde himself, possibly with a few elements derived from the translations of Douglas and Beardsley.

Few people in the English-speaking world can have seen a production of *Salome*; and, perhaps, not so many more have read it. The curtain rises on a great terrace of the palace of Herod of Judea. Moonlight floods the scene. Narraboth, a young Syrian, captain of the guard, whose royal father had been defeated in battle by Herod and whose mother had been given as a slave to Herodias, is talking to the queen's page. Also on the stage are soldiers guarding an ancient cistern in which the prophet Jokanaan is imprisoned. The young Syrian is aflame with passionate love for the princess Salome, daughter of Herodias and step-daughter of Herod:

> *The Young Syrian*: How beautiful is the Princess Salome tonight!
> *The Page of Herodias*: Look at the moon! How strange the moon seems! She is like a woman rising from a tomb. She is like a dead woman. You would fancy she was looking for dead things.
> *The Young Syrian*: She has a strange look. She is like a little princess who wears a yellow veil, and whose feet are of silver. She is like a princess who has little white doves for feet. You would fancy she was dancing.
> *The Page of Herodias*: She is like a woman who is dead. She moves very slowly.

Our attention is then drawn to the soldiers who remark on the howling of the Jews who sound like wild beasts. From the cistern comes the voice of the Baptist (Jokanaan) crying out against the wickedness of this world, the fate which will befall Herod, and the sinfulness of the incestuous relationship between Herod and Herodias. Mingled with these prophecies of doom are others relating to the coming of the Messiah:

> After me shall come another mightier than I. I am not worthy so much as to unloose the latchet of his shoes. When he cometh

69

the solitary places shall be glad. They shall blossom like the lily. The eyes of the blind shall see the day, and the ears of the deaf shall be opened. The new-born child shall put his hand upon the dragon's lair, he shall lead the lions by their manes.

The cistern has had a previous occupant. Herod had imprisoned his own elder brother there for twelve years before executing him. The brother's crime was to have possessed a wife whom Herod desired and whom he has since married—Herodias. The present occupant of the cistern, Jokanaan, who has come out of the desert, cannot be spoken to but neither can he be silenced: his denunciations and prophecies are not without their effect on the superstitious Herod.

Salome enters, having slipped away from the banquet to the cool and quiet of the terrace. Hearing the voice of Jokanaan she is at once fascinated and persuades the young Syrian to have him brought out of the cistern. The pale face of the prophet gleaming in the moonlight, his white body in its roughly woven and ragged garments, his dark tangled hair and beard, and his cold aloofness arouse her lusts. The more he upbraids and curses her the more she begs to be allowed to kiss him:

Salome: Let me kiss thy mouth.
Jokanaan: Cursed be thou! Daughter of an incestuous mother, be thou accursed!
Salome: I will kiss thy mouth, Jokanaan.

In the anguish of his despairing love for Salome the young Syrian kills himself and falls at her feet. His death is unnoticed and unmourned except by the page of Herodias who speaks a moving threnody over his corpse. Jokanaan, resolute and defiant, returns to the cistern.

Herod enters. He slips in the blood of the dead Syrian. With his claim that this is an evil omen we begin to see the credulous and unscrupulous, sadistic and malevolent nature of the tyrant. Everything is interpreted by him as an omen, usually bad. At the same time he is relentless in his pursuit of Salome, never for once taking his eyes off her. He wishes her to dance for him. To achieve this aim he will promise her everything and anything she wishes. She begins to put aside her sullen indifference:

Herod: Dance for me, Salome, I beseech you. If you dance for me you may ask of me what you will, and I will give it to you, even unto the half of my kingdom.

Salome: Will you indeed give me whatsoever I shall ask, Tetrarch?

Herodias: Do not dance, my daughter.

Herod: Everything, even the half of my kingdom.

Salome: You swear it, Tetrarch?

Herod: I swear it, Salome.

Herodias: Do not dance, my daughter.

Salome: By what will you swear, Tetrarch?

Herod: By my life, by my crown, by my gods. Whatsoever you desire I will give it you, even to the half of my kingdom, if you will but dance for me. Salome, Salome, dance for me!

Salome: You have sworn, Tetrarch.

Herod: I have sworn, Salome.

Having obtained Herod's promise, Salome sends for perfumes and her seven veils. She has her sandals removed in order to dance with bare feet. Then she dances. Herod is carried away with ecstatic delight:

Herod: . . . Come near, Salome, come near, that I may give you your reward. Ah! I pay the dancers well. I will pay thee royally. I will give thee whatsoever thy soul desireth. What wouldst thou have?

Salome: I would that they presently bring me in a silver charger.

Herod: In a silver charger? Surely, yes, in a silver charger. She is charming, is she not? What is it you would have in a silver charger, O, sweet and fair Salome, you who are fairer than all the daughters of Judea? What would you have them bring thee in a silver charger? Tell me. Whatsoever it may be, they shall give it to you. My treasures belong to thee. What is it, Salome?

Salome: The head of Jokanaan.

Herod recoils in horror at this suggestion. He is able to set Jews and Nazarenes at odds with each other, to tyrannise his kingdom, but he cannot persuade Salome to change her demand. He offers her his peacocks, his jewels, even half his kingdom in place of the head of the holy man of whose strange, foreboding words he is, apparently, afraid. Salome will not yield. Encouraged by her mother, she remains obdurate in her perverse request. Unwillingly, seeing everywhere around him omens of disaster, Herod takes from his finger the ring of death, indicating that one of his soldiers is to give it to Namaan, the negro executioner, who then descends into the cistern. Salome hangs over the side of the cistern urging him on to the fatal task until, at last, his arm rises above the edge, supporting on a silver shield the head of Jokanaan. Salome hungrily seizes it. Herod hides his face in his robe. Herodias smiles and fans herself. The Nazarenes kneel and begin to pray. Salome continues with a horrifying monologue:

> I, I saw thee, Jokanaan, and I loved thee. Oh, how I loved thee! I loved thee yet, Jokanaan, I love thee only . . . I am athirst for thy beauty; I am hungry for thy body; and neither wine nor fruits can appease my desire. What shall I do now, Jokanaan? Neither the floods nor the great waters can quench my passion. I was a princess, and thou didst scorn me. I was a virgin, and thou didst take my virginity from me. I was chaste, and thou didst fill my veins with fire . . . Ah! ah! wherefore didst thou not look at me. Jokanaan? If thou hadst looked at me thou hadst loved me. Well I know that thou wouldst have loved me, and the mystery of love is greater than the mystery of death. Love only should one consider.

Herod withdraws into his palace. He calls upon the slaves to extinguish their torches, the stars to disappear, the moon to which he has constantly referred to hide itself. Fearful of what may happen he calls upon Herodias to hide herself away with him. A great black cloud passes in front of the moon and completely hides its light. In the darkness is heard the exultant voice of Salome as she boasts, 'I have kissed thy mouth, Jokanaan.' A ray of moonlight falls on her. Herod turns at the top of the stairs. 'Kill that woman,' he cries; and the soldiers advance and crush beneath their shields Salome, daughter of Herodias and Princess of Judea.

This brief summary does not take into account such vivid scenes as, for instance, those in which Herod baits the Christians, Nazarenes, Pharisees, and other religious fanatics nor does it show the extraordinary range of moods, but it does at least indicate the varied acting parts. Nothing is known of Wilde's ideas on casting this drama but there seems to have been a tradition that the page of Herodias was to have been played by a girl thus adding a Shakespearian piquancy to the opening scene between the page and the young Syrian. It might be possible to extend the decadent sexual undertones of the play still further by casting another girl as the

Syrian, as Beardsley appears to suggest in his illustrations. Although both Salome and Herodias have important parts and would seem on first reading to dominate the drama, Wilde was equally fascinated by the characters of Jokanaan and Herod. Yet in performance the denunciations, prophecies and curses of Jokanaan tend to monotony and little that is attractive comes through in his character. It is enough (and more difficult than may at first be imagined) to have an actor who is tall, raven-locked, pale, thin, even emaciated, beautiful and golden-voiced with an ability to remember long and repetitive speeches with unhelpful cues. It is worth noting that when Richard Strauss came to write his opera of the same name he changed the usual order by which the leading rôle is written for a tenor and made Jokanaan a bass-baritone. The majority of reviews have singled out for mention the actors and singers who have taken the rôle of Herod. Of the performance by the singer Burrian who took the part of Herod in the first production of the opera at Dresden, Sir Arnold Bax wrote in his autobiographical *Farewell my Youth* (1943), that he 'created a quite horrifying Herod, slobbering with lust, and apparently decomposing before our disgusted but fascinated eyes' (p. 33). Wilde himself seems to have glimpsed the possibilities of the part when he said to Beerbohm Tree, celebrated for his gallery of eccentric stage portrayals, that 'As Herod in my *Salome*, you would be admirable.' At the first (private) English performance it was the actor who played Herod, Robert Farquharson, who was singled out for praise. The part offers tremendous scope to an actor who is prepared to exploit the hysteria, the cunning, the fear of old age, as well as the terror, the love of power, and the levantine treachery of the tyrant. Wilde has brilliantly underlined the sadistic bestiality of the man as well as the ruthless opportunism of the politician, the callous husband as well as the sensual stepfather. Herod is, in fact, the most totally conceived of Wilde's male characters. Others are wittier, others are more definitely serious in intention and creation, but none are so memorable. And although *Salome* is a short play, the rôle of Herod is of marathon length. He is well contrasted with Herodias, a similarly evil character of a different, more brutal nature. During the course of the play Wilde shows us Herod in the midst of the Jews and Nazarenes, cleverly setting them at odds with one another, searching for in-

73

THE PLAYS OF OSCAR WILDE

formation (not about first-born sons but about the whereabouts of the new prophet who is restoring men to life—Herod has no intention of letting any of his murdered political rivals return from the grave to oppose him), and displaying his own basic superstitious religiosity, while at the same time Herodias is calling her slave girl to her and striking her with a feathered fan. The juxtaposition of the two incidents is not casual: Wilde wants us to see the direct, callous and unrestrained character of Herodias contrasted with the cunning deviousness of the husband. The play is built up on such juxtapositions or counterpointings. Herodias has even fewer scruples than Herod (who stole her, as she claims, from the arms of her first husband) about using the lives of others for her own ends: Salome is as much the victim of her mother's jealousy and hostility to her husband as she is of Herod's irrational and reckess lust, fear of old age and relentless cruelty.

But it was the character of Salome herself which must have first inspired Wilde: a superhuman task for the actress who must bewitch as much by the beauty of her voice as the sinuous and virginal beauty of her naked body. From her first entrance she must show that she is aware that she fascinates Herod, but she must also show the insatiable and paradoxical nature of her lust for Jokanaan whose body, as virginal as her own, repels and attracts her. Her guileless and petulant viciousness, revealed when she demands the prophet's head, must certainly alienate the audience although not to the extent that they do not feel a random pity at her death. There are, of course, other aspects of her character to be considered later.

Failing to win any support from the literary and theatrical establishment in London, Wilde determined to have his play published in the original French version. A copy (for which Marcel Schwob seems to have corrected the final proofs) was sent to the Librairie de l'Art Indépendant;[19] and on 22 February 1893 it was published simultaneously in an edition of 650 copies by the Librairie de l'Art Indépendant and Elkin Mathews and John Lane in London. Wilde had copies sent to Edmund Gosse, Bernard Shaw and William Archer. The English version came out almost a year later on 9 February 1894 in an edition of 600 copies published by Elkin Mathews and John Lane with decorations supplied by Aubrey Beardsley. All this must have given Wilde tremendous satisfaction

74

—was he not, probably, the first British writer of note to have published a work in French—French of his own writing and not merely translated?

As for the notorious decorations—it would be inaccurate to describe them as illustrations—it is known that it was Robert Ross who persuaded Wilde to give Aubrey Beardsley the opportunity to show his genius.[20] At that time Beardsley was twenty-one years old, a brilliant, malicious, salacious, and sickly young man with only five years of life left to him. A letter which he wrote to Ross in 1893 indicates some of the difficulties Wilde was encountering in connection with these decorations and the jealousy which existed between Douglas and himself. He confides:

> I suppose you've heard all about the *Salome* row. I can tell you I had a warm time of it between Lane and Oscar and Co. For one week the numbers of telegraphs and messenger boys who came to the door was simply scandalous. I really don't quite know how the matter really stands now. Anyhow Bosies's name is not to turn up on the title. The book will be out soon after Xmas. I have withdrawn three of the illustrations and supplied their places with three new ones (simply beautiful and quite irrelevant).
>
> (*Letters*, 344)

Wilde disliked all of Beardsley's illustrations, claiming that they were Japanese while his play was Byzantine. To other friends he remarked, 'They are like the naughty scribbles a precocious schoolboy makes on the margins of his copybooks,' and 'They are cruel and evil, and so like dear Aubrey, who has a face like a silver hatchet, with grass-green hair.' Yet Wilde had written in the copy of the 1893 edition of *Salome* which he had sent to Beardsley: 'For Aubrey: for the only artist who, besides myself, knows what the dance of the seven veils is, and can see that invisible dance. Oscar.'[21] Aware that Beardsley did not care for him at all and that there was no love lost between them, Wilde behaved with his customary generosity and courtesy to the young artist giving him the first great opportunity of his artistic career. It did him little good since the public looked for evil in Beardsley's decorations to *Salome* and finding little there that was comprehensible to their eyes concluded that the evil must lie in Wilde's text. In his malicious way Max Beerbohm used to remark that *Salome* was only the material which had served to inspire the drawings: 'I have just been reading it again—and like it immensely—there is much, I think, in it that is beautiful, much lovely writing—I almost wonder Oscar doesn't dramatise it' (*op. cit.*, 183).

Beardsley's work was surely meant to mock at Wilde, for the author is caricatured in at least four drawings: in 'The Woman in the Moon', Wilde is the moon; in 'A Platonic Lament', he is embodied in a fragment of the sky asleep over the ghoulish scene of the nude Salome leaning over the body of Jokanaan and gripping his head between her eager hands; in the 'Eyes of Herod' he is shown as a long-haired and bearded figure gazing through the candles' flames at Salome; and in 'Enter Herodias' he is pictured as the showman-jester carrying a caduceus. In the end it must have seemed to Wilde that his text was in danger of becoming a mere accompaniment to the drawings which were, in any case, free and fantastic improvisations on the moods aroused in Beardsley by the play. But Wilde did not seriously object to them. He was, as Beardsley slyly indicated in 'Enter Herodias', a showman in whom there was sufficient acumen to recognise the value of the publicity afforded by the decorations. Holbrook Jackson wrote that Wilde was not at all put out by Beardsley's malice.

> . . . possibly because he was a showman as well as an artist, and recognised the advantage of having his play decorated, even a little outrageously, by the most discussed artist of the moment. So Herod, Herodias, and even the Moon, which plays a leading part in the drama, were allowed to appear with the author's features . . .
> (Introduction to The Limited Editions Club edition of *Salome*, 1938, 13–14)

Beardsley had the last word. In a drawing entitled 'Oscar Wilde at Work' he made a private satirical comment on Wilde's boast that he never had to look up anything so perfect was his memory and so wide his range of learning, for he shows the playwright at work in his study, writing at a desk piled high with large volumes which include a 'Family Bible', a *Dorian Gray*, *Trois Contes* by Flaubert, volumes of Swinburne and Gautier, the *Histories of Josephus*, a French dictionary and a 'First Course in French' and also 'French verbs at a Glance'!

Before going on to discuss the play's sources it may be interesting to mention yet another metamorphosis of this play, not in this case from words to drawings but from the spoken to the sung word. There is a general rule that anything which is too silly, too indecent or too shocking to be spoken may be safely sung without offence to anyone. This was the case with *Salome* as most music-lovers are aware. Its text seemed ideally suited for transformation into an opera. The first musician on the scene was a young French naval officer called Marriotte but apart from one performance at Lyons, his native town, the operatic version he made has languished in obscurity. This lack of success was not entirely due to the quality of his music but also because he had simply omitted to secure the exclusive rights to the text which had meanwhile been obtained by the German composer Richard Strauss.

In 1905 Richard Strauss, general music director of the Berlin Royal Opera House, let it be known that he was preparing a work of a very special kind, an opera to be based on an abridged German version of *Salome* made by Hedwig Lachmann. Even before the first notes of the score had been sounded in the opera house, *Salome* had become the subject of heated controversy. Following its premiere on 9 December 1905 on the stage of the Dresden Royal Opera it was branded by some critics as 'monstrous' and praised by others as 'revolutionary, a work of obvious beauty'. With such wild reactions the opera's success was inevitable and before long, following the triumphs of Wittich in the part of Salome, there was a queue of prima-donnas all over the world pressing to be allowed to divest themselves of the notorious seven veils and to caress the Baptist's severed head while struggling vocally through Strauss's dissonant harmonies: Destinn in Berlin, Krusceniski at La Scala, and Fremstad and Garden (singing the rôle in French) at New York. After the performance at the Metropolitan Opera the music critic of the *New York Tribune*, Henry Krehbiel, declared that it 'left the listeners staring at each other with starting eyeballs and wrecked nerves'.

Strauss had become obsessed by the manner in which Wilde treated Salome's passion for Jokanaan and created a score in which the sounds of an ancient Eastern biblical land are hardly heard in the tempestuous flow of frenzied harmonies and erotic modulations. He said that he felt urged to create some truly exotic harmonies, particularly in the unusual cadences, like the iridescence of shot silk. The desire to produce the most sharply defined characters possible, decided him to use bi-tonality. Strauss added that he had been led 'to the use of the most daring harmonic innovations, psychological polyphony, taxing the listening capacity of modern ears to the limit'.

There are few set pieces in the opera of *Salome*, apart from the quintet of the Jews and the celebrated dance of the seven veils, frequently performed on its own as a concert piece. The single act form of the original drama which Strauss retained and the wonderful opportunities provided by the rôle of Salome herself contributed to the impact of the opera as well as the symphonic treatment of the orchestral score in a manner derived from Wagner and the remarkable exploitation of tone colour. Strauss interwove the voices in a subtle and sparse manner which he described as 'neuro-contrapuntal', enabling him to conjure up for the audience the fatal power of Salome's lust, the rancorous disputes of the Jews and Nazarenes and Pharisees the depraved brazenness of Herodias, the earnest fervour of the Baptist, the whining cunning of Herod, and the decadent viciousness of his court. In other words, Strauss utilised to the full the unique and imaginative realisation of the legend by Wilde; and in this way a second masterpiece gained life, never ceasing to thrill in the opera house, even convincing us by purely musical means that the mature lady on the stage is in reality an eighteen-year-old princess of Judea.

Masterpiece or not, it was unlikely that Strauss's opera would ever be heard in an English theatre. The improving hand of the Censor had already been to work on the performance of another opera on a similar theme: a licence had been granted for a performance of Massenet's *Hérodiade* at Covent Garden in 1904 on condition that the title be changed to *Salome*! However, the action had to be transferred to Ethiopia and Herod and Herodias transformed into two hitherto unknown biblical characters called Moreame and Mesotoade. Thus, when, in 1910, Beecham thought of producing Strauss's *Salome* at Covent Garden he was lost as to what to do, for he knew that the composer was not the kind of man to allow any meddling with his work. In the event, conscious of his musical reputation and, more probably, of his firm's donations to party political funds, he turned to the Prime Minister who arranged to allow its presentation. The minimum of alterations was required. Jokanaan whose name would be a source of direct offence to the public (or so the Censor thought) had to be renamed 'The Prophet' which means he could have been Muhamed himself as far as the more ignorant members of the public were concerned— except that representations of Muhamed were also forbidden for fear of giving offence to Britain's Muslim allies. There were other 'safeguards', as the Censor called his petty changes, notably the omission of Jokanaan's head carried on a silver charger. At the actual performance as Sir Thomas related in his autobiography *A Mingled Chime* (1944) the singers at Covent Garden slipped back into the original text and nobody noticed anything objectionable, least of all the Lord Chamberlain who congratulated him on the way in which he had met all the Censor's demands.[22]

The mention of Beardsley's drawings and Strauss's opera are not irrelevant to criticism of *Salome*, for it is a play which drew on many cultural elements and forces. The subject was popular among the *fin-de-siècle* writers and artists, especially among the so-called decadents to whom Wilde wished desperately to belong, for his ambition was to be accepted as a man of letters of European fame which meant, in his view, to be accepted as an equal by the major French writers of his day. Deliberately or otherwise, his *Salome* crowns a long period of European interest in the legends of Herod, Herodias and Salome. Mario Praz has pointed out that most literary versions of the biblical legend owe their inspiration to Heinrich Heine's poem 'Atta Troll' (1841), in which Herodias is enamoured of John the Baptist and is overwhelmed at his execution—which she does not originate—and grasps his severed head in frenzied sorrow. But Wilde was more likely to have been acquainted with French treatments of the story. There was almost certainly the inspiration of the seductive Carthaginian priestess in Flaubert's *Salammbô* (1862), and of his *Tentation de Saint Antoine* (1874). The poet Mallarmé, so greatly admired by Wilde, also fell a victim to this French passion for the erotically oriental and began his dramatic poem *Hérodiade* in 1864, worked on it until 1869 when commonsense and his fastidious sense of the correct took over, and he relinquished the work although it circulated in manuscript until its publication in 1898. Théodore de Banville, a

79

lesser poet of the time, dedicated to Herodias one of the sonnets in his sequence *Les Princesses* (1874). Thirteen years later Jules Laforgue wrote in his *Moralités Légendaires* of a modern Salome whose lips bore a corrosive poison. Even in Germany there was interest in the subject and in Wagner's *Parsifal* (1882) we are told by the magician Klingsor that his creature, the penitent-temptress Kundry, was in a former life the princess Herodias—between whom and Salome there is much confusion in early legends. The theme of the original seductress (of a vaguely biblical nature) was also taken up by Massenet in his operas *Thais* (1894), based on the novel by Anatole France published in 1889, and *Hérodiade* (1889) of an even earlier date.

It may be that the inspiration which was immediate, pervasive and enduring was that of Gustave Moreau, the symbolist painter, who from 1876 exhibited a number of works, religious, mystic and erotic, of Salome dancing or gazing in wonder at the decapitated body or severed head of the Baptist floating in space. Behind Moreau's vision of the young princess may have been the sonnet by Baudelaire in his *Les Fleurs du Mal* ('Spleen et Idéal, XXVII) which begins:

> Avec ses vêtements ondoyants et nacrés,
> Méme quand elle marche on croirait qu'elle danse.

Moreau's *Salomé dansant*, exhibited at the Salon in 1876, was to inspire a much-quoted description in J. K. Huysman's novel *À Rebours* (1884), well-known to Wilde, when the hero, Des Esseintes, sees Salome not as the dancing girl of the New Testament story, but as

> in some way, the symbolic deity of indestructable lust, the Goddess of immortal Hystera, the accursed Beauty exalted above all other beauties ... the monstrous Beast ...

The fact is that Wilde actually created the characters of his play, rolling several historical Herods into one and using the biblical narrative as the slenderest of bases for his plot—as Beardsley indicated by placing the *Histories* of Josephus among the reference works on Wilde's desk. Salome and Herodias are almost original creations—previous writers having shown Herodias as enamoured of the Baptist with Salome taking a minor part in the action. The point to bear in mind, however, is the wise comment of Mario Praz in *The Romantic Agony* (reprint, 1966):

> The Salomes of Flaubert, of Moreau, Laforgue and Mallarmé are known only to students of literature and connoisseurs, but the *Salome* of the genial comedian Wilde is known to all the world. (337).

As for the extraordinary style in which the play is written it may have had its origin, as has already been suggested, in Wilde's limited command of French as a theatrical language. It may also have been influenced by the repetitive incantations adopted by Maurice Maeterlinck, then considered the most serious and important dramatist in Europe, in his drama *La Princesse Maleine* (1889) and *Les Sept Princesses* (1891). Critics spoke of this style as 'childish prattle', a phrase that has elements of descriptive truth but which reveals an inability to comprehend how effective such language can be when employed in the theatre at the hands of a master: and, after all, the illogicality of men and women of all stations of life speaking in blank verse has never been questioned in the drama of the past.

Whether or not *Salome* is an as yet unacknowledged masterpiece—and the claim is justified—there can be no denying that it has many remarkable features, several of them extraordinary for their day, such as the contrast of sounds (and of action, as has already been instanced) which is so distinctive a feature of the play. The whispered, dreamy and yet urgent dialogues between Narraboth and the page of Herodias alternate with the coarse, loud mockery of the soldiers, the Cappadocian and the Nubian. Salome's hysterical entreaties contrast with the fiery but stern tirades of Jokanaan. Two critics of the time commented on the musical aspects of the drama. In the short-lived journal which he founded at Oxford, *The Spirit Lamp*, Lord Alfred Douglas wrote:

> One thing strikes one very forcibly in the treatment, the musical form of it. Again and again it seems to one that in reading one is *listening*; listening, not to the author, not to the direct unfolding of a plot, but to the tones of different instruments, suggesting, suggesting always indirectly, till one feels that by shutting one's eyes one can best catch the suggestion.
>
> (4 May 1893, iv, 1, 21–27)

In the review *Black and White,* William Archer made much the same kind of argument:

> There is at least as much musical as pictorial quality in *Salome.* It is by methods borrowed from music that Mr. Wilde, without sacrificing its suppleness, imparts to his prose the firm texture, so to speak, of verse. (4)

It is a matter of theatrical history that *Salome* with the music of Richard Strauss has proved itself a major work in the repertoire of twentieth-century opera. Strauss had been struck by the novel plot and by Wilde's stagecraft, but actually inspired by the words. Critics have suggested that *Salome* is basically an opera libretto which is an erroneous view since it is a major work in its own right possessing a verbal quality which is akin to music but not of it. The play may be said to embody the statement of the writer and teacher who so deeply influenced Wilde at Oxford, Walter Pater, that all art tends to the condition of music.

There is an extraordinary use of what might be called *leit motiv* throughout. The soldiers and their companions drink wine, and discuss the Tetrarch, local gods, Jokanaan, the first husband of Herodias, and the huge negro executioner, whereas Narraboth and the page talk entirely of the moon which for the page is like a dead woman and for Narraboth like a princess dressed in white. When Salome enters, conscious of the Tetrarch's lecherous stare, she looks at the moon and finds it virginal. Herod stares at the moon which he declares to be a woman, drunken and naked, reeling through the clouds in search of lovers. Jokanaan prophesies that the moon will turn red as blood, which, indeed, it later appears to do. These references to the moon throughout the drama are transmuted and transformed as in Wagnerian music-drama by the people into whose mouths the sentiments are put. For not only do the attitudes towards the moon reveal the characters of the speakers but they serve to move on the drama, increasing the tension and supplying feverish hints as to the outcome. Arthur Ransome writes in his *Oscar Wilde: A Critical Study* (1912) of the cumulative weight of these short contradictory sentences,

> that fall like continual drops of water on a stone, never argue, are never loud enough to be quarrelsome, and sometimes amuse

themselves by reflecting, as if in a box of mirrors, a single object in a hundred ways (161).

From the opening of the play to the execution of Salome at the end one feels a deliberate ritualistic element. Wilde brilliantly balances this element, generally linguistic in nature, with startling realism of action, the one acting against the other in shaping the drama. When the action is ritualistic it is surpassingly effective, as when the arm of the negro executioner rises from the cistern supporting on a charger of silver the head of Jokanaan: here the gesture, almost priestlike, has, despite its horror, a strange perverse beauty. Silences have their parts to play in this balancing of dramatic antagonisms. So, too, do repetitions. Usually Wilde begins by using fairly short sentences until he comes to the pleading entreaties of Herod when the sentences become long and comparatively involved—not, however, with any loss of theatrical intelligibility. And words, in this play, are of the greatest significance because they are the drama, the characters most frequently expressing themselves in words rather than in action: indeed, much of the structure and movement of the play arises from the fact that the speech, as Ransome argues, 'maps out by avoidance what is really said' (op. cit., 144) and the conflicts do not express themselves in action but in being unmoved by action. Derived as the verbal effects may be from Maeterlinck, Wilde puts the 'brief melodious phrases, the chiming repetitions, the fugal effects beloved by the Belgian poet' to superlative effect, although Maeterlinck's plays are notorious for their tepid rigidity rather than for the frenzied lust which lurks in Wilde's play.[23] A striking illustration of this point occurs in the last pages when Herod announces that he is happy: 'Tonight I am happy, I am exceeding happy. Never have I been so happy.' In the background we hear the soldiers murmuring, 'The Tetrarch has a sombre look. Has he not a sombre look? Yes, he has a sombre look.'

On the other hand, Wilde gives his characters speeches which might be described as heavily embroidered, so replete are they with adjectives and unfamiliar words. The most famous is the one in which Herod implores Salome to dance for him and offers her his rarest treasures:

. . . I have jewels hidden in this place—jewels that thy mother even has never seen; jewels that are marvellous to look at. I have a collar of pearls, set in four rows. They are like unto moons chained with rays of silver. They are even as half a hundred moons caught in a golden net. On the ivory breast of a queen they have rested. Thou shalt be as fair as a queen when thou wearest them. I have amethysts of two kinds: one that is black like wine, and one that is red like wine that one has coloured with water. I have topazes yellow as are the eyes of tigers, and topazes that are pink as the eyes of a wood-pigeon, and green topazes that are as the eyes of cats. I have opals that burn always, with a flame that is cold as ice, opals that make sad men's minds, and are afraid of the shadows. I have onyxes like the eyeballs of a dead woman. I have moonstones that change when the moon changes, and are wan when they see the sun. I have sapphires big like eggs, and as blue as blue flowers. The sea wanders within them, and the moon comes never to trouble the blue of their waves. I have chrysolites and beryls, and chrysoprases and rubies; I have sardonyx and hyacinth stones, and stones of chalcedony, and I will give them all unto thee, all, and other things will I add to them. The King of the Indies has but even now sent me four fans fashioned from the feathers of parrots, and the King of Numidia a garment of ostrich feathers. I have a crystal, into which it is not lawful for a woman to look, nor may young men behold it until they have been beaten with rods. In a coffer of nacre I have three wonderful turquoises. He who wears them on his forehead can imagine things which are not, and he who carries them in his hand can turn the fruitful woman into a woman that is barren. These are great treasures. They are treasures above all price. But this is not all. In an ebony coffer I have two cups of amber that are like apples of pure gold. If an enemy pour poison into these cups they become like apples of silver. In a coffer incrusted with amber I have sandals incrusted with glass. I have mantles that have been brought from the land of the Seres, and bracelets decked about with carbuncles and with jade that come from the city of Euphrates. What desirest thou more than this, Salome? . . .

This is exactly the kind of oriental junk with which Sarah Bernhardt loved to adorn herself for the benefit of painters and photographers, at the same time reclining alongside a panther or two; and it is the sort of thing which Wilde's friend, the French novelist Pierre Loti, might have picked up in the bazaars of Istanbul or

Cairo. It is also—which is the exact point that Wilde is making—
the kind of treasure which a superstitious and sadistic paranoiac
like Herod would have collected in his palace. Wilde must surely
have intended the contrast (in this play of contrasts) between the
scintillating effect of the long list of precious and rare stones
and other riches, and the tawdry nature of the absurd talismans
which Herod has gathered about him—and the efficacy of which
he seems never to have tested. It has been suggested that Wilde
nearly always keeps apart his two styles of writing—the one gor-
geous, jewelled and poetic, the other cynical, paradoxical and
witty: it is impossible not to believe that Wilde did not have his
tongue in his cheek when he wrote a speech such as this and that
he was not here combining his two styles for an ironic purpose.
And that purpose is surely to present Herod not as an heroic figure,
but as a petty tyrant every bit as mad and as cruel as his step-
daughter and wife.

In this play Wilde by-passed the trap which awaits most writers
who seek to emulate Shakespeare or continue what is called 'the
poetic tradition of English drama'—and into which he had himself fallen with *The Duchess of Padua*. The trap is simply to believe
that the language of the Elizabethans can be revived as can the
vocabulary and style of the blank verse which was their favourite
dramatic medium; by attempting to do so modern writers can only
produce dramas which are anachronistic and still-born. Wilde
turned his back on blank verse and created a style, a prose style,
which is poetic, musical even, and which is a perfect vehicle for the
action, a new kind of dramatic language which drew for its
strength on another source of linguistic inspiration in English, on
another tradition entirely divorced from that of Shakespearian
blank verse, the revised version of the Bible. That is not to say he
slavishly imitated the Bible, for his originality becomes clear when
the speeches of Jokanaan, for example, are compared with those of
the other characters: the prophet speaks in a rhetorical style which
draws heavily on the Old Testament—his words to Salome have
been described as biblical insult—while the soldiers and royal characters talk in a manner which is basically close to everyday speech
although supported, as it were, by the Song of Solomon and the
Psalms of David. In every case the language is refined and purified
to create the maximum dramatic effect by the simplest of verbal

means. And the pauses, the silences and the repetitions which Wilde introduced and exploited have become the basic technical weapons of the modern theatre, particularly in the plays of Pinter and Beckett. No other play of the nineteenth century, it can be safely argued, is so revolutionary in style and technique.

Wilde did not neglect the visual side of *Salome*. The proposals made in connection with its production by Sarah Bernhardt have already been mentioned but the play carries within it a basic contrast of colour by which Wilde must have intended to symbolise the major conflict. The colours are red and white, the colours of blood and of innocence. When Herod first enters he slips on the blood of the young Syrian who has killed himself for love of Salome: it is an evil omen, says Herod. And from then onwards the colour becomes of increasing significance as even the moon turns red. On the other hand, Salome's feet are like little white doves and the moon is initially virginal and white. The costumes of the characters are also intended to produce a varied and exotic effect since Wilde carefully specifies the origin of the various types on the stage. There is contrast of sounds, of voices, and of physical groups: at times the stage is almost empty, at other times it is a mass of writhing and gesticulating figures. The appearance of Jokanaan's bloody head, on a silver charger, supported by the bare arm of the negro executioner, one of the few incidents from the play actually illustrated by Beardsley, is a masterstroke of visual drama. But even this horrifying moment is to be surpassed. As Salome kisses the severed head, Herod flees into his palace and then in a spasm of jealousy and remorse and tyrannical but calculated paranoia orders his soldiers, 'Kill that woman!' whereupon we should see a wall of gleaming shields close in on the oblivious and demented girl and crush her to death. No more horrifying stroke of stagecraft is to be seen in the dramatic theatre—a fitting end to this drama of lust, seething hatred, malevolence, superstition, and obsessive violence.

In the few descriptions of *Salome* that are to be found there is no mention of one of its most vital characteristics, the element of wit which pervades the play from first to last. Wilde himself used to parody lines from the play; but was less happy when his friends did so. Yet the reader (or audience) can never escape the uncomfortable sensation that the author is actually parodying the action, the words, the characters, the whole *ensemble* of the drama. This suspicion of parody, however faint, produces an intentional distancing, a deliberate alienation, which far from allowing us to dismiss the drama serves to increase the total effect of decadence. It is surely this very quality to which Mario Praz is referring when he writes that *Salome*

> reduces the voluptuous orient of Flaubert's *Tentation* to the level of a nursery tale. It is childish but it is also humoristic, with a humour which one can with difficulty believe to be unintentional, so much does Wilde's play resemble a parody of the whole of the material used by the Decadents, and of the stammering mannerism of Maeterlinck's dramas and, as a parody, *Salomé* comes very near to being a masterpiece.
>
> *(op. cit.,* 332)

Seen in this light, Herod's long speech offering his treasures to Salome, followed as it is by the brevity and unexpectedness of his 'Kill that woman' is a form of wit, grotesque, depraved and black —and yet wit. The structure of the play tends to this end: while it is an accepted matter of fact that most dramas contain a hero and a heroine and a villain, *Salome* has three villains and a hero-saint, all of whom are parodied by Wilde, the good no less than the bad.

To some extent the unusual characterisation of *Salome* represents a partial solution to a dramatic problem which had troubled Wilde in *Vera* and *The Duchess of Padua* and which he never quite resolved. The irony inherent in his nature, his irrepressible wit, his sense of fun, his keen feel for social injustice, always threaten to disrupt the plots of his dramas especially when he incarnates himself as a Prince Paul or a Duke of Padua. The comments of these characters, and their cynical wit which is too pointed and overbearing for the lesser needs of the action, represent an anarchic element within the dramatist himself which he had to suppress or integrate within the plot before he could produce a successful play. In *Salome* he simplifies the problem by a bold experiment: all his major characters comment on their action either in words or by their deeds. Ultimately none of them believe in anything except their own unrestricted wills: they are, like Wilde himself, anarchic, giving nothing to the laws of man or god and certainly not to the needs of others. Wilde joined together several historical Herods and Tetrarchs to make the Herod of his drama : the savage hatred between Herod and Herodias is not to be found in other works on the subject. The name 'Salome' is not to be found in the Gospels and the actual story is merely a brief anecdote in the 14th chapter of the Gospel of St. Matthew and the 6th chapter of St. John, although the story of Salome (or, in some accounts, Herodias) dancing before the Tetrarch Herod and demanding as her reward the head of John the Baptist on a charger is widespread and belongs to any writer who cares to use it. Wilde not only made Salome the central character of her drama but supplied the intense motivation which other writers who used the legend failed to supply, for in no other version does Salome profess her love for Jokanaan only to meet with fanatic abuse. Her demand for his head (aesthetically set on a silver charger) is as much a comment on her nature as is Herod's command for her to be put to death a comment on his: both are capable of acting in a totally unexpected (and anarchic) manner. Her death is a dreadful parody of Isolda's dying into love at the end of Wagner's opera of *Tristan and Isolda*. She does not, in Wilde's play, lust for Jokanaan's living body; she wants to transform him into a love-object, set on the silver charger, much as a butterfly collector impales his catches on pins before sealing them in glass show-cases. For Salome is the incarnate spirit of the aesthetic woman; remote, desirable, a rapacious *belle dame sans merci* from whom no man is safe (and her character probably reveals much about Wilde's wavering sexual tendencies at this period in his life), but, at the same time, a creature which can be destroyed as easily as it is made. He even removes her from the realm of logic, of rationality, from words which might be used to criticise, to evaluate her actions, to call her to account, for it is not by words that she seduces Herod but by the mute appeal of her body as she dances and when she is finally destroyed it is beneath the silent and relentless impetus of the shields of her stepfather's soldiers.

Salome represents a major achievement in Wilde's career as a dramatist. It was a failure in the theatre of his day; he never saw it performed. After his death it was to be recognised in Europe, especially in Germany, as a masterpiece. He had tried writing plays for actresses, for the *monstres sacrés* of his day and had failed. This was natural, for he was familiar neither with their audiences nor their companies nor, at base, with the actresses for whom he had chosen to write. More than this, he had not come to terms with the British theatre at the end of the nineteenth century, a period of great artistic and commercial vitality. He was to adapt himself to these requirements and to win his greatest popular successes; but the literary and artistic originality of *Salome* was never to be surpassed by him in the remaining years of his career as a dramatist. The last word may be left with Arthur Ransome, an early and perceptive admirer of this play:

> . . . when the play is done, when we return to it in our waking dreams, we return to that elevation only given by the beautiful, undisturbed by the vividness, the clearness with which we realise the motive of passion playing its part in that deeper motive of doom, that fills the room in which we read, or the theatre in which we listen, with the beating of the wings of the angel of death.
>
> (*op. cit.*, 165)

NOTES

1. The custom of writing works in French for translation into English seems a peculiarly Hibernian one, to judge by the practice of another Irish writer of domestic comedies, Samuel Beckett.
2. French poet and writer. He founded the review *La Conque* to which Hérédia, Leconte de Lisle, Maeterlinck, Verlaine, Mallarmé, Gide, Moréas and Swinburne contributed.
3. Stuart Fitzrandolph Merrill (1863–1915): American poet who lived in Paris and wrote in French. Wilde first met him in 1890 in London. Merrill and his wife were staunch friends of Wilde. Adolphe Retté (1863–1910): French symbolist poet.
4. It is interesting to compare the play with Ionesco's *Bald Prima-Donna* in which text-book phrases and exercises are used to express an overwhelming sense of tedium.
5. Paul Duval, pseudonym Jean Lorrain (1856–1906): French symbolist poet and writer.
6. The Palace Theatre had been opened by Richard D'Oyly Carte for the presentation of 'English Grand Opera', a commodity that was in such short supply that a full season never materialised. The theatre was too

large for domestic drama, but its size, newness, and attractiveness, made it a suitable *lieu* for Bernhardt's grandiose productions.

7. Artist and writer. He designed many stage costumes but was to score his greatest success with his children's play *Pinkie and the Fairies* produced by Beerbohm Tree in 1908.

8. Artist, writer, book and stage designer. He and his friend Charles Hazlewood Shannon designed and decorated many of Wilde's books.

9. Playwright and novelist whose works on rural life were especially popular in the 1920s.

10. Artist and writer; the son of a Bradford wool-merchant, he studied at the Slade and later in Paris. He wrote on Wilde and other friends in the first volume of his *Men and Memories* (1931).

11. Charles Brookfield (1860–1912): English actor. James H. Glover (1861–1931): Irish musician and writer. Charles Hawtrey (1858–1923): English actor of light comedy and manager. Brookfield and Hawtrey have been accused of collecting evidence against Wilde on behalf of the Marquis of Queensberry, in this way securing the downfall of the man who had generously obtained them parts in his plays.

12. English actor-manager. Half-brother of the cartoonist and writer Max Beerbohm.

13. When Piggot died in 1895 Shaw wrote a savage obituary in the Saturday *Review*, reprinted in *Our Theatres in the Nineties*, (1954) Vol. I, 48–55.

14. Archer (1856–1924) was a Scots author, critic, and translator of Ibsen's plays.

15. Aurélien-Marie Lugné-Poe (1869–1940): French actor-manager. Lugné-Poe produced himself as Herod and Lina Munte as Salome.

16. Eleanora Duse (1861–1924): great Italian actress of distinction, frequently compared with Bernhardt. Wilde did not care for her style of acting.

17. It was reported in the early summer of 1973 that entertainments committees of two Northern seaside resorts, Lytham St. Anne's and Llandudno, had refused to allow performances of *Salome* on the grounds of its indecency.

18. Beardsley was an artist and writer, associated with the *Yellow Book* (1894) and the *Savoy* (1896).

19. Schwob was a French symbolist writer to whom Wilde dedicated his poem 'The Sphinx'.

20. Art-critic and literary journalist of Canadian descent.

21. In the inscribed copy: Sterling Library, University of London; quoted in Stanley Weintraub, *Beardsley, A Biography* (1967), 56.

22. Other works of a religious or semi-religious nature were also banned. Rostand's *La Samaritaine* (1897) in which Bernhardt had one of her greatest successes as Photine, the woman of Samaria converted by the teaching of Jesus, and which she revived each Easter was never allowed in England. Bernhardt's great rival, Eleanora Duse, fared no better

with her production of D'Annunzio's *La Città Morta* (1903) which was refused a licence. Nor would the censor permit the production of Maeterlinck's *Monna Vanna* in 1902.

23. Wilde may have begun *Salome* before he had either read or heard of Maeterlinck's dramas. For a valuable account of the forces which may have been operating in Wilde's mind at the time of writing the play see: Richard Ellmann, 'Overtures to *Salome*', *Oscar Wilde: Twentieth Century Views* (1969), 73–91.

4

Lady Windermere's Fan

Biographers of Oscar Wilde frequently mention with incredulous awe the large sums of money he was earning at the time of his downfall in 1895 but only four years earlier he was living in straitened circumstances, hard-pressed for cash, with a wife and two children to support. In 1891 it was imperative for him to get money from somewhere. Knowing full well that large amounts were to be made in the commercial theatre, then at the heights of its prosperity, Wilde set about making his fortune there, turning his back on the art theatre, the literary theatre, and temporarily abandoning thoughts of literary prestige in Europe and America. This surely explains why, as writers have stressed, Wilde was unaccountably unwilling to write a play for the actor-manager George Alexander, for while laziness, as always with him, may have played some part, it was more that it cost him some pains to give up his ambitions in the realm of serious drama. Confident that Wilde could write an effective commercial play and equally confident that it would confirm the quality of his management, at a time when he had just leased the St. James's Theatre, and badly needed a financial success, Alexander showered letter after letter on the reluctant playwright. A normally cautious man, Alexander also made an advance of £100 in royalties to the playwright whose only answer was that he was in what he called 'the invention period'. Whenever they met, Wilde chattered away with charm and wit and equanimity but never actually delivered the much-desired script. Eventually the following conversation took place:

> When am I going to see that play, Oscar?
> My dear Alec, you may see any play you wish to see. You have only to go to the theatre where it is being performed, and I am sure they will give you admirable seats.

You know perfectly well what play I mean.
How can I know if you keep it secret?
The play you are writing for me.
Oh that! My dear Alec, it isn't written yet, so how can you possibly see it?

(Pearson, 221)

When exactly Wilde decided to settle down to the serious business of writing a play for the London stage and to set his cerebral and imaginative faculties in motion is uncertain. Hesketh Pearson says that he wrestled with his theme during the late summer of 1891 at Windermere in what he improbably describes as a cottage. If Wilde did any wrestling in the Lake District at this time it was not with the play which was probably already being typed out so that in the early autumn he was able to send a preliminary copy (the play was then called A Good Woman) to the American dramatist and theatrical manager Augustin Daly whose company, with Ada Rehan as its star, was performing in London.[1] Wilde was far from scrupulous in his dealings with managers, a sensible attitude to adopt in the light of his previous experiences, and his attempt to place the drama with Daly and the suggestion that Ada Rehan should play the leading part of Mrs. Erlynne hardly indicates a firm commitment to Alexander about whose prospects as a theatre manager Wilde was not entirely confident and for whose methods of production he did not care. However, the play was finally handed over to him with the words that it was 'one of those modern drawing-room plays with pink lampshades', which is exactly what it was in most respects.

Alexander was delighted to have the play and still more delighted when on a brief reading he discovered its merits, notably that it appeared, as he thought, sensational without being serious, interesting without being disturbing, and quite, quite witty. He was so pleased that he offered to buy the play outright for £1,000. Wilde knew his man:

Do you really mean to say that you will give me a thousand pounds for it?
I will, certainly.
Then, my dear Alec, I have such complete faith in your excellent judgement that I cannot but refuse your generous offer.

93

He was right to do so. The play netted him seven thousand pounds during its first run.[2] However, as will be seen, relations between Alexander and the playwright were unhappy, not least on the personal plane; and as he had foreseen Wilde was to be troubled by changes suggested by Alexander during rehearsals. During the autumn he was in Paris finishing his *Salome* and had little time to spare for revisions of the new play although he was trying at the same time to interest Coquelin *aîné*, the celebrated actor of the Comédie Française, in a French translation and production.

On 20 February 1892 the new play now called *Lady Windermere's Fan* was produced at the St. James's Theatre, with Alexander as Lord Windermere, Marion Terry as Mrs. Erlynne, R. H. Vincent as Lord Augustus Lorton, Lily Hanbury as Lady Windermere, and Nutcombe Gould as Lord Darlington. It ran to packed houses for five months until 29 July, was taken on tour, and returned to the St. James's on 31 October. The first American production opened in New York almost a year later on 6 February 1893 and despite the customary reservations of the critics a successful run of several months followed.

The first performance in London fell on a Saturday. The theatre was crowded with the most fashionable figures from society and the arts. Wilde contrived to turn the event into a *succès de scandale* as well as of *estime*: well prepared to take a curtain call—he was by now a noted man-about-town if not yet an admired writer—he quickly acceded to the cries of 'author' by leaving his wife in the box they shared and coming on to the stage where he stood smiling and holding a cigarette in his hand—insolently, some critics were to complain. 'Ladies and gentlemen', he began, 'I have enjoyed this evening *immensely*. The actors have given us a *charming* rendering of a *delightful* play, and your appreciation has been most *intelligent*. I congratulate you on the *great* success of your performance, which persuades me that you think *almost* as highly of the play as I do myself.' (A member of the theatre staff took down Wilde's speech in shorthand; this is probably the only accurate account of any of his utterances.) When stopped in the street and asked how the play was doing he replied, 'Capitally', adding in a serious tone, 'I am told that royalty is turned away nightly.' On yet another occasion he was heard to ponder aloud the proposition that there might possibly be wittier men than the author of *Lady Windermere's Fan* but if there were he had yet to meet one. Audiences recognised that it was without doubt the wittiest and best constructed play seen on the English stage for over a hundred years; and that it earned Wilde an honourable place in the distinguished line of comic dramatists, all of them Irish, descending in time from Congreve, Sheridan, and Goldsmith.

Full employment in the theatre of the time was ensured by this play. There are four acts and three changes of scenery although Wilde respected the Aristotelean principle of unity of time by making the events take place within twenty-four hours, beginning on a Tuesday afternoon at five o'clock and ending the next day at 1.30 p.m.—a twenty-four hours crowded with incident, as Lady Bracknell might have observed. In addition, there is a cast of sixteen with parts equally distributed between men and women.

The first act introduces several threads which are to become important in the dramatic texture of the play. It is the afternoon of Lady Windermere's twenty-first birthday. She is giving a party that evening to celebrate her coming of age. Flowers have been sent up from the country house at Selby, an idyllic spot which is contrasted as a place of innocent happiness with the sinister sophistication of life in London. Lord Darlington, a close friend, calls, is shown a fan which is a birthday gift from her husband, is given tea, and is chided for paying extravagant compliments the previous evening. Lord Darlington's reply perhaps represents the author's views as well as his own: 'Nowadays we are all of us so hard up, that the only pleasant things to pay *are* compliments. They're the only things we *can* pay.' Lady Windermere emphasises that her mother died when she was young and that she has been brought up by her father's elder sister who taught her the difference between right and wrong and that any form of moral compromise was evil. For a young woman, married only two years, with a child of six months, she displays an excessive amount of rectitude. Lord Darlington mischievously suggests that if in the case of a young married couple the husband was found associating with a woman of doubtful character then the wife might have the right to console herself with another man. Lord Darlington describes himself as a man who can resist everything except temptation; and

95

establishes himself as a wit of the same order as Wilde himself
and the direct literary descendant of Prince Paul Maraloffski and
the Duke of Padua. The tête-à-tête is interrupted by the arrival
of the Duchess of Berwick and her daughter Lady Agatha Carlisle[8]
who is sent to look at photographs of Switzerland—'such a pure
taste'—and then to look at the sunset from the terrace—'such re-
finement of feeling'—while her mother informs Lady Darlington
that her husband is paying frequent visits to Mrs. Erlynne, a
woman with half a dozen pasts, all of which fit, and that he seems
to be giving her money. When her visitors have gone Lady Windermere is drawn to the bureau where her husband's bank book is
kept and finds nothing in the book to suggest that he has been
paying out sums of money. She then finds another book and sees
entries which indicate the payment of money to Mrs. Erlynne.
When her husband enters almost immediately she taxes him with
this evidence but he protests the innocence of his relationship with
this woman who, he says, lost everything years ago and whom he
wishes to help and restore to a position in society. Indeed, he wishes
his wife to invite her to their reception that evening. Lady Windermere refuses and says she will strike Mrs. Erlynne with the fan
given her by her husband if this woman dares to cross their thres-
hold. She sweeps out in a cloud of righteous indignation:

> Lord Windermere (calling after her): Margaret! Margaret! (A
> pause.) My God! What shall I do? I dare not tell her who this
> woman really is. The shame would kill her. (Sinks down in a
> chair and buries his face in his hands.)

In the second act Lady Windermere receives her guests before
they pass into the adjoining ballroom where an orchestra is playing. She toys nervously with her fan. When Mrs. Erlynne does
finally arrive, very beautifully dressed and very dignified in manner,
Lady Windermere is so confused that she drops the fan and bows
coldly to her. The wicked Lord Darlington exploits her distress,
asking her to leave the house with him that night, a suggestion
which she indignantly repudiates. He leaves. After overhearing a
conversation during which Mrs. Erlynne tells Lord Windermere
that she has decided to accept Lord Augustus Lorton's offer of
marriage and wants him to settle two thousand five hundred pounds
a year on her without divulging that he is the donor, Lady Winder-

mere scribbles a note, puts it in an envelope, leaves it on the table, and goes out. Mrs. Erlynne enters and asks for Lady Windermere. Seeing the envelope addressed to Lord Windermere on the table she impulsively opens it, and then sits down with a shudder of fear. There follows a speech and an episode which caused bitterness between Wilde and Alexander:

> *Mrs. Erlynne*: Oh, how terrible! The same words that twenty years ago I wrote to her father! And how bitterly I have been punished for it! No; my punishment, my real punishment is tonight, is now!

When Lord Windermere comes in she tells him that his wife has a headache, has retired to bed, and does not wish to be disturbed. She orders Lord Augustus Lorton to take Lord Windermere down to his club at once and to keep him there for the rest of the night. She then sets off resolutely, leaving behind her a bewildered suitor.

In the third act Lady Windermere has reached Lord Darlington's rooms. Mrs. Erlynne enters with the letter which she proceeds to burn, explaining that there is no romantic attachment between herself and Lord Windermere, that he loves his wife alone and that she must return to him at once. Her pleading is in vain. She begs Lady Windermere to remember the child she is going to abandon whereupon the young woman relents, holds out her hands to her, helplessly, as a child might do, and asks to be taken home. As they are about to leave they hear Lord Darlington and his friends, Lord Windermere among them, arriving in the next room. Mrs. Erlynne pushes Lady Windermere behind one of the curtains and slips into the next room as the men enter. Finding the fan one of them charges Lord Darlington with having a woman in his rooms. Aghast, Lord Windermere recognises the fan as the one he has given his wife, and determines to search the room beginning with the curtained windows. Mrs. Erlynne distracts him by entering and calling his name. She claims she has taken the fan in error from the reception. The men, taken by surprise at the implications of these events, look at each other in surprise, anger, and cynical amusement. Meanwhile, Lady Windermere has managed to slip away unseen.

The fourth act takes place next morning. Lord and Lady Windermere are reconciled but still unhappy in different ways and for different reasons. Lady Windermere believes that Mrs. Erlynne must have revealed the truth about the previous evening in order to protect her own reputation and is bewildered when her husband repudiates Mrs. Erlynne, the woman for whose sake he seemed previously to be risking the wellbeing of their marriage. Lady Windermere now defends her and says she wants her to come to their home. She is about to confess everything when a servant enters with the fan and a written message from Mrs. Erlynne. Asked up, she explains that she is leaving England at once and would appreciate a photograph of Lady Windermere. While his wife is out of the room looking for a suitable one, Lord Windermere berates Mrs. Erlynne. It was only at this point that the first-night audience learned the guilty secret:

> *Lord Windermere*: Rather than my wife should know—that the mother whom she was taught to consider as dead, the mother whom she has mourned as dead, is living—a divorced woman, going about under an assumed name, a bad woman preying upon life, as I know you now to be—rather than that I was ready to supply you with money to pay bill after bill, extravagance after extravagance, to risk what occurred yesterday, the first quarrel I have ever had with my wife. You don't understand what that means to me. How could you? But I tell you that the only bitter words that ever came from those sweet lips of hers were on your account, and I hate to see you next to her. You sully the innocence that is in her. And then I used to think that with all your faults you were frank and honest. You are not.

For a time Mrs. Erlynne is reduced to abjection. She admits that only once in her life—the previous evening—has she known a mother's feelings. She recovers sufficiently to state that she does not see herself as a woman with a grown-up daughter:

> Margaret is twenty-one, and I have never admitted that I am more than twenty-nine, or thirty at the most. Twenty-nine when there are pink shades, thirty when there are not.

She has decided to leave her daughter happy in her illusions of a dead and unstained mother. When Lord Windermere threatens to tell his wife the truth, Mrs. Erlynne says it is she who will decide what is to be revealed if she can bring herself to do so before she leaves the house—if not then she will keep silence for ever. At this point Lady Windermere returns with the photograph. Mrs. Erlynne asks Lord Windermere to go and see if her carriage has come and while he is out of the room she advises her daughter (without revealing their true relationship) never again to yield to temptation. She makes one last request: that she may retain the fan which she has already returned since it carries a name they share—Margaret—and to this Lady Windermere gladly accedes. The carriage and Lord Augustus Lorton arrive. He greets Mrs. Erlynne coldly but is persuaded to escort her to her carriage. She looks for the last time on her daughter and leaves. Moments later Lord Augustus Lorton returns to say that everything has been explained. Both the Windermeres are horror-stricken. But 'everything' only means that Mrs. Erlynne has explained that she had decided the previous evening to accept him, had gone to his club in vain, and then gone on to Lord Darlington's rooms to tell him this good news. As a condition of her acceptance of his hand they must live out of England:

> Lord Windermere: Well, you are certainly marrying a very clever woman!
> Lady Windermere (taking her husband's hand): Ah, you're marrying a very good woman!
>
> Curtain

From manuscripts and letters we are able to glean a deal of information about the writing of Lady Windermere's Fan, particularly in relation to alterations which were made during rehearsals. It must always be remembered that although he deliberately gave the impression of careless amateurism and disliked the word 'author' believing it lowered his social status Wilde was a careful and painstaking writer. Autograph drafts of Lady Windermere's Fan were presented to the British Museum by Robert Ross; and the University of Texas holds a corrected typescript. In its final form the play was published in 1893 by Elkin Mathews and John Lane in an ordinary and large paper edition with decorative devices by Charles Shannon, both dedicated by the author 'to the dear Memory of Robert Earl of Lytton in Affection and Admiration'.[4] For Speranza, his mother, he wrote in a large paper copy (now at the University of Texas) the dedication, 'To my dear wonderful mother, with my love, Oscar Wilde '93'. It was his mother incidentally, who was responsible for changing the play's name: she had read in a Sunday newspaper that he was calling his play *A Good Woman* and wrote to him shortly before the opening night that she did not like the title, adding, "It is mawkish. No one cares for a good woman. *A Noble Woman* would be better.'[5]

Wilde was obliged to make two changes in the construction of the play to suit the requirements of George Alexander who thought, probably correctly, that as an actor and as a manager he knew better than Wilde. In both cases the writer unwillingly acceded. Hesketh Pearson states, somewhat inaccurately:

> Wilde entertained views of his own which conflicted with the actor's, and stuck to them stubbornly. For example, at every rehearsal of Act 2 it was pointed out to him that the curtain should be brought down on something more effective than the usual dramatic outburst. He treated the suggestion with disdain, and Alexander was galled by his 'damned Irish obstinacy'. At length he consented to try a light ending, and rather to his annoyance found that it was a great improvement.
>
> (Pearson, 221–222)

It will be remembered that at the end of the second act after Mrs. Erlynne has read the letter Lady Windermere has left to say she is leaving to live with Lord Darlington she is terrified that her daughter has made the same mistake as she made years ago and rushes off to Lord Darlington's rooms in pursuit of her. Before she does so she commands her suitor Lord Augustus Lorton to keep Lord Windermere engaged at his club—in order, of course, that he should continue to think his wife has gone to bed early— and in the meantime she will follow Lady Windermere and persuade her to return home. Wilde wanted to end the act with Mrs. Erlynne rushing off, distracted and horror-stricken, but Alexander wanted a rather more comic curtain; so eventually a compromise was reached and Lord Augustus, absolutely at a loss as to what is happening, is left alone on the stage and comments:

> *Lord Augustus*: Well, really I might be her husband already. Positively I might. (*Follows her in a bewildered manner.*)

One cannot help feeling that Wilde's instinct for the dramatic situation, exaggerated as was that situation, was not entirely at fault. In a letter to Alexander written towards the end of the rehearsals he makes a convincing defence—and, incidentally, reveals how basically reasonable he was despite his occasional fits of petulance:

> With regard to the speech of Mrs. Erlynne at the end of Act II, you must remember that until Wednesday night Mrs. Erlynne rushed off the stage leaving Lord Augustus in a state of bewilderment. Such are the stage directions in the play. When the alteration in the business was made I don't know, but I should have been informed at once. It came on me with the shock of a surprise. I don't in any degree object to it. It is a different effect, that is all. It does not alter the psychological lines of the play . . . To reproach me on Wednesday for not having written a speech for a situation on which I was not consulted and of which I was quite unaware was, of course, a wrong thing to do. With regard to the new speech written yesterday, personally I think it adequate. I want Mrs. Erlynne's whole scene with Lord Augustus to be a "tornado" scene, and the thing to go as quickly as possible. However, I will think over the speech, and talk it over with Miss Terry.

(Letters, 308)

The other change required by Alexander was crucial. For the first few performances of *Lady Windermere's Fan* the secret of Mrs. Erlynne's relationship with Lady Windermere was not revealed until the last act although Alexander had wanted the audience to be informed much earlier. He tried to impress this on Wilde over and over again but without gaining his point. Wilde also had a point:

> An equally good play could be written in which the audience would know beforehand who Mrs. Erlynne really was, but it would require completely different dialogue, and completely different situations. I have built my house on a certain foundation, and this foundation cannot be altered. I can say no more.

(Letters, 309)

His stagecraft was not deficient and he had calculated the effect he wished to obtain:

> . . . about the disclosure of the secret of the play in the second act, had I intended to let out the secret, which is the element of

suspense and curiosity, a quality so essentially dramatic, I would have written the play on entirely different lines. I would have made Mrs. Erlynne a vulgar horrid woman and struck out the incident of the fan. The audience must not know till the last act that the woman Lady Windermere proposed to strike with her fan was her own mother. The note would be too harsh, too horrible. When they learn it, it is after Lady Windermere has left her husband's house, to seek the protection of another man, and their interest is concentrated on Mrs. Erlynne, to whom dramatically speaking belongs the last act. Also it would destroy the dramatic wonder excited by the incident of Mrs. Erlynne taking the letter and opening it and sacrificing herself in the third act. If they knew Mrs. Erlynne was the mother, there would be no surprise in her sacrifice—it would be expected. But in my play the sacrifice is dramatic and unexpected.

(Letters, 308)

Eventually, probably by the fourth or fifth night, Wilde rewrote Mrs. Erlynne's speech towards the end of the second act so that the audience became aware of the true relationship. In reply to a suggestion in the St. James's Gazette that he had made the changes because of press criticism he wrote to the editor on 26 February:

> . . . all my friends, without exception, were of opinion that the psychological interest of the second act would be greatly increased by the disclosure of the actual relationship existing between Lady Windermere and Mrs. Erlynne—an opinion, I may add, that had previously been strongly held and urged by Mr. Alexander. As to those of us who do not look on a play as a mere question of pantomime and clowning, psychological interest is everything. I determined consequently to make a change in the precise moment of revelation.

(Letters, 313)

Purposely it may be, the disclosure comes so suddenly and unexpectedly at the very end of the act that the audience hardly has time to appreciate the new development. On the printed page the whole episode of Mrs. Erlynne's concern for her daughter's happiness and reputation, and the self-discovery of her maternal feelings in the process may seem over-dramatic, but in the reality of performance it affords the actress a fine opportunity to play for the audience's sympathy albeit in a rhetorical fashion. The play is so brilliantly written, so sparkling in style and so full of incident that any weakness of plot—for instance, as to where exactly the disclosure comes—is of little significance. Wilde's concern with psychological truth was a new departure in the theatre: during April 1891 he saw two performances of Ibsen's *Hedda Gabler* which may have intensified his sense of the need for psychological truth in drama. And Wilde was right in one essential respect: he had written a play called *A Good Woman* in which, quite logically, the interest was to be concentrated on Mrs. Erlynne, *a bad woman*. Thus, the tension would be increased by holding audiences in suspense as long as possible even if they actually suspected the relationship from early in the play. The changes he made served to turn it from *A Good Woman* into *Lady Windermere's Fan*, a memorable title but one which does not commit the writer to a moral viewpoint or indicate the central motive of the action, and which leaves the audience free to judge the play without any pre-conditioning. Some writers have mistakenly increased her wickedness. H. Montgomery Hyde, writes in his *Oscar Wilde* (1976): 'the fact that Lady Windermere was Mrs. Erlynne's illegitimate daughter, which has been hinted at in the first act, was disclosed to the audience in the second!' (138). There is no hint in the play that Lady Windermere was illegitimate.

The critics gave the play what is called 'a mixed reception'. Clement Scott writing in the *Daily Telegraph* was too flabbergasted by Wilde's 'insolent effrontery' in smoking on the stage before an audience to say anything worthwhile about the play itself: Scott also happened to be a major defender of censorship in the theatre. 'I will show you and prove to you', he pictured Wilde as saying to himself,

> ... to what an extent bad manners are not only recognised but endorsed in this wholly free and unrestrained age. I will do on the stage of a public theatre what I should not dare do at a mass meeting in the Park. I will uncover my head in the presence of refined women, but I refuse to put down my cigarette.
>
> (*Illustrated London News*, 27 February 1892, c. 278)[6]

William Archer, entirely opposed to Scott, and a powerful intellect in the world of theatrical criticism, admired *Lady Windermere's*

Fan, as did the equally influential literary and dramatic critic, A. B. Walkley who wrote in the *Speaker*:

> Here is a gentleman who devotes brilliant talents, a splendid audacity, an agreeable charlatanry and a hundred-Barnum-power of advertisement, to making a change in old customs and preventing life from being monotonous. He does this in innumerable ways—by his writings, his talk, his person, his clothes, and everything that is his. He has aimed at doing it in his play *Lady Windermere's Fan*, and has been, to my mind, entirely successful.

> (V, 27 February 1892, 257–258)

These sympathetic critics were not blind to what Shaw described (in another context) as Sardoodledum, that is, the tirades, strong situations, striking exits and curtain lines, and manœuvring of the plot associated with such French dramatists as Sardou, Scribe, Augier and others. Wilde had no cause to worry: the play was a runaway success. In any case, he had no great opinion of theatrical criticism other than his own. On being told that theatrical critics could be bought, he reflected a moment, and said, 'Perhaps you are right. But judging from their appearance, most of them cannot be at all expensive.' In a letter to the editor of the *St. James's Gazette* he reflected on the culture, courtesy and critical acumen displayed in such papers as the *Referee*, *Reynolds*, and the *Sunday Sun*, with reference to his play, and commented:

> When criticism becomes in England a real art, as it should be, and when none but those of artistic instinct and artistic cultivation is allowed to write about works of art, artists will no doubt read criticisms with a certain amount of intellectual interest. As things are at present, the criticisms of ordinary newspapers are of no interest whatsoever ...

> (*Letters*, 313)

Such words were to cost Wilde dear in the bitter days of his trial and the years of self-imposed exile. Perhaps the words which pleased him best were his mother's: 'You have had a splendid success and I am very happy and very proud of you.'

As we have seen Wilde faced difficulties with his plot during rehearsals and performances and made several changes which seem of less consequence to us today. The plot has been criticised on grounds of improbability which if accepted would mean that quite a number of plays of this and of all periods are equally at fault. Medical evidence would dash to pieces a good deal of the plot of Ibsen's *Ghosts*: and it is difficult to understand why if Gertrude can describe Ophelia's death by drowning in such detail she did nothing about pulling the poor girl out of the water. It is all too easy to confuse the improbabilities of the everyday world with dramatic improbabilities; they are not the same thing at all, the one calling for suspicion or investigation, the other for an agreeable suspension of disbelief. The principal difficulty of *Lady Windermere's Fan* does not rest in Mrs. Erlynne's sacrifice but in that the audience has to accept that Lady Windermere has been reared in total ignorance of her mother—that she has never seen a painting or a photograph of her—which is probable in the kind of family to which she belongs—and that she has never inquired about her grave—an absolute improbability in an age given to weddings and wakes, feasts, fasts, and funerals. Whether or not Mrs. Erlynne's admission to twenty-nine if the lamps have pink shades and thirty when they have not is ever believed by the men around her, she must be attractive enough for Lady Windermere (and others) to believe she is a rival for her husband's love and for Lord Augustus to fall in love with her. The situation is not dissimilar from that between Jocasta and Oedipus in *Oedipus Rex* or Hamlet and Gertrude, where the age differences between mothers and sons must appear slight, however improbably so. Mrs. Erlynne must also have changed so much that she is not recognised by any of her former acquaintances or friends in London society. Her new name must be socially acceptable and yet not arouse suspicion as to her past. The drama proceeds at such a pace—here Wilde's skill is used most effectively—that the audience has little time for criticism or fault-finding. The central situation of a daughter behaving badly, with some justification it must be admitted, towards a woman whom she believes is her husband's mistress but who is her mother, and that same mother's sacrifice of her newly-gained respectability to save her daughter's reputation is sufficiently vital to command an audience's whole attention.

The characterisation is generally adequate. If the parts of Lord and Lady Windermere read thinly on the printed page, they are surprisingly effective on the stage, provided the players are well cast in terms of youth, graceful movement, breeding, handsome looks and good speech. The parts act themselves with the minimum of artifice. Presumably Wilde wrote the part of Lord Windermere with Alexander in mind and exactly fitted it to his good looks, fair hair, and honest-jawed but rather dull expression. Lily Hanbury was a demurely sweet English beauty—exactly Lady Windermere. Or so the character would appear on a superficial reading of the play. But Lady Windermere and Mrs. Erlynne are not only (falsely) opposing antagonists, the white and the black of the drama, but also mother and daughter! No doubt Wilde stressed Lady Windermere's youth in order that he might also make Mrs. Erlynne youthfully attractive; but is not the fact that Lady Windermere at twenty is already a wife and a mother indicative of the same passionate attitude to life and love which led her mother at much the same age to abandon her home, her husband and her child? In brief, if Lady Windermere has a complexion of roses and cream she must also have dimples of steel.

Mrs. Erlynne was played by Marion Terry, sister of the more famous Ellen, both of them great friends of Wilde. He provided a superb part for an actress of a kind that has, unfortunately, more or less vanished from the stage. She must be able to carry her gowns with style; she must bear herself well; she must be able to speak with brilliant and scintillating clarity; she must be seductive, pathetic, young, middle-aged, witty, winning and handsome. In the favourite term of the period, a 'stunner'. She—and all the other characters—must have supreme style. For the success of the drama Mrs. Erlynne must be able to move from brazen defiance to tear-provoking pathos. In the first act she plays at blackmail; in the last at suffering motherhood incarnate, having sacrificed herself without a moment's hesitation on behalf of her erring daughter. When she asks for the photograph she must appeal to every mother in the audience. Despite the facts that she has run away from her home, abandoned her baby daughter, broken her husband's heart, and is blackmailing Lord Windermere—her daughter's husband— the audience's sympathy is always with her. As G. B. Shaw remarked, in Wilde's early plays:

> . . . the chivalry of the eighteenth-century Irishman and the romance of the disciple of Théophile Gautier (Oscar was old-

fashioned in the Irish way, except as a critic of morals) not only gave a certain kindness and gallantry to the serious passages and to the handling of the women, but provided that proximity of emotion without which laughter, however irresistible, is destructive and sinister.

(S. Weintraub, compiler, Shaw, An Autobiography, 1969, 249–250)

In making a grand marriage, admittedly to a rather stupid aristocrat, Mrs. Erlynne retrieves all her earlier losses and is able to walk off the stage with her head held high, as had many another such 'fallen' woman in late Victorian society.[7]

Lord Darlington is the kind of part which Wilde wrote for himself; and could clearly have been prevailed upon to impersonate at the drop of a hat. He might have done so all the more happily since he had small confidence in the abilities of actors to remember or speak his lines: actors were, as he remarked in an interview, 'terribly creative . . . terribly creative'. Lord Darlington is the witty man-about-town *par excellence*, a variation upon the cynical but amusing mouthpiece of his own humorous, cynical outlook on life which he had first created in Prince Paul in *Vera*. In fact, at least one of the Prince's epigrams is repeated in *Lady Windermere's Fan*: 'Experience, the name men give to their mistakes.' From Lord Darlington's lips come some of Wilde's best-known epigrams, such as, 'Nowadays to be intelligible is to be found out,' or a cynic is 'a man who knows the price of everything and the value of nothing'. He is sufficiently charming to be a passing temptation to Lady Windermere although hardly wicked enough to be taken seriously as the villain of the play, for Wilde was clever enough to know he was purveying social comedy and not realistic tragedy. The difficulty with the part is that away from his epigrams and absurdly romantic declarations to Lady Windermere he has no basic character, for the simple reason that he exists only as a potential threat to her virtue. Her motives in going to his rooms are neither erotic nor romantic—at any rate we are not meant to think so—but are the result of an understandable fit of pique. Once she eschews the temptation to run away with him or, rather, is persuaded to repent of her hasty action, and once Mrs. Erlynne has had the chance to show her basic and strong maternal love, there is no longer any reason for Lord Darlington's

107

existence: like Bunbury in *The Importance of Being Earnest* he has to fade out of the play with some loss to its merriment but with considerable gain to its concision and its dramatic strength. Had Wilde made only a little more of him the balance of the play would have been irrevocably upset; it is he who would have proved the real danger to society and not Mrs. Erlynne whose morality is as conventional as that of her daughter and son-in-law.

The minor characters such as the Duchess of Berwick—mother of Lady Agatha Carlisle and sister to Lord Augustus Lorton— Lady Plymdale, and Lady Stutfield serve much the same purpose as Mrs. Candour and her friends in *The School for Scandal* by chattering and gossiping with sharp and malicious delight and passing on useful information in the process. Wilde borrowed this device from Sheridan and used it again in his next two plays. These minor characters are decorative, amusing and pad out the body of the play. They are also a headache to the producer who is trying to economise in terms of wardrobe and actresses.

In fact, a number of difficulties which could not have been foreseen by Wilde face the modern producer who wishes to present *Lady Windermere's Fan.* To begin with, apart from the fact that there are few actors and actresses who possess sufficient style either of speech or carriage to play the leading rôles let alone the minor ones, even those of servants, few theatrical wardrobes carry enough well-fitting costumes for the cast. The costumes, as always in Wilde and, it may be said, in all plays of this period, must represent hours of work on the part of dress-makers, tailors, fitters and sewing-machines. It was not a period which believed in concealing the pains which were taken in the construction of women's clothes —the idea was to exploit lace, silk, ribbons, tucks, pleats, embroidery, beads, brilliants, foliage, flowers and plumage, every fabric and device known to the dressmakers and milliners. Such clothes were designed to proclaim that their wearers were above everyday toil. Light colours were especially popular since they needed more frequent laundering—which more ordinary mortals could not afford. The sexual, physical attractiveness on which Wilde's women characters depend for their power is expressed in their clothes, the armour in which they fought their campaigns on the battlefields of social adventure, social prestige and social success, rather than in their actual persons. Facial make-up was not encouraged yet modern actresses will insist upon wearing inordinate amounts of make-up when no respectable woman of the period used anything more than a little rice powder, did not surround the eyes with inches of glittering blues and greens and certainly never painted the lips a brilliant red. When Marion Terry (who took the part of Mrs. Erlynne in the play) once dipped her hair in henna and wore a little make-up she aroused the shocked disapproval of society; and there were ladies who declared in public that they would certainly not attend performances in which a made-up woman took part. Those society women (and others) who were fortunate enough to have been born with fine complexions and strikingly florid colouring were able to pass as beauties and outshine the pallid faces around them. Photographs of Lily Langtry, the great beauty of the time who attended the first performances of Wilde's plays, show a bold-featured woman who appears to be quite lacking in any beauty of face or figure: they fail to show the brilliance of her colouring and the glow of her skin which entranced the men around her, lovers of blood-stock all, and which gave her such an advantage over other women for whom there could be no respectable recourse to artificial means to beauty. Wilde adored Lily Langtry; and there can be no doubt that it was such a character as hers which went into the creation of Mrs. Erlynne and other adventuresses. The settings, too, must be superlatively luxurious. Two shabby settees and a few miscellaneous pieces borrowed from a well-disposed antique shop are entirely inadequate to suggest the splendour of a London house such as that of Lady Windermere—richness and extravagance of satin, silk, velvet, bronze and gilt which can be characterised as *Louis* without the specification of *quatorze*, *quinze* or *seize*. Three settings and four changes of scenery are a burden to any producer; and, unfortunately, beyond the capacity of most amateur groups; and the fact that Wilde's comedies are successfully presented in very inadequate settings is a tribute to the strength and vitality of his writing.

Wilde was shrewd enough to realise that he was living in a period of some elegance in terms of clothing and interior decoration, and cleverly varies the action between different times of the day and night which affords the actors and actresses several opportunities for change of costume. The audience, in evening dress and tiaras and, sometimes, with buttonholes of green carnations, must have recognised with approbation on the stage a mirror to their own opulence. Wilde had also seen the end of the old rough-and-ready stock companies and the vast improvements in stage speech and deportment brought about by the Bancrofts and other players which meant he could find a cast which could impersonate the lords and ladies of London society and carry off the character-isations with complete success. The audience was treated to a theatrical picture of society, an exaggerated but true one. Mrs. Erlynne, like other of Wilde's female characters, had her counter-part among the mistresses and companions of the Prince of Wales; and she was by no means an improbable figure in that age of outrageous cocottes and ladies of pleasure. We find confirmation of all this in an account written by Florence Alexander of her husband's theatre:

> First nights at the St. James's Theatre were great events . . . I sat in my box sick with anxiety, and between the acts I used to put on an apron and go behind the scenes to place all the little things on the stage myself until the men got used to it. I arranged the flowers; in those days we had so much detail, and I loved to make things look real. I ordered the gowns to suit the decorations of the scene so that nothing clashed or was ugly . . . Our first nights . . . were like brilliant parties. Everybody knew everybody, everybody put on their best clothes, everybody wished us success. When I entered my box on a first night I always had a reception from the gallery. I do not know why, but I did. They were always so pleased and so kind to me.
>
> (A. E. W. Mason, *Sir George Alexander and the St. James's Theatre*, 1935, 227–228)

This sense of *rapport* between management and all sections of the audience also extended to the actors and to the playwrights. Wilde who had a very real feeling for beauty both on and off the stage shared in this sensation of being at a brilliant party. At the first night of *Lady Windermere's Fan* he sat in a box with his wife Constance who wore, we are told, a 'pale brocaded gown made after the fashion of Charles I's time, with its tabbed bodice, slashed sleeves, and garniture of old lace and pearls'. Thus, in a real sense, Wilde was able to play the parts of host and master-magician at the same time in a gathering which delighted his taste for social life. His appearance on the stage, at the end of the play, with a cigarette in his hand, was perfectly appropriate: he was in his own drawing-room, a situation only possible in the reformed and renovated theatres of the 1890s.

This sympathetic atmosphere is particularly significant in relation to Wilde's remark that *Lady Windermere's Fan* was one of those modern drawing-room plays with pink lampshades, for it was the first of three plays set in contemporary society and linked not only by pink lampshades but by a common theme, that of a guilty secret. However preposterous the plot, however insidiously critical of society and morals, Wilde knew there would not be a demur from the audience if the visual ensemble was sufficiently charming and the wit sufficiently amusing. His play belonged, superficially at least, to the type served up at the St. James's under the management of George Alexander, purporting to deal with life as lived by the upper classes. Peers of the realm, in Wilde's plays particularly, were as common on the stage as they were in the stalls; but few of those in the stalls spoke as wittily as those on the stage, although some, as Wilde was to learn to his cost, behaved even more outrageously. The middle-class members of his audiences fondly cherished as scandalous truth what was essentially social mockery on Wilde's part: it was not so much the basic situation of a society woman who has run away from her husband and child that interested him as the way in which she is able to manipulate society for her own ends. *Lady Windermere's Fan* is not serious drama but social comedy seasoned with sensational elements which, it must be admitted, are not without theatrical and emotional impact. It has been said of the audiences at the St. James's that:

> Alexander catered for their dramatic taste much as the Savoy Hotel catered for their gastronomic taste: the dramas, like dishes, were pleasant to the palate and left nothing disagreeable in the mind or the mouth. In a typical St. James's play the humorous characters were delightfully playful, the serious characters charmingly sentimental, and the plot savoured of scandal without being objectionably truthful. Adultery was invariably touched on and inevitably touched up . . .
>
> (Hesketh Pearson, *The Last Actor-Managers*, 1950, 23)

This atmosphere, carefully nurtured by the Alexanders, made possible the success of *Lady Windermere's Fan* as a comedy, just as the sophistication of the audience enabled its author to move into the sphere of social satire where his strong feeling for social justice went comparatively unremarked. The fact is, by customary standards, the leading characters are detestable. Mrs. Erlynne knows, as did many a woman in the audience, that the wages of sin are not death but a comfortable private income and an aristocratic husband and a desirable place in the highest society—abroad. She does not hesitate to stoop to blackmail; and she freely admits that she has never experienced maternal feelings. Lady Windermere, too, has few scruples about leaving her husband and placing herself under the protection of Lord Darlington. That gentleman has no scruples about doing anything to his own advantage, least of all in making advances to his friend's young wife. Lord Windermere deceives his wife as to Mrs. Erlynne's identity and himself as to her character. Almost everyone in the play is an unrepentant casuist. Critics who castigated Wilde for writing a sentimental melodrama akin to *East Lynne* with its notorious lines of 'Dead! Dead! And never called me Mother!,' forget that he makes it absolutely clear that for the greater part of twenty years Mrs. Erlynne has never even wished anyone to call her mother! He slyly introduces us to a world, a mirror world, to the aristocratic section of society that flocked to the St. James's (and other popular and fashionable theatres), in which self-interest and self-protection direct every action. That he has some compassion for Mrs. Erlynne is obvious; and, indeed, that kind and tolerant humour for which he was famous embraces all his characters without, however, sugaring their weaknesses. This is why *Lady Windermere's Fan* must be considered with respect: it is an indirect indictment of a heartless and mercenary society of which the fan, an extravagant and useless toy, is so accurate a symbol.

The year after *Lady Windermere's Fan*, in 1893, Alexander scored another tremendous hit with *The Second Mrs. Tanqueray* by Arthur Pinero, in which Mrs. Patrick Campbell began her tempestuous career. Pinero's drama, despite its faults, has always been considered the first notably serious British play of the nineteenth century, but there can be no doubt that the way to the writing of this social drama, then thought utterly daring but now seen as utterly boring, had been eased by the success of Wilde's play which gained Alexander a permanent position as a manager in the London theatrical world and ensured the prosperity of his theatre. More important, it gave Wilde the confidence and incentive to persevere in playwriting, an activity in which he had hitherto had little encouragement. A. B. Walkley wrote of *Lady Windermere's Fan* that, 'The man or woman who does not chuckle with delight at the good things which abound . . . should consult a physician at once' (*Speaker*, 27 February 1892, V. 257–258), not appreciating that Wilde was himself acting as a physician, giving an indirect but serious diagnosis of the society around him. Those pink shades which were so advantageous to Mrs. Erlynne's complexion cast too soft a glow over Wilde's first social comedy, obscuring its satirical ironies but bringing into delightful prominence its undeniable wit and humour.

NOTES

1. Daly was to have a theatre named after him in London and New York. His leading lady was Ada Rehan (1860–1916): American actress of Irish descent.

2. Alexander bought the acting rights of *Lady Windermere's Fan* and *The Importance of Being Earnest* at the time of Wilde's bankruptcy. He passed on sums of money to Wilde and bequeathed the rights to Wilde's eldest son.

3. Wilde had a taste for naming his characters after places where he stayed when writing a particular play.

4. Edward Robert Bulwer, first Earl of Lytton (1831–1891): formerly Viceroy of India, latterly British Ambassador in Paris where he entertained Wilde. He wrote verse using the *nom-de-plume* of 'Owen Meredith'.

5. Thomas Hardy's novel *Tess of the Durbervilles*, subtitled *A Pure Woman*, had created a sensation when it appeared in book form in 1891. Did it influence Wilde's choice of title, one wonders?

6. Scott was a drama critic of the *Daily Telegraph* from 1872–1898, and a translator and adapter of plays.

7. In his *The Devil's Disciple* (1897), correctly described as a melodrama, Shaw wrote something of a variation on *Lady Windermere's Fan* except that in his play a man whom the society of the time condemns as wicked sacrifices himself somewhat illogically on behalf of a good woman.

5

A Woman of No Importance

Towards the end of the summer of 1892, flushed with the success of *Lady Windermere's Fan* and outraged by the banning of *Salome*, Wilde went to Germany, to the spa town of Homburg, near Frankfurt, and took the health cure. When he returned to England, presumably reduced in pocket if not in weight, he rented a house at Felbrigg, near Cromer, Norfolk, where he began on a new play. Early in September he said in a letter that two acts had been typed out, the third was almost finished, and that he expected to have the whole play ready within ten days or a fortnight. Wilde was always over-optimistic about the time it took him to write his plays and as late as February of the following year he was writing to Lady Mount-Temple, who was distantly related to his wife and whose house at Babbacombe Cliff, Torquay, he had rented, that he was working on his new play in her boudoir, a room called Wonderland (*Letters*, 328). He had told her in the previous November when he was negotiating to take the house that he wanted to write *two* plays, one of them in blank verse.

It should be noted that Wilde was not writing for George Alexander as might have been expected after the triumph of *Lady Windermere's Fan* but for Herbert Beerbohm Tree who had installed himself as an actor-manager at the Haymarket, one of London's most important and historic theatres, and who presented throughout his career a wide variety of plays such as Alexander would never have risked. Alexander was the matinée idol of the day, basically stodgy and ultra-cautious, in whom a love of the theatre and a desire for prosperous respectability were placidly and successfully combined, whereas Tree, like Irving, adored the actor's life, delighted in make-up, wigs and costumes, and in indulging his love of grotesque character parts of which the most popular was that of Svengali in an adaptation of Du Maurier's *Trilby*, although he also essayed Shylock, Falstaff, and other Shakespearian characters. He seemed unlikely to fit into a social comedy such as Wilde had in mind but producing himself in the straight part of Lord Illingworth in the new play Wilde wrote for him, eventually to be called *A Woman of No Importance*, he scored a triumph for which he was ever after grateful to the dramatist whose name he refused to vilify in the dark days that lay ahead. Wilde seemed to have faint hopes that he would eventually present *Salome*, taking the part of Herod. It was to Tree, incidentally, that Shaw turned for the first production of his *Pygmalion* in which Tree was brilliant as Professor Higgins as was the somewhat mature Mrs. Patrick Campbell as Eliza Doolittle.

Later in September, before he had quite finished the play, Wilde went up to Glasgow where Tree was on tour with his Haymarket company and read him those parts he had completed. Tree was delighted with what he considered 'a great modern play'. In response to his congratulations to the author on his management of the plot he received the reply:

> Plots are tedious. Anyone can invent them. Life is full of them. Indeed one has to elbow one's way through them as they crowd across one's path. I took the plot of this play from *The Family Herald*, which took it—wisely, I feel—from my novel *The Picture of Dorian Gray*. People love a wicked aristocrat who seduces a virtuous maiden, and they love a virtuous maiden for being seduced by a wicked aristocrat. I have given them what they like, so that they may learn to appreciate what I like to give them.
>
> (Hesketh Pearson, *Beerbohm Tree*, 1956, 67)

Rehearsals in March and April of the following year did not proceed much more smoothly than they had done with Alexander. In a not unusual burst of extravagance Wilde moved from the expensive Savoy Hotel to the even more expensive Hotel Albermarle from where he kept an eye on the play which Tree produced, as he said, 'with interference' from the author.

A Woman of No Importance opened at the Haymarket Theatre on 19 April 1893 with a distinguished cast which included Beerbohm Tree, Fred Terry (brother of Marion who had played Mrs. Erlynne at the St. James's), Julia Neilson, Mrs. Tree, and Rose

Leclercq. In the cast was Mrs. Beere, who had vainly undertaken to present *Vera* in 1881. Apart from a break of three nights it ran until 16 August.[1] The run was actually shorter by some weeks than that of *Lady Windermere's Fan* but Wilde had no cause for complaint—he said he used to draw one hundred and seventy to nearly two hundred pounds a week during its run in London. He also drew money from the provincial tours and amateur performances. On 11 December 1893 the play opened in New York where the audiences gave it a somewhat tepid reception, possibly because they thought it was poking fun at Americans abroad.

On the first night Wilde did not repeat the behaviour for which he had been censured by Clement Scott on the first night of *Lady Windermere's Fan*. In reply to the many calls of 'Author' he stood up in his box and announced in the gravest of tones, 'Ladies and gentlemen, I regret to inform you that Mr. Oscar Wilde is not in the house.' It was a suitable ending to an evening of sparkling epigrams and sentimental sardoodling which was not, however, without a degree of serious intent.

Beerbohm Tree's management was famed for the lavishness of its stage settings and costumes; and Wilde, naturally, took full advantage of the fact. *A Woman of No Importance* has four acts each with a different setting, although the action of the play takes place within twenty-four hours either at or near Hunstanton Chase, an English country house. This means that the cast of fifteen has ample excuse for frequent changes of costume.

On the terrace of Hunstanton Chase, we find Lady Caroline Pontefract quizzing Hester Worsley, an orphaned American heiress who is visiting England for the first time. Rather like some of Henry James's heroines, she is critical of English institutions which she considers out-dated and of English society which she considers unfair to women. She is full of admiration for a young man called Gerald Arbuthnot:

> *Lady Caroline*: Ah, yes! the young man who has a post in a bank. Lady Hunstanton is most kind in asking him here, and Lord Illingworth seems to have taken quite a fancy to him.

Gerald enters almost directly with the news that Lord Illingworth has just offered to make him his secretary which represents his first step into political and social life. Lady Hunstanton writes to ask his mother, a retiring woman who is devoted to good works, to come to dinner that evening. Later Mrs. Arbuthnot replies to the effect that she will not come to dinner but that she will come up from the village in the evening.[2] Lord Illingworth happens to see this letter lying on the table and says that the handwriting reminds him of a woman he used to know years ago, a woman of no importance.

The next act is set in the drawing-room of Hunstanton Chase where the lamps, presumably in pink shades, have been lit. Coffee is served and the ladies talk among themselves—or, rather, fire off epigram after epigram about marriage and the troubles of the married state. Hester sets out to be a wet blanket, preaching several unwelcome sermons on the wicked inequalities in English social and economic life and, more to the central issue of the play, on punishment for sin; and by sin she means sexual irregularity. However, she has a stance of her own on this subject:

> You are unjust to women in England. And till you count what is a shame in a woman to be an infamy in a man, you will always be unjust, and Right, that pillar of fire, and Wrong, that pillar of cloud, will be made dim to your eyes, or be not seen at all, or if seen, not regarded.

Meanwhile Mrs. Arbuthnot has entered from the terrace. When the men join the ladies she recognises Lord Illingworth as her former lover. Alone, they have a conversation in which we learn that Lord Illingworth, then a younger son with no expectation of succeeding to the title and family wealth, had had an affair with Mrs. Arbuthnot (a name which she has adopted arbitrarily) when he was twenty as the result of which she bore him a son. His father had told him it was his duty to marry the young woman but his mother tried in vain to buy her off with six hundred pounds a year and advised him not to marry her. Mrs. Arbuthnot disappeared with the child. Lord Illingworth, who has already taken Gerald under his protection and who is unmarried, now feels an even stronger duty towards him. Mrs. Arbuthnot pleads to be allowed to keep Gerald by her side. The act ends with Lord Illingworth presuming he has won the struggle, slight as it has been, to keep Gerald as his own.

Act III does not advance the action a great deal. Mrs. Arbuthnot begs Gerald to stay with her. Without revealing that she is the woman concerned she tells Gerald how Lord Illingworth, then George Harford, made love to a young woman, persuaded her to leave her father's house, and when she became pregnant refused to marry her. Her son's answer is appropriate:

> My dear mother, it all sounds very tragic, of course. But I dare say the girl was just as much to blame as Lord Illingworth was. —After all, would a really nice girl, a girl with any nice feelings at all, go away from her home with a man to whom she was not married, and live with him as his wife? No nice girl would.

He refuses to believe any ill of Lord Illingworth. At that very moment, however, Hester rushes in to seek Gerald's protection, saying that she has been horribly insulted by Lord Illingworth. Quite beside himself with rage Gerald threatens to kill him whereupon we get the *denoument* for which we have had to sit through the whole act:

> *Mrs. Arbuthnot*: Gerald!
> *Gerald*: Let me go, I say!
> *Mrs. Arbuthnot*: Stop, Gerald, stop! He is your own father!
> *Gerald clutches his mother's hands and looks into her face. She sinks slowly on the ground in shame. Hester steals towards the door. Lord Illingworth frowns and bites his lips. After a while Gerald raises his mother up, puts his arm round her, and leads her from the room.*
>
> *Curtain*

In the last act, set in Mrs. Arbuthnot's comfortable home at Wrockley, we find Mrs. Allonby and Lady Hunstanton who comment:

> Most women in London, nowadays, seem to furnish their rooms with nothing but orchids, foreigners, and French novels. But here we have the room of a sweet saint. Fresh natural flowers, books that don't shock one, pictures that one can look at without blushing.

They have come to see if Mrs. Arbuthnot has recovered from her sudden indisposition of the previous evening and when they find she has a headache they regretfully depart. Gerald writes a letter which he proffers for his mother's approval: it is a sensible document in which he orders Lord Illingworth to marry his mother and put right the wrong he did her so many years ago. To his astonishment his mother says she will not marry his father. She remarks on the cruelty of women to each other, singling out the words of Hester:

> A woman who has sinned should be punished . . . She shouldn't be allowed to come into the society of good men and women . . . And the man should be punished in the same way . . . it is right that the sins of the parents should be visited on the children. It is a just law. It is God's law.

Ironically, in this play of ironies, Hester overhears this conversation from the terrace and eventually runs in to support Mrs. Arbuthnot in her resolve not to marry Lord Illingworth, for that, she says, 'would be real dishonour, the first you have ever known . . .'. It emerges that she loves and has always loved Gerald: in fact, they love each other. They agree to marry. Mrs. Arbuthnot is to be with them: 'For a little then: and if you let me, near you always.' The two young people go into the garden. Lord Illingworth is shown in. He finds he has lost his son to the Puritan, as he has nicknamed Hester, and addresses Mrs. Arbuthnot rather distastefully:

> . . . Must be strolling back to Hunstanton. Don't suppose I shall see you there again. I'm sorry, I am, really. It's been an amusing experience to have met you amongst people of one's own rank, and treated quite seriously too, one's mistress and one's—
> *Mrs. Arbuthnot snatches up glove and strikes Lord Illingworth across the face with it. Lord Illingworth starts. He is dazed by the insult of his punishment. Then he controls himself and goes to window and looks out at his son. Sighs and leaves the room.*

Gerald and Hester then enter. Gerald finds Lord Illingworth's glove lying on the floor, and picks it up:

> *Gerald*: Hallo, mother, whose glove is this? You have had a visitor. Who was it?
> *Mrs. Arbuthnot (turning round)*: Oh! no one. No one in particular. A man of no importance.
>
> *Curtain*

A *Woman of No Importance* was published by John Lane in October 1893, and dedicated to Gladys Countess de Grey. The original typescript with Wilde's autograph changes and corrections is in the Clark Library at the University of California, Los Angeles.

Another typescript and autograph drafts are in the British Museum where they were presented by Robert Ross. They bear out what we already know from Wilde's correspondence; that he completed the first two acts with comparative ease and then found difficulty in completing the rest of the play.

Speranza wrote to her son of his plays that they all wanted 'more plot and more human feeling, so in your next strengthen the plot and heighten the human interest'. He said himself:

> I wrote the first act of A Woman of No Importance in answer to the critics who said that Lady Windermere's Fan lacked action. In the act in question there is absolutely no action at all. It is a perfect act.
>
> (Pearson, 237)

Nevertheless, the plot is weak, and is, in fact, practically non-existent. The incident, such as it is, of a woman meeting a former lover and being involved in a tug-of-war over their child does not offer sufficient action or opportunity for development to fill four acts. At Tree's request Wilde cut out a diatribe against puritanism and substituted a number of epigrams. On another occasion when a scene proved unsatisfactory during rehearsals Wilde retired into a corner of the theatre and shortly emerged with a completely new scene bristling with wit and epigram. Despite this apparently casual attitude to dramatic construction, we know from the notes Wilde scribbled on his copy of the play during rehearsals that he was keenly aware of the effects which he wished to obtain and also of the dangers of over-emphasis which would reveal the play's weaknesses, hence such words of admonition as, 'false exit', 'far too theatrical', and 'Tree not emphasise this'.

An initial weakness of construction is that whilst there are reversals of attitude there are none of any importance in the plot; and such as there are of both varieties are concentrated in the last act. Normally, a dramatist seeks to introduce a new character, frequently with a different attitude or viewpoint, later in the play so as to provide variety and contrast or a fresh development in the plot. Hester, the American heiress, would have been the ideal candidate for this task but Wilde's anxiety to make his social attitudes clear from the beginning of the play obliges him to introduce her early in Act I, and thus he denies sufficient interest to the

succeeding acts. Yet another weakness arises from the scene at
the end of Act I when Lord Illingworth and Mrs. Allonby chat
together about the attitudes of men and women towards each
other: the conversation turns into a duel of wits from which Mrs.
Allonby emerges undefeated—which, perhaps, implies that Mrs.
Arbuthnot's yielding to Lord Illingworth years ago was as much
the consequences of her own emotional nature and her own desires
as the importunities of Lord Illingworth.[3] But it is apparent to
the audience that Lord Illingworth and Mrs. Allonby are actually
flirting with each other and that there is a clear degree of sexual
attraction between them: since Wilde does not exploit this further
he has only managed to set the audience off on a false trail which
is not directly relevant to the action although it does emphasise
the moral ambivalences of a society which is prompt to condemn
a 'sinner' like Mrs. Arbuthnot whilst ignoring equally culpable behaviour provided it is discreetly conducted and not brought out
into the open. Hunstanton Chase is to be seen as representative of
superficial moral respectability whilst Mrs. Arbuthnot's home at
Wrockley seems quite sure in its attitudes despite its being a house
of 'sin'.

William Archer singled out for special praise the scene between
Lord Illingworth and Mrs. Arbuthnot at the end of the second
act, describing it as:

> the most virile and intelligent—yes, I mean it, the most intelli-
> gent piece of English dramatic writing of our day. It is the work
> of a man who knows life, and knows how to transfer it to the
> stage. There is no situation-hunting, no posturing. The interest
> of the scene arises from emotion based upon thought, thought
> thrilled with emotion. There is nothing conventional in it, nothing
> insincere. In a word, it is a piece of adult art.
>
> (The World, 26 April 1893)

This is the scene, it will be remembered. where Lord Illingworth
claims his son as his own and promises a brilliant future for him,
away from his mother. Mrs. Arbuthnot, on the other hand, pleads
to be allowed to keep Gerald by her side.

> Leave me the little vineyard of my life; leave me the walled-in
> garden and the well of water; the ewe-lamb God sent me, in pity or
> in wrath, oh! leave me that. George, don't take Gerald from me.

121

Archer possibly knew more about Ibsen and the advanced theatre than any other man in England so that it is extraordinary to find him praising this scene in such sincere and glowing terms. Did it remind him, one wonders, of the scenes between Mrs. Alving and her son Oswald in *Ghosts*, another dramatic display of maternal egotism? The answer may be that whereas we are repelled by the language of the scene between Mrs. Arbuthnot and Lord Illingworth—repelled by the gross sentimentality of the language, that is—Archer saw in it a defence of a woman's right to lead her own life in a conscientious disregard of conventional morality. This was an attitude he admired in Ibsen's heroines. In fact, the greater part of Archer's review of *A Woman of No Importance* is given to an attack on the character of Mrs. Arbuthnot as drawn by Wilde and suggesting that she should have been given a share of 'sad, half-smiling dignity and wisdom'. In other words, the nearer Mrs. Arbuthnot's character resembles that of an Ibsen heroine the more successful Wilde has been:

> the play would have been a much more accomplished work of art if the character of Mrs. Arbuthnot had been pitched in another key. And I am not without a suspicion that Mr. Wilde's original design was something like what I have indicated.
>
> *(ibid.)*

Despite Archer's advocacy the scene, necessary to the action as it is, does represent a weakness to contemporary audiences who find its sentimental language difficult to swallow. Another major weakness, this time of actual construction, is Hester's hysterical complaint of having been insulted by Lord Illingworth, for this comes as too violent a shock, Wilde never having prepared us previously for this aspect of his character: the audience knows that it is merely a device to prepare them for the reversals of the finale.

The characterisation of the play is no more than adequate. Tree had good reason to be pleased with the part of Lord Illingworth, for he dominates the action whenever he appears. Into his mouth Wilde puts his most scintillating epigrams:

> I adore simple pleasures. They are the last refuge of the complex. But, if you wish, let us stay here. Yes, let us stay here. The Book of Life begins with a man and a woman in a garden.
> *Mrs. Allonby*: It ends with Revelations.

The other characters, as in this example, merely serve as foils. Neither Mrs. Arbuthnot nor Gerald has much life—at any rate, in relation to the plot, although their attitudes deserve study. In fact, the weakness of the characterisation obliges us to reflect on what exactly Wilde was up to. He seems to give us the stock characters of nineteenth-century drama, the basic characters of the problem play, but without in the least convincing us that they have any life apart from the immediate scenes in which they appear. Mrs. Arbuthnot may be classified as the Wronged Woman and the Loving Mother and as Virtue Redeemed. She is even the Fallen Woman. Hester is True Love Overcoming. Lord Illingworth is The Wicked Lord or The Victor Vanquished. And so on.

The real problem of the play is not that set out on the stage but one inherent in Wilde the man as distinct from Wilde the dramatist: on one side he is writing a social comedy geared to the tastes and requirements of the commercial theatre of the 1890s, and on the other he is attempting to explore a number of social and moral wrongs although, unfortunately, not in any specific way.[4] In earlier plays he used the cynical comments of characters such as Prince Paul or Lord Darlington to criticise social situations or to mock the pretensions of other characters within the drama. Lord Illingworth is such a type of commentator, an acute social observer with no illusions as to his class or society in general:

> *Kelvil*: Still our East End is a very important problem.
> *Lord Illingworth*: Quite so. It is the problem of slavery. And we try to solve it by amusing the slaves.

> Discontent is the first step in the progress of a man or a nation.

> We in the House of Lords are never in touch with public opinion. That makes us a civilised body.

Logically his views should be opposed in some measure by Mrs. Allonby, or by a woman of impeccably virtuous social character such as Lady Hunstanton, or even by Mrs. Arbuthnot, although her values are, as we shall see, extremely individual and as anarchic as his. Instead Wilde resorts to the literary device of introducing an alien, a foreigner, an intruder upon the social scenes, the *mores* of which are unfamiliar to her, who is thus able to comment on actions, themes and topics with freedom and propriety. The character he uses for this purpose is Hester, the American heiress, the Puritan, who not only carries the burden of being the attractive female juvenile lead (to use the theatrical jargon of the period) but also of rather stridently asserting values which are, in part, those of Wilde:

> *Lady Caroline*: In my young days, Miss Worsley, one never met anyone in society who worked for their living. It was not considered the thing.
> *Hester*: In America those are the people we respect most.

> *Lady Hunstanton*: . . . I am afraid in England we have too many artificial social barriers. We don't see as much as we should of the middle and lower classes.
> *Hester*: In America we have no lower classes.

> *Hester*: You rich people in England, you don't know how you are living. How could you know? You shut out from your society the gentle and the good. You laugh at the simple and the pure. Living as you all do, on others and by them, you sneer at self-sacrifice, and if you throw bread to the poor, it is merely to keep them quiet for a season . . .

These quotations indicate some of the themes which Wilde wished to exploit without sufficient opportunity in the dramatic form he had chosen, although that is not to say his inadequate explorations—what, in fact, he leaves unsaid—do not add a dimension, a strength, a width of argument, to his plays and elevate them above the commercial successes of the theatres of the nineties with their simple, tract-like plots. Despite its Sardoodledum, its use of apparently stock characters and situation, this play has a unity of tone and incident: there is no deliberate contravention of the theatrical conventions of the *genre*, and on one plane it passes as an ordinary social comedy, a comedy more distinguished than most by wit, intellectual calibre, and dramatic instinct, Hester's seriousness threatens this unity: at any moment she may descend to cloud the sunlit lawns of Hunstanton. The reader will recognise in her a resurrected Vera in whose person truth speaks. But Wilde was too astute, too avid for popular success and financial gain, to allow her *persona* complete freedom, and at the end of the play elevates her on the one hand into a *dea ex machina* and on the other transforms her into the redeeming heroine. Yet it is possible to be too exacting in standards of judging this and other of Wilde's social comedies. Vincent O'Sullivan makes two observations which are worth considering in relation to the observations which have been made about Wilde's management of the plot and the inconsistencies of his characterisation:

> His best personages are conducted through the drama with such vigour and logic that it becomes impossible to escape their particular truth. This is especially true of A Woman of No Importance.
>
> (op. cit., 205)

O'Sullivan's second point reminds us of the popular base of these plays, their rootedness in everyday feeling, emotion and thought:

> . . . it was just the coarse strain in Wilde which made the popularity of his plays. He was sentimental in his dramas—not aristocratic.
>
> (ibid., 204)

And here O'Sullivan is using the term 'sentimental' in its best sense, as relating to emotions shared by each and every member of his audience. Thus it is that Wilde succeeds in the play he sets out to write—but considerably at the expense of certain truths about which he felt deeply as we know from his letters and other writings, notably The Soul of Man Under Socialism.

Yet it cannot be denied that the ostensible theme of A Woman of No Importance, the sexual exploitation of women, attracted Wilde's sympathies and that the dialogue in the play is also closely related to it. In fact, comparatively little else is discussed in the four acts. Instead of A Good Woman, Wilde might primarily have thought of calling his play Theme and Variations; instead, as we know, he called it A Woman of No Importance although it demonstrates that it is the man who is of no importance either as mate, husband or father. It is not generally realised that it is the women and not Lord Illingworth whose standards are least morally sensitive:

> Lady Caroline: . . . I regard Henry as infamous, absolutely infamous. But I am bound to state . . . that he is excellent company, and he has one of the best cooks in London, and after a good dinner one can forgive anybody, even one's own relations.

125

> *Mrs. Allonby*: . . . How can a woman be expected to be happy with a man who insists on treating her as if she was a perfectly rational being?

Lord Illingworth is absolutely aware of the strength of women:

> . . . to the philosopher . . . women represent the triumph of matter over mind.

> The history of women is the history of the worst form of tyranny the world has ever known. The tyranny of the weak over the strong. It is the only tyranny that lasts.

> . . . Women are a fascinatingly wilful sex. Every woman is a rebel, and usually in wild revolt against herself.

Here it is opportune to examine the character of the Woman of No Importance herself. She is not a conventional female character, resolutely defying stock characterisation as a Fallen Woman. Wilde tells us through the action that she is a woman of some social standing, that she is accepted as a friend by the aristocratic ladies at Hunstanton Chase, and that she is by no means poverty stricken. When we are shown her home in the last act it proves to be comfortably and tastefully furnished with a maid in waiting. Mrs. Arbuthnot is never described as badly dressed. We know that Lord Illingworth's mother had offered to settle the considerable sum of six hundred pounds a year on her but she had refused and disappeared with the child. In the second act Mrs. Arbuthnot states her initial argument: she has cared for her son for twenty years and she is not prepared to surrender him to the man who has ruined her life by refusing to marry her even after she had given birth to the child:

> My son—to go away with the man who spoiled my youth, who ruined my life, who has tainted every moment of my days? You don't realise what my past has been in suffering and in shame.

To this Lord Illingworth retorts that Gerald's future is more important than her past, that the real question is what is best for their son's future, and that her position is illogical in that she would allow her son to go away with a complete stranger but not with his own father. However, her argument is soon to be challenged by Gerald, her own son, who, on learning the truth about his parentage, reacts by writing to his father to tell him that he must marry his mother and make an honest woman of her in the eyes of the world. Here, then, is the opportunity for which Mrs. Arbuthnot has waited twenty years, the opportunity to marry the father of her child, the man she once loved. In sending this ultimatum to his father Gerald is concerned solely with his mother:

> . . . It is to take away the bitterness out of your life, to take away the shadow that lies on your name, that this marriage must take place. It is a duty that you owe, not merely to yourself, but to all other women—yes; to all the other women in the world, lest he betray more.

Appeals to general benevolence have no attraction for Mrs. Arbuthnot who replies:

> I owe nothing to other women. There is not one of them to help me. There is not one woman in the world to whom I could go for pity, if I would take it, or for sympathy, if I could win it. Women are hard on each other.

Lord Illingworth has warned her that, 'Children begin by loving their parents. After a time they judge them. Rarely, if ever, do they forgive them,' an aphorism she is later to use against him. But for a time the words ring true as when Gerald is shocked by his mother's refusal to take up a conventional social stance by marrying his father:

> Mrs. Arbuthnot: What son has even asked of his mother to make so hideous a sacrifice? None.
> Gerald: What mother has ever refused to marry the father of her own child? None.
> Mrs. Arbuthnot: Let me be the first, then. I will not do it.

Mrs. Arbuthnot has, in fact, been driven to search deep into her own inner feelings: she now realises, for the first time, that her life has been based on a falsehood, that far from wishing the father of her child to marry her she wishes nothing of the sort. Her purpose in life is motherhood unadulterated by marriage. In this sense Mrs. Arbuthnot's stance is close to that taken up by the suffragettes and, still further on in the century, by the various women's liberation movements: for the late eighteen-nineties her views were revolutionary although obscured by the use of such words as 'sin', 'the mire of my life', 'sinner', and so on. It can be argued that Mrs. Arbuthnot, like Mrs. Erlynne (and Mrs. Cheveley in *An Ideal Husband* and all the women in *The Importance of Being Earnest*), is a study in female obsessiveness, all of them linked, perhaps, with the outsize personality of his mother Speranza. In Wilde's plays, generally, the men are impotent triflers, the women domineering, powerful, ruthless, self-possessed and absolutely determined in their obsessive desires and loves, whether of money, marriage, social standing, or a son.

Mrs. Arbuthnot explains her position clearly, neither excusing herself nor apologising. She possesses a surprising degree of self-knowledge:

> No, Gerald, no ceremony, Church-hallowed or State-made, shall ever bind me to George Harford. It may be that I am too bound to him already, who, robbing me, yet left me richer, so that in the mire of my life I found the pearl of price, or what I thought would be so . . . You thought I was happier working amongst the poor. That was my mission, you imagined. It was not, but where else was I to go? The sick do not ask if the hand that smooths their pillow is pure, nor the dying care if the lips that touch their brow have known the kiss of sin. It was you I thought of all the time; I gave to them the love you did not need; lavished on them a love that was not theirs . . . And you thought I spent too much of my time in going to Church, and in Church duties. But where else could I turn? God's house is the only house where sinners are made welcome, and you were always in my heart, Gerald, too much in my heart. For, though day after day, at morn or evensong, I have knelt in God's house, I have never repented of my sin. How could I repent of my sin when you, my love, were its fruit. Even now that you are bitter to me I cannot repent. I do not. You are more to me than innocence. I would rather be your mother—oh! much rather!—than have been always pure.

A little later she is to tell Lord Illingworth:

> We women live by our emotions and for them. By our passions, and for them, if you will. I have two passions, Lord Illingworth: my love of him, my hate of you. You cannot kill those. They feed each other.

Her final act of rejection, her last act of revenge, is not her striking him across the face with her glove but her dismissal of him as 'A man of no importance', an example of Wilde's words going far beyond the rather melodramatic gesture. The ultimate secret is not that Mrs. Arbuthnot is an unmarried mother but that she loves her sin—to use the language of conventional morality—and would not have it otherwise: she cannot and will not repent. Nor will she satisfy the calls of society and religion by marrying the father of her child, even when that marriage would bring her the additional bonuses of social recognition and a title.[5] Both Lord Illingworth and Gerald see marriage as the only possible solution for the problems created by her existence in society as an unmarried mother: she absolutely refuses any such solution. The whole course of the drama has tended to this end—to self-recognition, the recognition of her own needs, attitudes and morality. In this sense she is akin to Mrs. Erlynne who has never wished to be loved as a mother and who has refused to recognise maternal feelings (until the occasion when she goes to the rescue of her daughter); Mrs. Arbuthnot has lived a life of resentment, always conscious of the wrong done her by Lord Illingworth when, as a young man, he refused to marry her, but eventually recognises that she does not want and probably never has wanted to marry him; she has only wanted to be a mother. Atonement does not exist for Lord Illingworth but neither does it exist for Mrs. Arbuthnot, simply because she does not believe in conventional morality. Moreover, like Mrs. Erlynne, she is selfish. Wilde never unmasks her egotism, her greedy determination to keep her son at her side even if it condemns him to a mediocre career in a small bank; and he does not enlarge upon her willing acceptance, through her son, of a place in the heartless and selfish society at Hunstanton Chase, or upon her relentless desire to be near her son once he is married. And it must be said that she has done well by him in leading to his hand an eminently acceptable American heiress!

These considerations are softened rather by Wilde's genial humour which was not much appreciated by contemporary critics, Archer among them—and his translations of Ibsen had not exactly exposed him to an inordinate amount of fun—who thought it was out of place in a serious drama. But with Wilde wit and fun were marks of grace, of a gentle forgiveness and understanding which he generously extended to all his characters. It must also be remembered that the play was written to the commission of Beerbohm Tree, himself a jolly man, full of jokes and humour, who began to sound more and more like Wilde who commented at last, 'Ah! every day dear Herbert becomes *de plus Oscarisé*,—it is a wonderful case of Nature imitating art.' It was perhaps his kindly temperament which inspired the abundant humour of the play; and his grotesqueries may be behind a different aspect of Wilde's comic invention in which he had not hitherto indulged. In Act II we meet The Ven. Archdeacon Daubeny, D.D., about whose wife Lady Hunstanton enquires:

> *Lady Hunstanton*: Ah, I am so sorry Mrs. Daubeny could not come with you tonight. Headache as usual, I suppose.
> *The Archdeacon*: Yes, Lady Hunstanton, a perfect martyr. But she is happiest alone. She is happiest alone.

We learn more and more from the Archdeacon about his wife:

> Her deafness is a great deprivation to her. She can't even hear my sermons now.

> The eyesight is rapidly going. But she's never morbid, never morbid.

> She was very deft with her needle once, quite a Dorcas. But the gout has crippled her fingers a good deal. She has not touched the tambour frame for nine or ten years. But she has many other amusements. She is very much interested in her own health.

> She used to be quite remarkable for her memory, but since her last attack she recalls chiefly the events of her early childhood. But she finds great pleasure in such retrospections, great pleasure.

> . . . Mrs. Daubeny never touches solids now. Lives entirely on jellies. But she is wonderfully cheerful, wonderfully cheerful. She has nothing to complain of.

Nowhere in comedy of the 1890s can be found a similar instance carried through the play of what is in essence a savage indignation at the state to which we must come, the terminal days of the human condition. But this bitter strand escapes in the thickly interwoven comic dialogue, most of it concerned with marriage and relations between man and wife or men and women and therefore supportive of the central plot.

It might be asked if *A Woman of No Importance* has a plot worthy of the name. It certainly has a theme, a number of highly dramatic situations, and, as has been indicated, quite a fair number of surprising reversals, a few of which, like Mrs. Arbuthnot's refusal to marry Lord Illingworth, run counter to the conventions of social drama. But the greater part of the play is talk, not action. When he is obliged to get the plot moving Wilde reluctantly tacks on to the end of the act another development. The characters are poorly balanced; and at the beginning of the play it looks as if Mrs. Allonby (who talks very much like a sophisticated woman with a past) is to take an important part in the action when, in fact, she remains a minor character. Wilde gives her a superfluity of epigrams from the moment of her entrance:

> I think to elope is cowardly. It's running away from danger. And danger has become so rare in modern life.

> The one advantage of playing with fire, Lady Caroline, is that one never gets even singed. It is the people who don't know how to play with it who get burned up.

> We have a far better time than they (men) have. There are far more things forbidden to us than are forbidden to them.

Another character who plays no part in the action is Mr. Kelvil, M.P. who is referred to throughout by Lady Caroline as Mr. Kettle. Unlike Mr. Pooter with whom he has points of resemblance he does not object to being misnamed; and although no cause of wit in himself is a cause of wit in others, for which purpose, no doubt, Wilde introduced him into the play. The more the play is examined the less important does the plot appear; and any degree of social verisimilitude it may possess is only incidental to the main purpose which is, surely, the investigation of Mrs. Arbuthnot's situation and character—and the original title of *A Good Woman* has ironical undertones in this respect. At the same time his portrayals of late Victorian society must have been sufficiently convincing to his audiences for them to have flocked to the theatre night after night, audiences which included all classes and degrees of society.[6] Wilde is experimenting with form in *A Woman of No Importance*, investigating how little plot he actually needed, even putting it aside at times, seeming to invite the audience to an amusing house-party during which they may have to suffer the slight but passing inconvenience of a number of somewhat tiresome episodes involving a mother, her son and her former lover which, however, he will do his best to enliven for their benefit by as many jokes and witticisms as he can conceive. That is, after all, the essence of social comedy. In this way *A Woman of No Importance* marks an advance on *Lady Windermere's Fan*; the sugar may be even sweeter but the pill is even more bitter; and the experience he gained prepares the way for *The Importance of Being Earnest*.

The public and the critics were at variance in their opinions of *A Woman of No Importance* since despite its long run the latter had little that was good to say about it. Max Beerbohm wrote to a friend:

> How the critics attack gentle Oscar! Have you, though, read Archer's very true and just critique? Walkley also is to the point, but the rest have scarcely tried to write on the play at all. They have simply abused Oscar.
>
> (Max Beerbohm—*Letters to Reggie Turner*, ed. Rupert Hart- Davis, 1964, 38)

The notice by William Archer, which has already been mentioned in connection with his praise of the scene between Lord Illingworth and Mrs. Arbuthnot, is kind if not thoroughly perceptive, since he fails to recognise that Wilde was evolving an original form of social comedy. Yet if he dislikes Wilde's wit, for us an enduring aspect of his playwriting, he appreciates other equally important qualities:

> It is not his wit, then, and still less his knack of paradox-twisting that makes me claim for him a place apart among living dramatists. It is the keenness of his intellect, the individuality of his point of view, the excellence of his verbal style, and above all the genuinely dramatic quality of his inspirations.
>
> (*The World*, 26 April 1893)

As for production much that has already been stated about *Lady Windermere's Fan* applies equally to this play: it might be summarised as style, style, and still more style. The play must be played straight and with the same consideration that is given to other plays with difficulties of text, construction or production—for instance, Constantine's suicide in *The Seagull* or the burning of the town in *The Three Sisters*. It abounds with humour and surprises of a kind that are not only unexpected but witty; and, excepting *The Importance of Being Earnest*, it is the most amusing of his plays. The student who ponders over a remark made by Wilde to an interviewer will be able to appreciate the spirit of *A Woman of No Importance*:

> Several plays have been written lately that deal with the monstrous injustice of the social code of morality at the present time. It is indeed a burning shame that there should be one law for men and another law for women. I think there should be no law for anybody . . .
>
> (Pearson, 251)

Least of all, perhaps, in the writing of social comedies.

NOTES

1. The play faced competition from Pinero's *The Second Mrs. Tanqueray*, which began its sensational career on 27 May 1893.
2. Is this, perhaps, an elaborate joke of Wilde's, a kind of pun created by inverting Alexander Pope's 'The Epistle to Arbuthnot' into the Epistle from Mrs. Arbuthnot? Her name has not got the regional links of the other characters in the play.
3. The part of Mrs. Arbuthnot was taken by Mrs. Bernard Beere who had undertaken to present *Vera* with herself as the tempestuous heroine twelve years earlier.
4. Bernard Shaw learned from Wilde, whose career he closely watched, that it was possible to exploit the strengths of the theatre of the '90s by writing plays which conformed to acceptable patterns, often using stock dramatic or comic situations, in order to express his own subversive socialist-social beliefs.
5. In *De Profundis* Wilde writes: 'I remember that as I was sitting in the Dock on the occasion of my last trial listening to Lockwood's appalling denunciation of me—like a thing out of Tacitus, like a passage in Dante, like one of Savonarola's indictments of the Popes of Rome—and being sickened with horror at what I heard, suddenly it occurred

to me How splendid it would be if I was saying all this about myself.'
Do not passages from Mrs. Arbuthnot's speech read, with minor changes
of wording, like a self-defence of his own innate sexual instincts?

6. A further irony may be reported: when the Prince of Wales went to a
performance he found the Royal Box had already been allotted to Lily
Langtry who offered to share it with him.

6

An Ideal Husband

Conscious that nothing succeeds so well as success, Wilde knew that he had to keep himself in the public eye if he was to progress in his career as a dramatist and ensure himself the high income necessary for the extravagant life to which he was becoming increasingly addicted. Potent as was his indolence, his emotional and financial needs were even more pressing and he realised that he must once again set pen to paper and produce another play, the form of literary production which now came easiest to him.

Thus in June 1893 he began to toy with the idea of a play, unnamed in his letters of the time, but presumably *An Ideal Husband*. He was then living at The Cottage, Goring-on-Thames, a rented house, where his life was, as he explained to a correspondent, 'divided in interest between paddling a canoe and planning a comedy—and finding that life in meadow and stream is far more complex than is life in streets and salons' (*Letters*, 342). 'Planning a comedy' is, perhaps, synonymous for thinking about a play, inventing witty lines, devising long and rhetorical speeches, creating dialogues, and actually putting off the laborious task of writing anything down on paper. Apart from a visit to Jersey in September to see a performance of *A Woman of No Importance* by Tree's touring company, he was free to settle down to writing—and in order to do so in peace and quiet—or so he claimed—he took rooms in a private hotel at 10–11 St. James's Place, London.[1] However, even in February 1894 he was describing the play as 'a little incomplete', which it probably was.

Wilde gave his own account of the circumstances in which the play was written in the long letter which he wrote to Douglas in January–March 1897 and which became known later as *De*

Profundis when it was published in an abbreviated version by Robert Ross in 1905. Douglas is reproached with having prevented him from writing and with making his life entirely sterile and unproductive:

> I remember, for instance, in September '93, to select merely one instance out of many, taking a set of chambers, purely in order to work undisturbed, as I had broken my contract with John Hare for whom I had promised to write a play, and who was pressing me on the subject. During the first week you kept away . . . In that week I wrote and completed in every detail, as it was ultimately performed, the first act of *An Ideal Husband*. The second week you returned and my work practically had to be given up . . . Of the appalling results of my friendship with you I don't speak at present. I am thinking merely of its quality while it lasted. It was intellectually degrading to me. You had the rudiments of an artistic temperament in its germ. But I met you either too late or too soon. I don't know which. When you were away I was all right. The moment, in the early December of the year to which I have been alluding, I had succeeded in inducing your mother to send you out of England, I collected again the torn and ravelled webs of my imagination, got my life back into my own hands, and not merely finished the three remaining acts of *An Ideal Husband*, but conceived the *Florentine Tragedy* and *La Sainte Courtisane*, when suddenly, unbidden, unwelcome, and under circumstances fatal to my happiness you returned. The two works left then imperfect I was unable to take up again. The mood that created them I could never recover.
>
> (*Letters*, 426–427)

Wilde is not telling the full truth here. Although there can be no doubt that his literary work was interrupted by those miserable scenes of petulance and anger which were a feature of his disastrous friendship with Douglas, there was evidence at his trial that he had received visits in these rooms from the young men he had picked up or met at particular private parties. But it is not unknown for writers and politicians and other semi-professional men to spend time with their mistresses or in search of *les filles* and still find time for their work and their families. If Wilde wasted time and energy with Douglas unwillingly, he wasted time and energy with these mercenary young men quite willingly; in either case he was quite free to choose his own way of life and had no right to complain as he did in so undignified a fashion in *De Pro-fundis*. More to the point he told a correspondent in January 1894 that he had written three acts of a play and that he would write the fourth act during the next fortnight, which, as we have seen, does not agree with this later account but which seems more likely, since the play was typed out by Mrs. Marshall's typing agency in the Strand by 19 February 1894 (*ibid*, 349).

The play suffered from the usual frustrations to which the minis-strations and interventions of actor-managers, producers and actors frequently give rise. It had been intended for the popular actor-manager John Hare, for whom the Garrick Theatre had been built by W. S. Gilbert. Wilde should have remembered that Hare had turned down a notable money-spinner of the time, Pinero's *The Second Mrs. Tanqueray*, as too daring; he now rejected Wilde's play on the grounds that the last act was unsatisfactory. Lewis Waller[2] who together with H. H. Morell had taken the Haymarket Theatre in Tree's absence on an American tour was badly in want of a success and was delighted to have the play which Wilde had called *An Ideal Husband*. Waller was a fine actor with a beautiful and clear voice and it was appropriate that he should cast him-self as Lord Chiltern while Charles Hawtrey took the part of Lord Goring. Julia Neilson was Lady Chiltern and Florence West had the important rôle of Mrs. Cheveley. Charles Brookfield who had written the burlesque on Wilde and who was to play such a male-volent part in the prosecution of the writer was pleased to accept the part of Lord Goring's servant. *An Ideal Husband* was advertised as the first play of the new season and went into rehearsal in the second half of December.

When the play opened on 3 January 1895 it was received with the greatest enthusiasm. The Prince of Wales was in a box and sent for Wilde after the performance to congratulate him. Wilde lamented that it had been too long and that he would certainly have to make cuts. 'Pray do not take out a single word,' the Prince exclaimed. The author, whose indolence was rarely appealed to in vain, willingly acceded to the royal behest. The play ran for one hundred and eleven performances before it was taken off on the day after Wilde's arrest. Actually it had been scheduled to end its run at the Haymarket about that time, but when revived at an other theatre could not continue in face of the public's righteous indignation and the sense of outrage whipped up by Wilde's trials and was taken off after a few days. In New York it began its run on 12 March 1895 with a more appreciative press and public than any of his plays had hitherto received.

An Ideal Husband is the last of Wilde's three plays with pink lampshades and a guilty secret. The plot is quite simple. In fact, it is rather too simple. Sir Robert Chiltern and his wife Gertrude are holding a reception at their home in Grosvenor Square. Lady Markby, one of the guests, has brought an acquaintance, Mrs. Cheveley, whom Lady Chiltern at once recognises as a former schoolfellow of dubious reputation. Mrs. Cheveley falls into conversation with Sir Robert during which he compliments her on the brilliant reputation she has acquired in society in Vienna where she has, apparently, lived for several years. He asks why she has returned to England, whether it is for politics or pleasure:

> *Mrs. Cheveley*: Politics are my only pleasure. You see, nowadays it is not fashionable to flirt till one is forty, or to be romantic till one is forty-five, so we poor women who are under thirty, or say we are, have nothing open to us but politics or philanthropy. And philanthropy seems to me to have become simply the refuge of those who wish to annoy their fellow-creatures. I prefer politics. I think they are more . . . becoming!
> *Sir Robert Chiltern*: A political life is a noble career!
> *Mrs. Cheveley*: Sometimes. And sometimes it is a clever game, Sir Robert.

This is an ominous note. Mrs. Cheveley mentions that she has invested heavily in an international company called the Argentine Canal Company on the advice of the late Baron Arnheim, a name at which Sir Robert starts. However, he denounces the scheme as fraudulent and says he intends to present a damning report on it to the House of Commons the next evening. Mrs. Cheveley advises him to do nothing of the sort. In fact, she advises him to withdraw the report on the grounds that the Commissioners who drew it up were mistaken or misinformed, and instead to tell the House that the government is reconsidering the scheme in view of the canal's tremendous importance. If he does so she will reward him handsomely. Sir Robert is outraged:

Sir Robert Chiltern: If you will allow me, I will call your carriage for you. You have lived so long abroad, Mrs. Cheveley, that you seem to be unable to realise that you are talking to an English gentleman.

Mrs. Cheveley: I realise that I am talking to a man who laid the foundation of his fortune by selling to a Stock Exchange speculator a Cabinet secret.

Mrs. Cheveley knows that as a poor but extremely ambitious young politician Sir Robert sold to Baron Arnheim a Cabinet secret—that the government was about to buy Suez Canal shares—which enabled the Baron and his associates to make a vast fortune, a considerable part of which they passed on to Sir Robert. As the last mistress of the Baron, Mrs. Cheveley has inherited a fortune and also the letter in which Sir Robert passed on the secret and which she now threatens to make public if he will not do as she requests. He must give his immediate consent so that she might telegraph to her associates in Vienna. Eventually, Sir Robert consents to withdraw the report. After Mrs. Cheveley has sent him to order her carriage she is approached by Lady Chiltern who asks her the nature of her business with her husband. Foolishly, Mrs. Cheveley says she has persuaded him to withdraw any opposition to the Argentine Canal Company scheme. Meanwhile the charming Lord Goring, a most eligible bachelor, has been flirting with Lord Chiltern's sister Mabel. They find lying on a sofa a brooch which can be transformed into a bracelet which is claimed by Lord Goring who says he gave it to someone years ago. When the guests have gone and she and her husband are alone together Lady Chiltern threatens to leave him if he does not write at once to Mrs. Cheveley saying he has changed his mind and will not support the Canal scheme. Near midnight as it is, he writes the letter which is dispatched by hand to Mrs. Cheveley's hotel.

In the second act Sir Robert confesses to Lord Goring. We learn that he received from the Baron the sum of one hundred and eleven thousand pounds, together with financial advice which enabled him almost to treble his fortune in five years. In an attempt to salve his conscience he has given large sums to charity. By a kind of strange coincidence peculiar to dramas of this kind it appears that Lord Goring was once briefly engaged to Mrs. Cheveley. Determined to thwart Mrs. Cheveley Sir Robert telegraphs the British Embassy in Vienna asking for a report on her. While he is out of the room his wife enters and tries to find from Lord Goring what is troubling her husband and whether he knows anything about his past. Lady Markby and Mrs. Cheveley call to ask if a diamond brooch belonging to the latter lady has been found. Mason, the butler, has no information of anyone having found it. While Lady Markby goes on to another engagement Mrs. Cheveley is persuaded to stay chiefly in order that Lady Chiltern might have the pleasure of telling her that it was she who forced her husband to write the letter in which he withdrew his support of the canal scheme. Mrs. Cheveley retaliates by revealing the nature of her hold over Sir Robert who enters the room unobserved and hears the conversation. Mrs. Cheveley departs a trifle unceremoniously. Lady Chiltern challenges her husband to tell the truth, listens to his confession of guilt, and refuses to accept any explanation. Sir Robert cries out against her false idealism in terms which were later to have still wider application to Wilde's own private life:

> *Sir Robert*: . . . And now what is there before me but public disgrace, ruin, terrible shame, the mockery of the world, a lonely, dishonoured life, a lonely dishonoured death, it may be, some day? Let women make no more ideals of men! Let them not put them on altars and bow before them or they may ruin other lives as completely as you—you whom I have so wildly loved—have ruined mine!

The last sentence is not, however, particularly applicable to either Sir Robert Chiltern or the author.

The third act is set in the home of Lord Goring who, in full evening dress, is just about to leave when his butler, Phipps, gives him a note from Lady Chiltern which reads, 'I want you. I trust you. I am coming to you.' No sooner has he read it than a visitor is announced, his father, Lord Caversham, who has come to persuade him to marry and settle down:

> *Lord Caversham*: . . . You have got to get married, and at once. Why, when I was your age, sir, I had been an inconsolable widower for three months, and was already paying my addresses to your admirable mother. Damme, sir, it is your duty to get married. You can't be always living for pleasure. Every man of position

is married nowadays. Bachelors are not fashionable any more. They are a damaged lot. Too much is known about them. You must get a wife, sir. Look where your friend Robert Chiltern has got by probity, hard work, and a sensible marriage with a good woman. Why don't you imitate him, sir? Why don't you take him for your model?

Since his father shows no intention of going, Lord Goring takes him into the library after telling Phipps that he is expecting a lady who is to be shown into the drawing-room. A lady does arrive: not the writer of the letter but Mrs. Cheveley. She examines the correspondence on the desk, reads the letter from Lady Chiltern, and hides it under the blotter. Phipps then ushers her into the drawing-room just as Lord Goring and his father emerge from the library. Eventually the old man departs to be replaced by Sir Robert who explains that a report has come from Vienna to say that nothing is known against Mrs. Cheveley there. In time, a noise is heard in the adjoining room whereupon Sir Robert throws open the door and discloses Mrs. Cheveley. He rushes from the house after accusing his friend of treachery. Mrs. Cheveley is in high spirits. She has lowered her sights: if Lord Goring will marry her—as he once intended—she will give him the letter in which Sir Robert compromised himself. Lord Goring refuses and producing the brooch which she had mislaid at Lady Chiltern's reception shapes it into a bracelet and clasps it on her arm. She struggles in vain to remove it. Lord Goring accuses her of having stolen it from his cousin, Mary Berkshire, to whom he had given it as a wedding present. He will call the police and denounce her unless she hands over the letter. This she does. The letter is burnt. Mrs. Cheveley then snatches up Lady Chiltern's letter from under the blotter:

Mrs. Cheveley: . . . I am going to send Robert Chiltern the love-letter his wife wrote to you tonight.
Lord Goring: Love-letter?
Mrs. Cheveley (*laughing*): 'I want you. I trust you. I am coming to you. Gertrude'.
Lord Goring: You wretched woman, must you always be thieving? Give me back that letter. I'll take it from you by force. You shall not leave my room till I have got it. (*He rushes towards her, but Mrs. Cheveley at once puts her hand on the electric bell*

that is on the table. The bell sounds with shrill reverberations, and Phipps enters.)
Mrs. Cheveley: Lord Goring merely rang that you should show me out. Good-night, Lord Goring.

For the fourth act we are returned to the Chilterns' home. Lord Goring and his father are there. Lord Caversham tells how Sir Robert Chiltern has made a brilliant speech in the House of Commons denouncing the Argentine Canal scheme, and then goes off to see the Prime Minister. Left alone with Mabel Chiltern in the room Lord Goring proposes and is accepted. When Mabel goes off to the conservatory Lady Chiltern enters and is told by Lord Goring that he has managed to destroy her husband's letter but that her own, apparently compromising, letter has been stolen. Sir Robert enters with the letter in his hand—mistakenly he supposes that the letter which Mrs. Cheveley (as we know) has sent him has actually come direct from his wife—after all, it bore neither date nor time. He is overwhelmed by this demonstration of her need for him. When Lord Goring, in his turn, goes off into the conservatory, Lady Chiltern tells her husband that he is safe: they are both agreed, however, that he should retire from public life. Lord Caversham enters with a letter offering him a seat in the Cabinet and is unpleasantly surprised when he finds the Chilterns united in a determination to refuse it. Sir Robert goes out to write a letter of refusal while Lord Goring steers his father off into the conservatory. He then tells Lady Chiltern that in encouraging her husband to leave public life she is unwittingly completing the evil work begun by Mrs. Cheveley. So moved is she by these pearls of worldly wisdom that when her husband returns with the letter of refusal she tears it up. Grateful as he is to Lord Goring for this latest intervention, Sir Robert refuses permission for him to marry Mabel because of the immoral implications of his finding Mrs. Cheveley in Lord Goring's home the previous evening. Lady Chiltern intervenes to say it was she whom Lord Goring had expected. At once all is forgiven by Sir Robert. It is to be hoped that the famous speech made in the House of Commons on the subject of the Argentine Canal scheme was of a somewhat better quality:

Sir Robert Chiltern: What! Had I fallen so low in your eyes that you thought that even for a moment I could have doubted your

142

goodness? Gertrude, Gertrude, you are to me the white image of all good things, and sin can never touch you. Arthur, you can go to Mabel, and you have my best wishes.

Lord Caversham, intimate of the Prime Minister and something of a Cabinet maker, a pinnacle of British political life, returns from the conservatory with Mabel Chiltern to hear that she and his son are to be married, and that Sir Robert Chiltern will, after all, accept a seat in the Cabinet. He threatens his son:

> Lord Caversham: If you don't make this young lady an ideal husband, I'll cut you off with a shilling.
> Mabel: An ideal husband! Oh, I don't think I should like that. It sounds like something in the next world.

An Ideal Husband is among the early autograph drafts in the British Museum; and there is an autograph draft and a typescript corrected by Wilde in the Clark Library of the University of California at Los Angeles. The play was first published in a limited edition in 1899, after Wilde had corrected the proofs and grumbled that it was worse than writing a new play.

The plot of An Ideal Husband is not without its elements of improbability and, unlike A Woman of No Importance, is overloaded by an excessive number of reversals and twists. Sometimes the plot verges on the nonsensical. Why, for instance, should Mrs. Cheveley hand over to Lord Goring the compromising letter written by Sir Robert Chiltern because he would otherwise hand her over to the police as a thief and yet walk out of his house, undenounced, with the bracelet still clasped on her arm? Again, the credibility of Mrs. Cheveley's identity, like that of Mrs. Erlynne, is rather suspect; and it is difficult to believe that a woman who was at school with Lady Chiltern and engaged to be married to Lord Goring should not have been extremely well-known in the closely-knit fabric of London aristocratic society. There seems no need to have telegraphed Vienna for details of her later career since a woman who had been the mistress of an international financier, who had been immensely enriched after his death, who dabbled in international finance, and who still retained links with London society—with Lady Markby at any rate—must have been recognised by many people. Unless Lord Goring is quite, quite old and, therefore, too old to become the husband of Mabel Chil-

tern, his engagement to Mrs. Cheveley must have been comparatively recent. And who was Mr. Cheveley—and how does he fit
into the picture? The critic A. B. Walkley was quite right, when
commenting on this play, to say that even Sardou had tired of
kleptomania as a theatrical device; but it cannot be denied that
Wilde uses the theft of the letter effectively. That there was a
similarity between Sardou's *Dora* and *An Ideal Husband* is undeniable, but a play can be interesting to the ordinary playgoer even
if the plot is not particularly original: as with Shakespeare, originality of plot, similarity of structure, and the use of dramatic devices
of a conventional nature are matters which concern professional
critics and scholars rather than the public which, by and large,
wishes to be interested and entertained.

Not unexpectedly, despite the fact that the critics charged him
with having stolen his adventures from Augier and his tirades from
Dumas *fils*, they did not comment on those elements of the play
which were individual to Wilde, notably the political background
which he treated in an ironical, cynical way which was quite
unique for the period. It is is arguably the most serious of Wilde's
social comedies, not because of its exploitation of the woman with
a 'past', but because of its political overtones. In his criticism of
the play A. B. Walkley stated that its plot was incredible because
it was most improbable that any of the politicians of the day
would behave in such a way: 'When Bulwer Lytton and Disraeli
wrote novels picturing politics as a drawing-room game of this
kind, they only distorted, not actually falsified, the facts,' he
stated, and added, 'But nowadays, of course, such a picture is
stark, staring nonsense' (Review signed A. B. W. in *Speaker*, 12
January 1895, iv, 43–44). The plain fact of the matter is that
Wilde was guilty of hardly any exaggeration, as political historians
would and should be the first to admit.

In the play Mrs. Cheveley tries to force Sir Robert Chiltern's
hand by threatening to reveal that he divulged the secret that the
British Government, of which he was a junior member, intended
to purchase Suez Canal shares, mercenary conduct on the part of
a civil servant which must have seemed impossible to innocent
dramatic and literary journalists. Historians, however, have always
known that the sources of all great wealth are vicious, tainted
and corrupt. What the public of Wilde's day did not know was that

Disraeli had been forced to borrow money from the Rothschilds in order to finance the government's purchase of Suez Canal shares and that this deal must certainly have strengthened the hands (and enlarged the funds) of the dealers in these and related shares. And this furtive financial intrigue had taken place only twenty years or so before *An Ideal Husband* had been written. The Prince of Wales himself relied heavily for his financial support on such men as the (imaginary) Baron Arnheim; his own chief supporters from whom he borrowed heavily were the financiers Baron Hirsch and Sir Ernest Cassell. It is said that at a ball the Prince of Wales playfully asked the lady with whom he was dancing, 'And now, what does Lady Salome want?' To which she replied, 'The head of Sir Ernest, sire.' At which the Prince stalked away in indignation. The financial adventures of Rhodes and other international crooks in Southern Africa was as skilfully veiled behind a patriotic flag in Wilde's day as it is in ours. In the second half of the nineteenth century the world of European finance, whether of notorious barons in Vienna or anonymous gnomes in Zurich, had begun to intrude more and more upon domestic politics.

It could only have been an earnest theatrical critic who could have been so naïve as to suppose that parliamentary and private secretaries were above the taints of bribery and corruption and that the realm of Victorian politics was pure and sinless. Wilde's portraits of Sir Robert, Mrs. Cheveley, and the late Baron Arnheim (who is only spoken of but whose character emerges clearly) are both just and exact; and the irony of the play is all the more cogent in our own day when cabinet ministers form family trusts to escape the taxation they thrust on others or have salaries paid abroad in tax-free havens or fly round the world in support of the latest Baron Arnheim Argentine Canal scheme, with no hesitation in speaking in support of such a scheme in which they will probably have a hefty investment themselves—continuing meanwhile to lecture the electorate on morality, honesty, patriotism, and honour.

As has been mentioned Wilde is said to have drawn his plots from French dramas either in the original or in translation but it may well be that he was partly inspired by a novel. *The Gilded Age* by Mark Twain and C. D. Warner, published in 1873, which is concerned with the wide-spread corruption in American life following the Civil War and the abolition of slavery and which has a scene between the adventuress Laura Hawkins and a Senator called Trollop in which she blackmails him into supporting a scheme in which she is financially interested. An extract shows a number of similarities with the scene between Mrs. Cheveley and Sir Robert Chiltern in the first act of *An Ideal Husband* although the language is different, naturally, since it takes place in Washington:

> "You know my bill—the Knobs University bill."
> "Ah, I believe it *is* your bill. I had forgotten. Yes. I know the bill."
> "Well, would you mind telling me your opinion of it?"
> "Indeed, since you seem to ask it without reserve, I am obliged to say that I do not regard it favourably. I have not seen the bill itself, but from what I can hear, it—well, it has a bad look about it. It—"
> "Speak it out—never fear."
> "Well, it—they say it contemplates a fraud upon the government."
> "Well?" said Laura tranquilly.
> "Well! *I* say 'well' too."
> "Well, suppose it *were* a fraud—which I feel able to deny—would it be the first one?"
> "You take a body's breath away! Would you—did you wish me to vote for it? Was that what you wanted to see me about?"
> "Your instinct is correct. I *did* want you—I *do* want you to vote for it."
> "Vote for a fr-for a measure which is generally believed to be at least questionable? I am afraid we cannot come to an understanding, Miss Hawkins."
> "No, I am afraid not—if you have resumed your principles, Mr. Trollop."

> (1903 edn., 255–256)

By reminding him that he has taken part in a fraud the investigation of which will destroy his career she is able to bring Trollop to heel much as Mrs. Cheveley is able to impose her will on Sir Robert by revealing his disclosure for financial gain of state secrets: and just as Mrs. Cheveley is defeated by the finding of the brooch which she had stolen years before so Laura is destroyed by her passion for a heartless married man who had seduced her years before.

Indeed, *The Gilded Age* could have aptly served as a sub-title for *An Ideal Husband*, for in this and his other plays Wilde realised a world of vulgar and tasteless luxury as well as of personal and national corruption, a world which was to reach its apotheosis during the Edwardian years when the most tasteless of objects was embellished with initials, real or false stones, silver or gold mountings and lavish workmanship, all paid for with the income from cheap and underpaid labour. It was the age in which Fabergé and his workmen created repulsive (and beautiful) objects of the greatest luxury and expense. Wilde's plots revolve round such items: in *Lady Windermere's Fan* it is the fan bearing Lady Windermere's Christian name which has been given to her as a birthday present by her husband, a miniature of her mother as a young woman, and a photograph of herself and her child; in *An Ideal Husband* it is a diamond brooch which can, improbably, be transformed into a bracelet; and in his last play *The Importance of Being Earnest* much of the first act is concerned with an engraved cigarette case.

In his letters Wilde speaks frequently of the wretched state of the workers in England, particularly stressing the misery of poor people in London; and it is impossible to believe that this generosity of compassion did not find a place in his dramatic work, too. On his release from prison he wrote to the press pleading that young children should not be imprisoned within grim prison walls, sometimes for offences on which they had not even been tried. His heart was with the weak and downtrodden. In *An Ideal Husband* Wilde at last found a vehicle for giving expression to the social sympathies first expressed in *Vera* and present, to some degree, in all the plays which followed it. It does credit to the Prince of Wales that he found no words of condemnation for the play, declared it was not a word too long, and probably relished the truth of the scene Wilde had depicted.

Wilde's mockery of conventional morality is equally biting as William Archer realised when he wrote of Sir Robert Chiltern:

> The thousands have increased and multiplied; he is wealthy, he is respected, he is Under-Secretary for Foreign Affairs, he is married to a wife who idolises and idealises him; and, not having stolen anything more in the interim, he is inclined to agree with

his wife and the world in regarding himself as the Bayard of Downing Street.

(*Pall Mall Gazette*, 10 January 1895)

Archer's comments are penetratingly satirical without being as perceptive as might be expected for he charges Wilde with having created a situation in which we find ourselves asking whether Sir Robert's old *peccadillo* ought to debar him from public life or whether it has strengthened his moral character and made him a better citizen of the world. Wilde, he believed, had answered the question for us by seeming to give a negative opinion while actually answering (within the fabric of the play) in the affirmative. Archer has not grasped the full irony of Wilde's plot. When Mrs. Cheveley threatens Sir Robert with the publication of the compromising letter he might possibly have answered, in the words of Wellington, 'Publish and be damned.' Had this been so—and, of course, it was not—Wilde would have had to devise another set of circumstances in order to rescue or damn Sir Robert. However, Sir Robert does not send Mrs. Cheveley packing and agrees with considerable alacrity to involve his country in a scheme which he himself describes as a swindle. He is quite prepared to sacrifice his country's honour to save his skin—and his fortune. Sir Robert is saved from personal disaster by the actions of Lord Goring who is adept at playing Mrs. Cheveley's game of theratening public disclosure. Once he has been saved by his friend, Sir Robert goes on to accept a post in the Cabinet. And with his wife's blessing. There is here a subtle twisting together of personal and public morality, both of them shams. Self-interest reigns. It is impossible to believe that Wilde did not contrive these turns of events without having his tongue prominently in his cheek.

If Sir Robert Chiltern shows himself a man who is honest only so long as it suits his convenience to be so, Lady Chiltern is hardly much better. After the disclosure of the letter to Baron Arnheim she looks at her husband 'with strange eyes, as though she was seeing him for the first time', and cries, 'Don't touch me!' Among other things she says a common thief were better than her dishonest husband. Later she uses the denial of her love as a weapon to make him agree to resign from public life. However, once the threat of exposure is safely behind them and a glittering career in the cabinet lies ahead, she feels love for him, 'Love, and only love'.

She adds that for them both a new life is beginning. Her inability to forgive Mrs. Cheveley's schoolgirl misdemeanours finds no counterpart in her attitude to her husband. So much for the morality of Lady Chiltern. A selfless word of pity or of compassionate understanding never passes her lips.

What Wilde demonstrates in this play is that the great secret of public success is simply never to be found out. *An Ideal Husband* does, in fact, enable us to rejoice over the escape of a sinner from the penalty of his sin through the trick of his friend with the diamond brooch-bracelet. This is not a convincing trick; and, perhaps, Wilde did not seriously intend it to be so. The action demonstrates the basic hypocrisy of English life. Mrs. Cheveley may seem to represent international and amoral finance forcing its way into English society and public life; but there can be no doubt that the ground had been well tilled and was ready for her activities. A further twist is given by the fact that Mrs. Cheveley is not actually an intruder—by birth and upbringing she is a member of English society and is, as the reply to Sir Robert's telegram to the Embassy at Vienna demonstrates, a leading and perfectly respectable member of society there, too. And Vienna under the Emperor Franz Joseph was, if anything, infinitely more rigid and righteous in its morality than was London. Mrs. Cheveley moves gracefully in both societies, in both capitals. Wilde could take dramatic cynicism no further.

Cynicism—for which dramatic irony is another term—is carried over into the stage directions supplied by Wilde in the printed text. We are so often told that it was G. B. Shaw who inaugurated the practice of printing lengthy stage directions to make his plays agreeably understandable to ordinary readers that it is not generally appreciated that this was also the custom with other dramatists, Wilde among them. He described the scenes in his *An Ideal Husband* in careful detail; and we know enough of the simple and carefully selected decorations and furnishings of his own home in Tite Street to appreciate that in this play he intended to convey an atmosphere of tasteless and expensive luxury. The octagon room at Sir Robert Chiltern's house in Grosvenor Square is furnished with a great chandelier, a large eighteenth-century French tapestry illustrating the Triumph of Love, from a design by Boucher, and a Louis Seize sofa—some of the glittering prizes, it is to be supposed, for which Sir Robert surrendered his honour years before. The tapestry after Boucher carries a sardonic message of the Game of Love which is to be played out between Sir Robert and Lady Chiltern, Lord Goring and Mabel Chiltern, with Mrs. Cheveley as the 'other woman'. But as these splendid decorations, obviously not inherited but acquired from expensive *antiquaires*, show it is not the triumph of love we witness in the drama but the triumph of money, ambition and corruption.

Wilde's stage directions also apply to the characters. Lady Chiltern is described as a woman of grave Greek beauty, Mrs. Marchmont and Lady Basildon would have pleased the brush of Watteau, and Mabel Chiltern is like a Tanagra statuette. Quite so. This was the effect at which these ladies aimed and, no doubt, succeeded in obtaining. The result, as can be seen in photographs of many late Victorian and Edwardian women, was that they would look as if they were in fancy-dress costumes which were as deceptive of their real interests, backgrounds and tastes as the guises of shepherdesses and milkmaids worn by Marie Antoinette and her ladies at the *petit hameau* of Versailles. Witty these ladies are (with the exception of Lady Chiltern), but the connection with Watteau and ancient Greece is remote: Lady Chiltern appears to have been reared on penny novelettes as her cries of 'Don't touch me!' reveal. She is a cousin of Shaw's Eliza Doolittle. With his acute awareness of appearances, especially the more superficial ones, of the lack of correlation between appearances and character, Wilde knew exactly the effect at which he was aiming with his stage directions—a society which was basically unstable and essentially *parvenu*.

The structure of the play is provided not by one but by two letters, which are cleverly balanced against each other. The first letter is that written by Sir Robert Chiltern years ago to Baron Arnheim and which is used by Mrs. Cheveley in her vain attempt to make him support the canal scheme in which she is financially interested; and the second is that written by Lady Chiltern to Lord Goring saying that she is coming to him and which is also used by Mrs. Cheveley. Both husband and wife are at risk through their epistolary addictions. Mrs. Cheveley is not successful in her use of either letter but does not seem to be particularly cast down.

Lord Goring who once knew her intimately (and who shares his father's pre-occupation with bonnets) says of her that she,

> is one of those very modern women of our time who find a new scandal as becoming as a new bonnet, and air them both in the Park every afternoon at five-thirty.

And although the device of the brooch which can be turned into a bracelet has been criticised as improbable—in the sense that a clever woman like Mrs. Cheveley would have acquired other jewels in the meantime and would have investigated the mechanism long ago—it belongs to the general ambivalence of the play, looking like one thing while it is really another. There is also a degree of irony in Mrs. Cheveley's being trapped (only temporarily, however) by a device which she stole years ago.

The rôles in this play are generously balanced. Mrs. Cheveley, the principal rôle, does not appear in the fourth and last act, but if she makes an impact from the first moment of her entrance she can dominate the action in the second and third acts. While the unscrupulous, calculating side of her nature should be upper-most during these scenes it should be remembered that when Sir Robert telegraphs Vienna he receives the reply that she has in-herited the great portion of Baron Arnheim's immense fortune and occupies a rather high position in society. This being so, Mrs. Cheveley must be acted as a woman of great intelligence, remark-able charm, striking beauty, and high breeding. In earlier days she has been engaged to Lord Goring which says much for her social position and attractiveness. If she threw him over in favour of a richer man she did no more—indeed, much less—than Sir Robert Chiltern who betrayed his country for money. She also struck a blow for the equality of the sexes in rejecting rather than being rejected. Lady Bracknell, it will be remembered, had no fortune either, but never dreamed of letting that get in the way of a good marriage. Mrs. Cheveley has little written in her lines to attract sympathy although her desire to return home to live in England and secure a personable husband in Lord Goring can be used to attract the audience's sympathy. The audience should feel that she is well able to take care of herself and that she is likely to burst upon the London scene in the near future as a countess or princess, if she can persuade someone to accept her proposals of marriage.

151

Mrs. Cheveley presents some problems to a thoughtful actress who tries to investigate her character. What kind of parents had she and where are they? How is it that she went to the same school as Lady Chiltern? Why and how did her character so quickly reveal itself as untruthful, dishonest, and so able to exert an evil influence on others? And can we believe this view of her which is derived, ironically, from Lady Chiltern? Why did she steal the diamond brooch? And why has she continued to wear it when a fortune such as hers would have enabled her to buy all the jewels she wanted? Does she still want money or does she want power? A thoroughly modern woman, she has been married to a Mr. Cheveley, has been the mistress of Baron Arnheim and the affianced of Lord Goring which seems a lot to have packed into a comparatively short life since it is unlikely that she is over thirty-four. But numerous ladies in late Victorian London, notably Mrs. Keppel and Lily Langtry, managed to live somewhat similar lives. A notable performer of the rôle was the late Martita Hunt whose very presence seemed in itself to answer the preceding questions and who scored a great success during the war years in an elegant production (appropriately at the St. James's Theatre) designed by Rex Whistler who was killed in action shortly afterwards. Martita Hunt possessed allure, abounding personality, and a suggestion of foreign blood which combined with a voice of impeccable clarity and a haunting range of tones made her the living incarnation of Mrs. Cheveley as described by Wilde:

> Lips very thin and highly-coloured, a line of scarlet on a pallid face. Venetian red hair, aquiline nose, and long throat. Rouge accentuates the natural paleness of her complexion. Grey-green eyes that move restlessly. She is in heliotrope, with diamonds. She looks rather like an orchid, and makes great demands on one's curiosity. In all her movements she is extremely graceful. A work of art, on the whole, but showing the influence of too many schools.

Lady Chiltern is quite different, 'a woman of grave Greek beauty, about twenty-seven years of age'. She is as hard as nails and must remain so, never playing for the audience's emotions in any way. Like Lady Windermere of *Lady Windermere's Fan* she is aggressively virtuous. In her character there is little feeling for others:

self-esteem and self-pity and self-righteousness are leading traits. Also like Lady Windermere her attempts to ameliorate the situation only make matters a good deal worse, rather suggesting that good women are rather more trouble than they are worth—which is part of Wilde's ironic comedy in the play. If the actress is ruthless enough to stress her initially unattractive qualities she will carry the audience with her at the big, dramatic moments, for they will sympathise with her predicament, sensing that she is a young wife on whom other blows will fall and whose character will gain in tolerance as the years go by. On the character of Lady Chiltern falls the burden of the irony of the play. As for Sir Robert Chiltern, it is enough that he should be played as an ostentatiously honest and upright politician—the more serious the better! Since Sir Robert is an actor and has acted a part for many years his part requires the minimum of stage artifice—which is why Lewis Waller proved excellent in the part as it was written (with his personality in mind) by Wilde.

Into the character of Lord Goring the author put much of the wit he saved or recorded from his own sparkling conversations: he is yet another of those cynical men-about-town whom we have traced back to Prince Paul. Wilde's own distinctive qualities as dandy, trifler and wit are all apparent in the character as is the good commonsense he showered upon his friends and upon which he occasionally acted himself. It must be remarked that Lord Goring, like Wilde himself, married a pretty but dull girl from a good family. Lord Goring's part is not the easiest in the play. He needs to attract and hold the amity of the audience if he is to carry off the rather brutal scene with Mrs. Cheveley in Act III with any degree of conviction; he must, therefore, avoid irritating the audience by displaying an excess of such flamboyant arrogance as Wilde showed in the last few years before his downfall. Friendship for Sir Robert Chiltern, respect for Lady Chiltern, and a quiet affection for Mabel Chiltern are the aspects to stress. Wilde's desscription is helpful both as to physique and character:

> Thirty-four, but always says he is younger . . . A flawless dandy, he would be annoyed if he were considered romantic. He plays with life, and is on perfectly good terms with the world. He is fond of being misunderstood. It gives him a post of vantage.

Unlike Prince Paul he is not destructive to the unity of the comedy, since in this the last of his problem dramas Wilde has found a theme and a plot which are sufficient in themselves as critical comments upon the fabric of British society and can therefore safely diminish the rôle of the interior commentator.

Mabel Chiltern—'A perfect example of the English type of prettiness, the apple-blossom type . . .' has very little to do in the play except to be charming, not always an easy task in the circumstances. Lord Caversham is sufficiently characterised, like Lord Augustus Lorton, to take a useful part in finalising the action: he is something of a magical godfather, bringing reconciliation, marriage and promotion and other worldly good things to the characters, acting as a kind of *alter ego* to Mrs. Cheveley, and providing a note of comedy which is reminiscent of the eighteenth-century comedy of manners:

> Never go anywhere now. Sick of London society. Shouldn't mind being introduced to my own tailor; he always votes on the right side. But object strongly to being sent down to dinner with my wife's milliner. Never could stand Lady Caversham's bonnets.

Like his other social comedies *An Ideal Husband* requires superlatively elegant settings, costumes, furnishings and properties. Wilde may be allowed to speak for himself in this respect, using the note he wrote in 1894 to the English actress Grace Hawthorne who wished to present his plays on a tour she was arranging:

> My plays are difficult plays to produce well: they require artistic setting on the stage, a good company that knows something of the style essential to high comedy, beautiful dresses, a sense of the luxury of modern life, and unless you are going out with a management that is able to pay well for things that are worth paying for, and to spend money in suitable presentation, it would be much better for you not to think of producing my plays . . .

> (*Letters*, 374)

This is especially true of *An Ideal Husband* which calls for three settings: the octagon room of Sir Robert Chiltern's house in Grosvenor Square, the morning-room in his home, and the library of Lord Goring's house in Curzon Street. For the last act we return to the morning-room of Sir Robert Chiltern's house. Wilde stipulates that the octagon room of the first act should be at the head of a staircase, but most designers disregard this direction since so few theatres are equipped with the means of building a staircase below stage level. It is far from easy to find the furniture and draperies which would be lavishly displayed in rooms such as those described in the play at the end of the nineteenth century.

Even if the settings do not prevent an insuperable problem, there remains the difficulty of finding fifteen actors and actresses who are sufficiently elegant and well-spoken to portray people from the very highest society. In addition, frequent changes of costume are made by these characters. If the producer cannot secure this impression of overwhelming luxury he had better not present this play, for otherwise the audience will be unable to appreciate the immense reward Sir Robert reaped when he passed on confidential information to Baron Arnheim. The nature of the Chilterns' decision not to repudiate their fortune or to resign from public life is, as Wilde intended, revealed in a cynical light when made against the background of these lavish and costly surroundings. The visual elements in Wilde's plays should never be disregarded. The characters, incidentally, present a convenient range of ages, for if they are old enough to have made mistakes they must also be young enough to have time to redeem them.

The critics reiterated their usual charges of lack of originality, cheap wit, and poor craftsmanship. H. G. Wells, in an unsigned review for the *Pall Mall Gazette* (whose permanent dramatic critic he was), thought that it was 'unquestionably very poor', but made a comment that was repeated in other words by his fellow critics:

> In many ways his new production is diverting, and even where the fun is not of the rarest character the play remains interesting. And among other things, it marks an interesting phase in the dramatic development of its author. Your common man begins in innocence, in his golden youth he wears his heart upon his sleeve; but Oscar Wilde is, so to speak, working his way to innocence, as others work towards experience—is sloughing his epigrams slowly but surely, and discovering to an appreciative world, beneath the attenuated veil of his wit, that he, too, has a heart.

> (4 January 1895, 3)

Clement Scott did not think the plot way very original and supposed that Wilde's success, such as it was, merely resulted from ephemeral fashion. A. B. Walkley, writing in the *Speaker*, said that Wilde's presentation of the world of political intrigue and scandal was stark, staring nonsense—which seems to show that no matter how able he was as a dramatic critic Walkley had no sense of political reality: political fortunes are not made by political rectitude but by political opportunism. The great thing about the play, according to Walkley, was that it was designed to fill the audience with joy over the escape of a sinner from the penalty of his sin through a trick with a diamond bracelet. Even Sardou, he said, had tired of such kleptodramatics. Only G. B. Shaw writing in the *Saturday Review* defended Wilde:

> Mr Oscar Wilde's new play at the Haymarket is a dangerous subject, because he has the property of making his critics dull. They laugh angrily at his epigrams, like a child who is coaxed into being amused in the very act of setting up a yell of rage and agony. They protest that the trick is obvious, and that such epigrams can be turned out by the score by any one lightminded enough to condescend to such frivolity. As far as I can ascertain, I am the only person in London who cannot sit down and write an Oscar Wilde play at will. The fact that his plays, though apparently lucrative, remain unique under these circumstances, says much for the self-denial of our scribes.
>
> (12 January 1895, 44–45)

When Wilde wrote to the artists Rickets and Shannon asking them to come to the first night of *An Ideal Husband* he confessed, 'It was written for ridiculous puppets to play, and the critics will say, "Ah, here is Oscar unlike himself!"'—though in reality I became engrossed in the writing of it, and it contains a great deal of the real Oscar' (*Pearson*, 250). The propensity for self-dramatisation which was so outstanding an aspect of Wilde's character and which manifests itself in all his plays is perhaps present most insidiously in this play. That it is a play about a guilty secret is true, only in this case the secret lies in the past of a distinguished man, not as in the case of the two previous plays, in the past of a comparatively obscure woman. This touches close on the secret private life of Wilde at this time, a secret life passed in private rooms and hotels, away from his home and his wife. And is there not a secret irony in the title of the play—*An Ideal Husband*—which the 'real Oscar' certainly was not?

Before taking leave of this play it is pertinent to note two elements which point to developments in his command of dramatic form and content. Although *An Ideal Husband* is his longest social comedy and has what might be described as a 'strong' plot, it contains several passages in which he plays with words almost entirely for their own sakes and with little or no reference to the dramatic content. No other dramatist of the day had the courage to tease the audience with words, with passages which are gems of the verbal *non sequitur*. The way ahead to *The Importance of Being Earnest* is clearly indicated in such an encounter as the following:

> *Lord Caversham*: . . . Want a serious conversation with you, sir.
> *Lord Goring*: My dear father! At this hour?
> *Lord Caversham*: Well, sir, it is only ten o'clock. What is your objection to the hour? I think the hour is an admirable hour.
> *Lord Goring*: Well, the fact is, father, this is not my day for talking seriously. I am very sorry, but it is not my day.
> *Lord Caversham*: What do you mean, sir?
> *Lord Goring*: During the Season, father, I only talk seriously on the first Tuesday in every month, from four to seven.
> *Lord Caversham*: Well, make it Tuesday, sir, make it Tuesday.
> *Lord Goring*: But it is after seven, father, and my doctor says I must not have any serious conversation after seven. It makes me talk in my sleep.

Not even Shaw, who alone rivals Wilde in the craft of comedy, could write dialogue as funny and as natural as this. It was not always easily achieved as a study of his manuscripts and revised prompt copies prove. A major reason for Wilde's continued success in the theatre—and one for which he is never given sufficient credit—is that he could write dialogue serious or amusing which on the lips of the actor becomes lively and accurate speech. He never stooped to speech littered with apostrophes to mark dropped consonants either at the beginning or end of words or other typographical devices of the 'realist' dramatist but his dialogue sounds extraordinarily convincing throughout: it does not need translation from the printed page because it lives both there and on the stage.

The last element concerns Wilde's plots which are always said to have been derived from Sardou or Scribe or Augier or other of the *boulevard* dramatists, a statement which it is extremely difficult to verify since the plays of these dramatists have absolutely disappeared from the stage whereas those of the 'derivative' Wilde are never absent from it for any length of time.[3] Wilde did care about his plots which, as we have seen, are less sentimental and more socially critical than is generally admitted. Yet he was also moving beyond the plot as a restraint and might well have eventually progressed to a new form of drama almost entirely without plot, much in line with a number of the supposed revolutionary developments in contemporary drama. John Russell Taylor says of his social comedies that they are:

> society dramas of a decidedly old-fashioned kind, littered with asides and soliloquies. What then saves them, for Shaw and for us. Primarily, I think, their entire shamelessness. Wilde does not give the impression, even for a moment, that he takes all this nonsense seriously. The plots are creaking old contrivances.
>
> (*op. cit.*, 89–90)

With due respect, it must be said that Wilde's three comedies with pink lampshades and secrets from the past are *not* littered with asides and soliloquies; and, in fact, there are no asides at all and no more soliloquies than can be found in the average play of the contemporary stage, where the device of a character reading a letter aloud or commenting in isolation on some aspect of the drama is far from uncommon. This emphasis on his plots diverts critical attention from a consideration of Wilde's merits as an important dramatist of his day and of today.[4]

An Ideal Husband is not the last of Wilde's comedies which pivot about a secret but it is the last in which the secret as such is taken seriously. He was restless, searching after new forms, experimenting with new techniques, yet staying within the bounds imposed by the commercial theatre of the 1890s. It marks yet another stage in his evolution as a dramatist while retaining its intrinsic value as a comedy which entertains, delights, intrigues and amuses audiences of today as much as it did the first-night audience in 1895.

NOTES

1. It is often forgotten that Wilde's income was not based totally on London performances but also on the numerous ones given by companies directed by London agents which toured the provinces. Then, as now, performances by amateurs provided a continuous and useful supply of cash.
2. Superb Shakespearian actor, especially of such rôles as Henry V where eloquence is needed, had taken over Tree's rôle of Lord Illingworth during a tour of *A Woman of No Importance* by Tree's company.
3. The author has, in fact, seen a performance of Sardou's *Madame Sans-Gêne* in Belgrade at the Jugoslavian National Theatre, given in Serbo-Croat, and can attest to very little laughter, very little action, and what seemed to be an inordinate amount of rhetorical dialogue. Visits to the plays of these once-celebrated French dramatists should be compulsory for those literary critics who accuse Wilde of borrowing from their great works.
4. The same writer summarises the plot of this play as, '. . . Sir Robert Chiltern, an ambitious and high-principled politician whose dark secret is that he once, in younger days, sold a state secret to a foreign power.'

7

The Importance of
Being Earnest

Wilde enjoyed popular success but enjoyed financial success even more; and comparing the enormous profitability of his plays with the bleak returns from his slight volumes of verse and prose must have been a sharp incentive to carry on writing for the theatre, an activity for which his love of words, flashing wit, and personal theatricality were most suitable and financially rewarding assets. By the beginning of 1894 he was juggling with several ideas at the same time, so that it is difficult to disentangle his projects. It seems likely that he was thinking about—greater precision is impossible —another social comedy of the 'pink lampshade' variety, a one-act play of a more 'literary' nature, and a light comedy or farce without, however, necessarily setting anything down in writing. That was the aspect of literature for which he cared least. The fact that the St. James's Theatre under Alexander had firmly established itself may have inclined his thoughts to the actor-manager whom he began to tempt about July 1894 with the promise of a play which would be all the sooner in making its appearance if an advance of money were forthcoming. This was a bad habit which he was to fall into with increasing shamelessness during his last years when his requests for money (and he certainly got through a lot during those allegedly penurious years abroad) were invariably accompanied by the promise of a play in return. In his letter to Alexander he said:

> The real charm of the play, if it is to have a charm, must be in the dialogue. The plot is slight, but, I think, adequate . . . Well, I think an amusing thing with lots of fun and wit might be made.

If you think so too, and care to have the refusal of it, do let me
know, and send me £150. If when the play is finished, you think
it too slight—not serious enough—of course you can have the
£150 back. I want to go away and write it, and it could be ready
in October, as I have nothing else to do . . . In the meantime,
my dear Aleck, I am so pressed for money that I don't know what
to do. Of course I am extravagant. You have always been a good
wise friend to me, so think what you can do.

(*Letters*, 359)

A little later he was still writing to Alexander suggesting he should
write yet another play for him, the plot of which he detailed. To
Lord Alfred Douglas he commented, 'My play is really very funny:
I am quite delighted with it' (*Letters*, 362). It is likely that the
'amusing thing' was to be *The Importance of Being Earnest* and
the second play *Mr. and Mrs. Daventry*.

The Importance of Being Earnest was written during August–
September 1894 when Wilde was staying with his family and
friends at the seaside town of Worthing, Sussex, where he had
rented a furnished house for the summer season at The Haven,
5 Esplanade. His son Vyvyan Holland remembered:

Wilde wrote the first draft in the summer and autumn of 1894,
at Worthing, where he had taken a house for my mother, my
brother and myself. I remember that time very well. He spent
the mornings writing, but most of the afternoons playing on the
beach with us.

(Explanatory *Foreword to the Original Four-Act Version of the*
Importance of Being Earnest, 1957, v)

Despite his ever-present financial difficulties the play was written
in a light-hearted atmosphere, as Wilde evidently realised when
he wrote to a correspondent:

I am in a very much worse state for money than I told you. But
am just finishing a new play which, as it is quite nonsensical and
has no serious interest, will I hope bring me in a lot of red gold.

(*Letters*, 364)

The play was finished within three weeks and submitted to George
Alexander who was evidently hesitant about producing the play
because Wilde wrote to him in September 1894 from Worthing:

My dear Aleck, I can't make out what could have become of your letter. I thought from your silence that you thought the play too farcical in incident for a comedy theatre like your own, or that you didn't like my asking you to give me some money. I thought of telegraphing to you, but then changed my mind.

As regards the American rights: when you go to the states, it won't be to produce a farcical comedy. You will go as a romantic actor of modern and costume pieces. My play, though the dialogue is sheer comedy, and the best I have ever written, is of course in idea farcical: it could not be made part of a repertoire of serious or classical pieces, except for fun—once—as Irving plays Jeremy Diddler to show the Bostonians how versatile he is, and how a man who can realise Hamlet for us, can yet hold his own with the best of fantastic farce-players.

I would be charmed to write a modern comedy-drama for you, and to give you rights on both sides of the disappointing Atlantic Ocean, but you, of all our young actors, should not go to America to play farcical comedy. You might just as well star at Philadelphia in *Dr. Bill*. Besides, I hope to make at least £3000 in the States with this play, so what sum could I ask you for, with reference to double rights? Something that you, as a sensible manager, would not dream of paying. No: I want to come back to you. I would like to have my play done by you (I must tell you candidly that the two young men's parts are equally good), but it would be neither for your artistic reputation as a star in the States, nor for my pecuniary advantage, for you to produce it for a couple of nights in each big American town. It would be throwing the thing away.

I may mention that the play is an admirable play. I can't come up to town. I have no money . . . Write me your views—about this whole business.

(*Letters*, 368–369)

This letter rather suggests that Alexander had not yet seen a copy of the play. But by insinuating that Alexander might not be a success in farcical comedy (and no actor can ever accept that he might not triumph in any kind of drama whatsoever), Wilde made sure that he would make some kind of nibble at the new play. However, we know that Wilde did not care for Alexander, that he had had his last two plays produced in other theatres, that he had hopes another actor-manager would take the new play, and, at the same time, probably wished Alexander to take (when finished)

Mr. and Mrs. Daventry which was the kind of play in vogue at the St. James's Theatre. Meanwhile the revised manuscript was sent for typing to Mrs. Marshall's typewriting agency, Wilde having found the writing of farcical comedy excellent for style but fatal to clarity of handwriting. It was typed out as *Lady Lancing* from 3–24 October and a copy sent to Alexander to whom Wilde wrote from Tite Street where he was recovering from what was ominously described as 'a sort of malarial fever':

> . . . I am quite well now, and, as you wished to see my somewhat farcical comedy, I send you the first copy of it. It is called *Lady Lancing* on the cover: but the real title is *The Importance of Being Earnest*. When you read the play, you will see the punning title's meaning. Of course, the play is not suitable to you at all: you are a romantic actor; the people it wants are actors like Wyndham and Hawtrey. Also, I would be sorry if you altered the definite artistic line of progress you have always followed at the St. James's. But, of course, read it, and let me know what you think about it. I have very good offers from America for it.
>
> (*Letters*, 375–376)

Alexander was not attracted by the play nor convinced by the 'very good offers from America' that Wilde spoke of and sent it to Charles Wyndham, the actor-manager. Two events now intervened: Wilde's *An Ideal Husband* began a triumphant run at the Haymarket Theatre on 3 January 1895, and Henry James's *Guy Domville* opened disastrously at the St. James's Theatre two days later and proved an instant failure. Alexander was an honourable man and kept *Guy Domville* in repertoire for a month but realised that a new play was essential. In desperation he remembered Wilde's farcical comedy, wrote to Wyndham asking for its return, and quickly put it into rehearsal. There were two difficulties. First, Wyndham agreed to surrender the play on condition that Wilde should write him another play before writing one for Alexander—who agreed to this condition with the reservation that the draft scenario—almost certainly of *Mr. and Mrs. Daventry*—which had been sent to him by Wilde from Worthing should not be the subject of this reservation. And, second, the play had been written in four acts and Alexander preferred a three-act play which could be preceded, as was customary, by a short curtain-raiser. Wilde re-

THE PLAYS OF OSCAR WILDE

vised the play and *The Importance of Being Earnest* took the form in which it is now generally presented.

Wilde was present at the first reading when the actors expressed the opinion that it would prove too subtle for the public. He continued to attend rehearsals and bombard the actors with suggestions until Alexander took him aside and told him that unless they were left alone the play would never be ready for the opening night. Wilde dutifully left for Algiers but not before giving an interview to the *St. James's Gazette*, a Conservative evening paper, in which he stated that Victor Hugo and Maeterlinck were the only dramatists of the century whose work had interested him. He had a witty revenge on Alexander when he returned to London for the dress rehearsal and shook the company by telling them that he supposed they would be starting rehearsals for the play on the following Monday. When asked by a press reporter whether it would be a success he answered, 'My dear fellow, you have got it wrong. The play *is* a success. The only question is whether the first night's audience will be one.'

The Importance of Being Earnest: A Trivial Comedy for Serious People, or, as Wilde also described it, a play written by a butterfly for butterflies, opened on the night of 14 February 1895, in the midst of a bitter snowstorm. With Alexander as John Worthing, Allan Aynesworth as Algernon Moncrieff, Irene Vanbrugh as Gwendolen Fairfax and Rose Leclercq as Lady Bracknell, it was from first to last a resounding triumph. Wilde turned to the actor Franklin Dyall and said, 'I don't think I shall take a call tonight. I took one only last month at the Haymarket, and one feels so much like a German band.' Years later Allan Aynesworth told Hesketh Pearson, 'In my fifty-three years of acting, I never remember a greater triumph than the first night of *The Importance of Being Earnest*. The audience rose in their seats and cheered and cheered again' (Pearson, 257). In general the critics were equally enthusiastic and the whole of London, social, literary, frivolous and serious, agreed that there was not a more amusing evening to be spent anywhere than at the St. James's Theatre.

Wilde now had two plays running at the same time to packed houses, money was pouring in, and a glittering future as playwright lay before him. But it is necessary here to recount events which took place on that first night and of which critics and audience were both unaware. Since 1891, as we have seen, Wilde had been intimate with Lord Alfred Douglas, a striking and gifted but tiresome and unbalanced young man, and had fallen foul of his father Lord Queensberry, perhaps the most uncouth and vicious nobleman in London. When he returned home for the dress rehearsal from Algiers where he had been travelling with Douglas he heard that Queensberry had booked a seat for the first night. Wilde wrote to R. V. Shone, business manager of the St. James's, asking him to write officially to Queensberry saying that the seat given to him had already been sold and returning his money. Not to be outdone, Queensberry presented himself at the theatre with a bouquet of carrots and turnips which he evidently intended to throw at Wilde when he took a curtain at the end of the play. Queensberry was ejected from the theatre and then tried to gain admission to the gallery and to pass through the stage door before retiring to his club. He had already created a stir in a London theatre when he went to a performance of Tennyson's *The Promise of May* in 1882 and not only flung a bouquet of vegetables at the cast but also made a speech in favour of atheism. What Wilde failed to realise was that Queensberry was as great a publicity-seeker as himself, that he was a relentless enemy, that he had some real paternal feelings, and that he was about to use his money effectively to bring Wilde low. As a result of his broodings, three days later, on 18 February, he presented himself at 4.30 p.m. at the Albermarle Club, produced a visiting card on which he had written, 'To Oscar Wilde posing as a somdomite', and gave it to the hall porter with the words, 'Give that to Oscar Wilde.' Ten days later Wilde went to the club where he was handed the card discreetly enclosed in an envelope. Anyone at all familiar with the tragedy which followed will know that this was the beginning of Wilde's downfall and the end of his career as a dramatist. Relentlessly and irresponsibly urged on by Douglas, one of literature's greatest pests, he foolishly decided to prosecute Queensberry with the unfortunate results that are now part of literary and legal history.

Despite Wilde's arrest on 5 April 1895 the play ran until 8 May, his name having been removed from the playbills and programmes—the subject of a protest by the playwright Sydney Grundy who wrote a letter on the subject to the *Daily Telegraph* on 8 April. The play ran for a total of eighty-six performances but Alexander lost the sum of two hundred and eighty-nine pounds, eight and fourpence during the run, attributing his loss to the scandal occasioned by the writer's trials. At the time of Wilde's bankruptcy he was able to buy the copyright of *The Importance of Being Earnest* for a minute sum. In 1902 he revived the play at the St. James's Theatre and although well received by critics and public is still did not make money. In 1909, on the second revival, it ran for eleven months and made a profit of over twenty-one thousand pounds, a very large sum of money for the time. Alexander wrote to Robert Ross with delight: 'You will be glad to hear that dear E has really caught on: we had splendid houses yesterday, and turned money away from the "pit and gallery"—how this would have pleased him (Wilde)!' (*Robert Ross: Friend of Friends*, ed. Margery Ross, 1952, 173). He put the play on again in 1911 and 1913. On his death Alexander bequeathed the copyright to Wilde's son Vyvyan whom it considerably enriched.

The reader may well wonder how the play fared in America since Wilde had so often insisted to Alexander that the managers there were crying out for it. The New York run opened on 22 April 1895, two days before Wilde's trial, and ran for a few weeks with no great public acclaim. When it closed there were no more productions of Wilde's plays for some ten years.

The plot of *The Importance of Being Earnest* is comparatively simple. In the morning-room of his flat in Half-Moon Street we find Algernon Moncrieff talking to his manservant Lane about the excessive amount of champagne which has been drunk, a dialogue which leads to the subject of marriage about which Algernon comments:

> Lane's views on marriage seem somewhat lax. Really, if the lower orders don't set us a good example, what on earth is the use of them? They seem, as a class, to have absolutely no sense of moral responsibility.

Algernon is joined by his friend Ernest Worthing who announces that he is in love with Algernon's cousin Gwendolen who is coming to tea with her mother Lady Bracknell. Algernon produces a cigarette case which Ernest Worthing left behind on a previous visit, and asks for an explanation of the inscription inside: 'From little Cecily with her fondest love to her dear Uncle Jack'. It turns out that Ernest is actually called Jack (or, more properly, John), that he was adopted at an early age by a Mr. Thomas Cardew who in his will made him guardian to his grand-daughter, Miss Cecily Cardew, who lives in the country under the charge of her governess, Miss Prism. In order to get up to London he has pretended to have a younger, wicked brother called Ernest who lives in the Albany (B.4, the Albany—a somewhat raffish address at the time) but has decided to bring the business to an end. Algernon then confesses that in order to get out of town he pretends to have an invalid friend called Bunbury to whose side he is frequently called. (In foreign language translations the play is frequently known as *Bunbury*). Lady Bracknell and Gwendolen arrive and take tea. Later, while Lady Bracknell is in the next room selecting music for her last reception of the season:

> French songs I cannot possibly allow. People always seem to think that they are improper, and either look shocked, which is vulgar, or laugh, which is worse. But German sounds a thoroughly respectable language, and indeed, I believe is so.

Jack takes the opportunity to propose to Gwendolen who is a very self-possessed young lady: however, she accepts him under the name of Ernest—'the only really safe name'. They are interrupted by Lady Bracknell who interviews Jack as a prospective son-in-law but on finding that he was a foundling—found in a hand-bag—at once dismisses him. She could not dream of allowing her only daughter—'a girl brought up with the utmost care—to marry into a cloak-room, and form an alliance with a parcel'. Gwendolen manages to have a last-minute conversation with Jack in which she says she may need to communicate with him urgently and requests his country address. This Algernon overhears. When, at the end of the act, he asks Lane to prepare his Bunbury outfit, we can be sure that mischief is afoot.

The second and third acts are set in the country, at the Manor House, Woolton. Wilde is writing a clever variation on the old theme of the corruption of the town and the innocence of the country, particularly as he sets Act Two in the garden amid roses, a large yew-tree, and basket chairs. In this Eden we find Cecily at her studies supervised by Miss Prism whose adoration of the

Rector, Canon Chasuble, is obvious. Algernon then enters in the guise of Jack's younger brother, the wicked Ernest, and begins at once to flirt with Cecily. Shortly afterwards, Jack is seen emerging from the back of the garden, dressed in the deepest mourning, with crepe hatband and black gloves. He announces the death of his wicked brother Ernest in Paris. A farcical situation ensues when Algernon and Jack face each other. When Algernon resumes his flirtation with Cecily he finds that she has always been determined to love someone by the name of Ernest: in consequence both he and Jack wish Canon Chasuble to christen them with the name of Ernest. While the two men are absent Gwendolen is shown in: jealousy and curiosity have brought her down into the country to find out more about Jack whom she knows only as Ernest. The two young women find that they seem to be engaged to an Ernest Worthing. After a scene of formal, restrained and ruthless bitchiness they join forces against Jack and Algernon who are left alone to eat muffins of which they are both extremely fond. Wilde may have derived some of this action from W. S. Gilbert's *Engaged* (1877; 1881).

The third and last act takes place in the drawing-room. Originally, Wilde set it in the garden and then moved it to a morning- or drawing-room. Lady Bracknell arrives. She refuses to allow a marriage with Algernon until she learns that Cecily is heiress to an immense fortune whereupon she sees in her many admirable qualities which she had hitherto overlooked. Jack takes his revenge by revealing that under the terms of her grandfather's will Cecily is not allowed to marry without the consent of her guardian until she is thirty-five. That does not seem an objection to Lady Bracknell:

> Thirty-five is a very attractive age. London society is full of women of the very highest birth who have, of their own free will, remained thirty-five for years . . . I see no reason why our dear Cecily should not be even still more attractive at the age you mention than she is at present. There will be a large accumulation of property.

However, Cecily shows a somewhat impatient nature by declaring that she cannot wait so long. The situation is resolved by the appearance of Miss Prism. It turns out that years before she had been in the employ of Lord Bracknell and had disappeared with a baby of the male sex in a perambulator. Miss Prism confesses that she put the manuscript of a novel on which she had been working in her few unoccupied hours in the perambulator and had placed the baby in a hand-bag which in a moment of mental abstraction she had deposited in the cloak-room of Victoria Station. Lady Bracknell solves the riddle of Jack's birth still further: he is the eldest son of her 'poor sister, Mrs. Moncrieff', and, therefore brother of Algernon. The baby deposited in the cloak-room at Victoria Station is none other than John Worthing J.P., who finds his place in society as Algernon's brother, Lady Bracknell's nephew, Gwendolen's cousin and fiancé, and Cecily's guardian and brother-in-law to be—since the play ends with declarations of love exchanged between Algernon and Cecily, Jack and Gwendolen, and Canon Chasuble and Miss Prism. The action takes place within twenty-four hours.

There are drafts in Wilde's hand of Acts III and IV of the original four-act version of the play in the British Museum; and Acts I and II are in the Arents Collection in the New York Public Library. Also in the British Museum is the licensing copy evidently typed in some haste by Miss Dickens's Type Writing Office and which was presumably received by the Lord Chamberlain's Office on 30 January 1895.[1] A rehearsal copy, also typed by Miss Dickens's office, bearing George Alexander's signature and bookplate, is in the Harvard Theatre Collection. The play itself was published by Smithers in February 1899 after Wilde had corrected a type-written script obtained from Alexander. He wrote to Smithers:

> Please have it type-written on thick good paper, *not* tissue, as I cannot correct tissue, and one should not waste tissue; so at least the doctors say.

> (*Letters*, 745)

In addition, there is a German translation of the four-act version, published in Leipzig in 1903, the Samuel French acting edition issued about 1903, and an early promptbook donated by Allan Aynesworth to the British Museum. These texts all vary considerably, in the actual dialogue as well as in the names and settings. For instance, in the text submitted to the Lord Chamberlain's office both Act II and Act III, as has already been mentioned, were set in the garden of the manor house and only in later versions was the action of Act III removed indoors—which movement, incidentally, has misled some producers into thinking that the act is taking place on the following morning. Lady Bracknell was then known (on the cover of the typescript) as Lady Lancing and (inside) as Lady Brancaster: only later was she given the name with which she now commands the stage. Algernon was called Montford, not Moncrieff. The rehearsal copy in the Harvard Theatre Collection shows evidence of Alexander's careful production methods, an interesting instance being the manner in which Jack enters in mourning from 'back of garden R. He goes C.', to be followed by Canon Chasuble and Miss Prism who 'both turn come down stage then towards C. See Jack for the first time.' In this way, the audience first becomes aware of the comedy of Jack's being dressed in mourning for an imaginary brother who is inside the house with Cecily—in the person of Algernon—and then the Canon and Miss Prism become aware of Jack: a carefully planned instance of a delayed reaction which increases the general sense of fun. This is surely an excellent proof of Wilde's visual sense— which Bernard Shaw, incidentally, tended to denigrate. It is also proof that an actor-manager like Alexander was capable of understanding the needs of the play and of thinking beyond his own particular rôle.[2] The various texts of The Importance of Being Earnest are extremely illuminating and have hardly received the critical attention they deserve.

The invaluable Hesketh Pearson tells us:

> At first the plot was far more complicated, dealing with a case of double identity, and was placed in the period of Sheridan. But the moment Wilde gave reign to his native genius, it burst through the style and costume of the eighteenth century and rioted in its own dimension.
>
> (Pearson, 252)

This must be hearsay since no text exists to substantiate the statement. We do know, however, that the play was first written in four acts—for which a text exists—but that Alexander insisted that Acts II and III should be compressed into a single act. The scene which was sacrificed showed Algernon being served with a writ for seven hundred and sixty-two pounds fourteen and two-pence on behalf of the Savoy Hotel Co. by a solicitor named Gribsby:

> *Gribsby*: I am sorry to disturb this pleasant family meeting, but time presses. We have to be at Holloway not later than four o'clock; otherwise it is difficult to obtain admission. The rules are very strict.
> *Algernon*: Holloway!
> *Gribsby*: It is at Holloway that detentions of this character take place always.
> *Algernon*: Well, I really am not going to be imprisoned in the suburbs for having dined in the West End. It is perfectly ridiculous.
> *Gribsby*: The bill is for suppers, not dinners.

Wilde is said to have asked Alexander if he realised what a sacrifice he was calling for in wanting the play abbreviated:

> 'You will be able to use it in another play,' replied Alexander.
> 'It may not fit into another play.'
> "What does it matter? You are clever enough to think of a hundred things just as good.'
> 'Of course I am', was the reply, 'A thousand if need be—but that is not the point. The scene you feel is superfluous cost me terrible exhausting labour and heart-rending nerve-wracking strain. You may not believe me, but I assure you on my honour that it must have taken fully five minutes to write.'

We can dismiss this as Wilde's tomfoolery since there is proof that Wilde revised the scene in question at least twice which hardly indicates a flippant attitude to play-writing. Vyvyan Holland, Wilde's son, attempted to reconstruct the four-act version in 1957, using the German translation of 1903 and various fragments but the result while amusing is not very convincing from a theatrical point of view (*op. cit.*). Although we lose a short act there is a clear gain in dramatic unity; and today even more than in Wilde's time audiences do not care to sit through any play that is longer than three short acts. Although Alexander disliked Wilde's presence at rehearsals it is possible to see that the comedy gained from the changes he made in the text, as the following example may show:

Licensing copy:
Lady Bracknell: Lady Bloxham? I don't know her. What number in Belgrave Square?

Rehearsal copy/first edition:
Lady Bracknell: Lady Bloxham? I don't know her.
Jack: Oh, she goes about very little. She's a lady considerably advanced in years.
Lady Bracknell: Ah, now-a-days that is no guarantee of respectability of character. What number in Belgrave Square?

The various scripts differ from each other, but serve to show that Wilde's added adornments during rehearsals, and later the proof sheets he corrected for Smithers' edition of 1899, which is now accepted as the standard version, are improvements (for further information on this see Joseph W. Donohue, Jr., 'The First Production of *The Importance of Being Earnest*: A Proposal for a Reconstructive Study' *Essays on Nineteenth Century British Theatre*, 1971, 134).

Although *The Importance of Being Earnest* is frequently described as a masterpiece of construction there is a clumsiness in the balance of events in the first act and those of the next two (which take place the following day) which the four-act version would have further emphasised. Part of the weakness of the first act derives from the late entry of Lady Bracknell whose dialogue intensifies the humour to a point from which it can only fall away after her exit. Contemporary critics stressed Wilde's indebtedness to the French theatre and to Beaumarchais among other writers of comedy—they would have done better to have mentioned Labiche whose *Celimaire* has some similarities with *The Importance of Being Earnest*; they also mentioned the influence of W. S. Gilbert and whether they meant Gilbert the dramatist or Gilbert the librettist is unimportant because in both capacities he was deservedly famous for his neat, farcical constructions. W. H. Auden states:

> . . . in 'The Importance of Being Earnest' Wilde succeeded—almost, it would seem, by accident, for he never realised its infinite superiority to all his other plays—in writing what is perhaps the only pure verbal opera in English. The solution that, deliberately or accidentally, he found was to subordinate every other

dramatic element to dialogue for its own sake and create a verbal universe in which the characters are determined by the kinds of things they say, and the plot is nothing but a succession of opportunities to say them.
(W. H. Auden, 'An Improbable Life', review of *The Letters of Oscar Wilde, New Yorker,* 9 March 1963; reprinted in Richard Ellman ed., *Wilde, A Collection of Critical Essays,* 1969, 135–36)

Auden seems here to have put his finger on a basic element in this comedy, although he does less than justice to the visual factors and to Wilde's sense of social justice which pervades the greater part of his work. Nevertheless, *The Importance of Being Earnest* can reasonably be described as a purely verbal opera, with all the fun and gaiety to be found in the comic operas of Gilbert and Sullivan but without any of the pathos or sympathetic studies of love to be found in those of Mozart. The play falls, as most producers from Alexander onward have realised, into set pieces: duets, trios, quartets, and septets, as well as into a number of arias of a varied and baroque nature.[8] Even the amusing mistake, vastly improbable as it was, whereby Jack Worthing, when a baby, was placed in a hand-bag and deposited in the cloak-room at Victoria Station and the manuscript of a three-decker novel put in his place in the basinette by the absent-minded Miss Prism has its counterpart in opera, serious and comic. The hero of *The Pirates of Penzance* when a boy was mistakenly apprenticed to a pirate instead of a pilot; and Azucena in *Il Trovatore* more tragically but hardly less improbably throws the wrong baby into the fire. The fact that Wilde did not care for music—and still less for opera— means he may have been more critically aware of the comic possibilities of most opera *libretti*; and it is this outrageous manipulation of plot which enables Eric Bentley to declare that he has 'no serious plot, no credible characters', although it must be stressed that his characters are as credible within their dramatic context as are any in opera ('The Importance of Being Earnest', *The Playwright as Thinker,* 1957 edn., 144). There is a greater truth than accuracy of character-drawing, and that is truth to the whole— in opera this is the music, and in Wilde's plays it is the verbal comedy.

The construction of the play also rests on a series of secrets. It has sometimes been remarked that Wilde's plays (his social comedies, at any rate) depend on secrets: but it would be nearer the truth to say that the action arises from disclosure or the fear of disclosure. Deception and deceit are, in any case, the basis of most comedy; and *The Importance of Being Earnest* is no exception. Algernon goes down into the country under the pretext of visiting an invalid friend called Bunbury, while John Worthing J.P., excuses his absences from his country home by claiming to have a profligate brother called Ernest who lives at B.4, The Albany, then a somewhat raffish place of residence and eminently suitable for a disreputable bachelor whose immigration to Australia is under consideration. While in town John Worthing (who prefers to call himself Jack) is known as Ernest. In the first act he tells Gwendolen that he is staying in town until Monday but retreats to the country the very next day, presumably to announce the death of his fictitious brother Ernest and also to have himself christened under that name. After having obtained Jack's country address on the pretext that she might have to communicate with him urgently and after having made sure that he is remaining in London, Gwendolen goes down into the country the very next day to investigate his home background. After having overheard the conversation between Jack and Gwendolen, Algernon notes down this address and, pretending to be the profligate brother Ernest, manages to slither (accompanied by three portmanteaus, a dressing case, two hat-boxes, and a large luncheon-basket) into the country home and meet Cecily. Lady Bracknell is no less guileful in this respect: by bribing Gwendolen's maid she manages to find out where she has vanished; and her own life has been touched by scandal and mystery (and coincidences are not supposed to happen in the best families) when her infant nephew disappeared, together with his nursemaid, and could not be recovered despite the elaborate investigations of the metropolitan police who succeeded only in finding the perambulator standing by itself in a remote corner of Bayswater. Miss Prism has lived with the guilty secret of her misdeed (and without her invaluable hand-bag) for nearly thirty years. But John Worthing, J.P., *alias* Jack Worthing *alias* Ernest Worthing, has lived with even greater scandals: those of his unknown parents, of his having been *found*—and of his having been found in the cloak-room of one of the larger London

THE IMPORTANCE OF BEING EARNEST

railway stations, places known before now to have concealed social indiscretions. In the four act version there is an even greater scandal, when Algernon masquerading as Ernest Worthing is served with the writ for his unpaid account at the instigation of the Savoy Hotel which seems to indicate that not only does John give himself up to a life of pleasure as Ernest but acts the part so fully as to run up debts in that name, a somewhat unnecessary course of action in view of his immense wealth. This wealth is also mysterious, for we learn little of the late Mr. Thomas Cardew, grandfather to Cecily and benefactor to John and who has left him a country house with about fifteen hundred acres attached to it, a town house at 149 Belgrave Square, and an income of between seven and eight thousand pounds a year. His lack of direct heirs is not referred to. It would have been interesting to know whether Mr. Cardew actually rose from the ranks of the aristocracy or was born in the purple of commerce: whatever the case he was in the exclusive Court Guides of the period and must have been among the wealthiest men in London. When John finds that the hand-bag in which he was found had belonged to Miss Prism he falls at her feet and calls her mother, willingly accepting that she was his unmarried mother. Of course, this is a piece of comic lunacy on Wilde's part—and to accept the fact that John is a bastard is a trifling matter after the various upheavals he has gone through. Nor is little Cecily above deceit, albeit of a petty kind, as when she tells Gwendolen that her engagement is to be announced in the local newspaper. The lives of the servants are no more impeccable: Lane, the manservant, was married in consequence of a misunderstanding between himself and a young person, a situation of which he speaks distantly. The entanglements of the plot proceed directly from Algernon's reading the inscription inside John's cigarette case—a clear parallel with the letters of *A Woman of No Importance* and *An Ideal Husband* and the fan (another useless object of luxury) of *Lady Windermere's Fan*—which he has been holding on to since John last dined at home with him. Another instance of near-kleptodramatics! Deception and misunderstandings are the essence of farce and, to a lesser extent, of comedy, so that it is wrong to regard those in *The Importance of Being Earnest* in too serious a light. But their existence as part of the dramatic situation must be noted by the conscientious reader and stressed by both actors and producers. Though they are decidedly comic they might very well have been tragic; and there is nothing funny about an arrest of any kind, as Wilde was to learn for himself only a few weeks after the first performance of the play.

'Today', writes Sir John Gielgud, 'we laugh at the very idea that such types could ever have existed . . .' and goes on to mention 'the ridiculously exaggerated values of birth, rank and fashion'. He sees a danger that contemporary actors will turn the comedy into wild caricature because they lack 'real types to draw from'. At the same time, he writes of 'the grave puppet characters . . .' who 'utter their delicate cadences and spin their web of preposterously elegant sophistication' (*Stage Directions*, 1963, 85). Sir John is an experienced producer of the play and as John Worthing gave a superlative performance which older critics considered superior to that of Alexander, and his views are, therefore, of importance. But surely he is mistaken in his general attitude, for the play deals with lasting verities and with attitudes which are still prevalent in English life.

In a manner not dissimilar from Shakespeare's comedies, *The Importance of Being Earnest* is concerned with young people, love and marriage; and as Shakespeare's comedies are generally set in the open air so Wilde sets his play in an English garden—in his first version three of the four acts were set there. At the end we are presented with declarations of love (which, it is to be presumed, imply proposals of marriage) by the two young couples as well as the older, graver Miss Prism and Canon Chasuble. The two young men are also, in a sense, regenerated by killing off their old Adams and seeking baptism—though not by total immersion. John soon declares his intention of killing off his brother and, in fact, announces that Ernest is 'Dead! . . . Quite dead', while Algernon kills off his *alter ego* Bunbury, 'Bunbury is dead . . . I killed Bunbury this afternoon . . . he was quite exploded.' If we take the intention of the two young men to be baptised as, in any sense, however comic, symbolic of their turning their backs on their old life and facing their new (married) life in an appropriate state of earnestness, we are reminded by Wilde that they are, in the Christian faith, already redeemed. The laughter arises not only from their casual attitude to christening but also from the different attitudes of Lady Bracknell and Canon Chasuble. Lady Bracknell does not underestimate the importance of christening, least of all in the financial sense, for she says that at John's birth he experienced it together with 'every luxury that money could buy', and his desire to be christened is described as 'grotesque and irreligious' and as an 'excess'—which, theologically speaking, it is. Canon Chasuble reinforces the theological attitudes when addressing Algernon, 'Yes, but you have been christened. That is the important thing.'

The Importance of Being Earnest is earnest in quite a different way in its attitudes to two very material substances, both, at times, interchangeable: money and food. Eating and drinking whether of champagne or tea, cucumber sandwiches and bread-and-butter, cake, tea-cake, muffins or crumpets, whether in Algernon's flat, at Willis's or in the country, is a near-continuous activity which ferociously engages the characters' attention and passions. Algernon tells us, 'When I am in really great trouble, as anyone who knows me intimately will tell you, I refuse everything except food and drink.' The emotional scenes are those involving food which is used as a weapon of warfare both personal and social. Thus cake is not eaten in the best houses any more (social aggrandisement); and, against her wishes Gwendolen is given cake and sugar is put in her tea (personal aggrandisement). The acquisitive instinct is aroused even more keenly by money, and Cecily's hundred and thirty thousand pounds—in the Funds. Lady Bracknell, indeed, rhapsodises on the subject: a large accumulation of property is eminently desirable even if the owner's youthful charms fade away during the process, for against human frailty is contrasted money, a real, solid quality, one of 'the qualities that last and improve with time'. As someone who before her marriage 'had no fortune of any kind' Lady Bracknell is clearly in a position to appreciate its value in others, as does her nephew Algernon who has nothing but his debts to rely on. The original four-act version, it should be remarked, had an act devoted to Algernon being arrested for the imaginary Ernest's debts.

Eric Bentley has pointed out that the very first scene between Algernon and his butler Lane is 'a prelude to the jokes against class society which run through the play' (op. cit., 143). Wilde, it is true, lets us see that Lane is not entirely defenceless; he establishes his right to help himself to the champagne in the blandest yet most defiant of fashions. Miss Prism reminds Cecily that watering the plants is a utilitarian (and, therefore, to be despised) occupation which belongs properly to the gardener. And Lady Bracknell believes that universal education is likely to result in 'acts of violence in Grosvenor Square'. The dialogue between Cecily and Gwendolen in the second act abounds with references to class, not the least being Gwendolen's assertion that she is happy to say she has never seen a spade. But so kind is Wilde's humour and his affection for these ruthless, acquisitive, snobbish characters all fighting for self-expression that he is content to establish the basic structure, the basic tone, and let the play speak for itself.

The Importance of Being Earnest is not a difficult play to present; it is modest in its requirements of settings and actors although they must, as in all of Wilde's plays, be elegantly dressed, carry themselves well, and speak graciously. Above all, they must wear authentic clothes. Comedy depends on a carefully regulated suspension of disbelief which will not be forthcoming if the characters are dressed like circus clowns. This authenticity must extend to the properties, especially in the second act when the tea-table should be an altar dedicated to the ritual of tea, with a glittering array of china, starched lace and linen cloth, silver, and a prodigality of food.

Wilde does not set difficult tasks for his actors and even the character of Lady Bracknell, although central to the drama, is comparatively easy to impersonate. Played as a refined aristocrat the character loses all impact, for if she is something more and something less than a representative of the upper classes, she is certainly not an aristocrat in whose veins runs the bluest of blood. Wilde was noted for his elaborate, whimsical and private jokes, among them a keen interest in the activities of Queen Victoria which in his last years he transferred to the Pope, and throughout his life he used to pretend that the Queen took an impassioned and anxious interest in the slightest circumstances of his life. Rushing away from a luncheon party he would excuse himself by saying that the Queen was in London and that he would not like to keep her waiting since she was dying to see him—and, it must be said, she probably would have died had she seen him engaged in some of his more riotously sexual activities. If Wilde seemed

178

to regard her as an institutional object of fun much as she was to those of her African subjects who thought she moved on castors he had actually begun the debunking that Lytton Strachey was to continue. It would have delighted Wilde had he known of the minute scribbled by the Queen in reaction to a request he made of her for any poetry she had written to be published in the woman's journal of which he was editor: 'Really, what will people not say and invent. Never could the Queen in her whole life write *one* line of *poetry* serious or comic or make a rhyme ever. This is therefore all *invention* and *myth*!' Lady Bracknell shares many of the attributes of her sovereign, not least her appreciation of German solemnity in music. The tomfoolery about missing trains and exposing oneself to comment on the platform is deliciously funny but only a *parvenu*, which Lady Bracknell was essentially, could have displayed such concern about social position. The secret of Edith Evans' triumph in the part (she said that she saw Lady Bracknell as the kind of woman who would ring the bell to bring you to put a single lump of coal on the fire) lay in the exact degree of flamboyant vulgarity she brought to it. At the same time, at heart, Lady Bracknell is a woman to whom money means infinitely more than birth—as it did in late nineteenth-century society. Miss Cardew is rejected as a wife for her nephew Algernon (penniless as he is), until it is revealed that she has a large fortune (in the funds) whereupon she instantly becomes attractive. John Worthing, found in a hand-bag and fortuitously adopted by Mr. Cardew, has no difficulty in making his way in London society, no doubt because of his inherited money. Lady Bracknell was herself without any money but this did not prevent her marrying Lord Bracknell. She despises land which gives one position but prevents one from keeping it up: she prefers money, especially in investments. She represents the new class which emerged in the last years of the reign of Victoria and which was to triumph at the court of King Edward; and the wonder is that she is not chasing an American heiress as a wife for her nephew rather than accepting an English girl from an undistinguished family. As it is, the recognition of John as her long-lost nephew Ernest, is a testimony to the strength of the English clan-structure, which, together with money, is where her basic interests lie. All of this is not to say that Lady Bracknell is not a gloriously funny and worthy member of the line of English stage eccentrics which includes Mistress Quickly, Mrs. Malaprop and Charley's Aunt. There are times as when she takes off on some gloriously dotty speech when we seem to be hearing Wilde himself speaking so that whilst avoiding any excessive suggestion of *travesti*, actresses playing the part might do worse than bear in mind the speaking voice and physical characteristics of Wilde, which Frank Harris described in his *Oscar Wilde* (1938 edn.): 'His whole face lit up as he spoke and one saw nothing but his soulful eyes, heard nothing but his musical tenor voice' (67). She is his greatest single creation in whom he managed to reconcile the qualities of wit and social observation he had previously tried to express through the characters of Lord Darlington and Prince Paul. Not only can she turn the social order upside down when she so wishes but even the physical one: both the number of John Worthing's house in Belgrave Square and the fashionableness of one side or the other can be changed if necessary, the (railway) line is immaterial, although she will not allow her daughter to 'marry into a cloak-room and form an alliance with a parcel'. Significantly, for her, marriage is an alliance (Lord Bracknell counting for very little in her own case); and society a battlefield on which triumphs are won not only by social position and material wealth but equally effectively by words.

Reviewers of the first performance in 1895 welcomed the play even if they expressed some reservations about Wilde's lack of seriousness. Archer wrote an article which is still useful for its description of Alexander's production, as in the following account of the play's funniest episode:

> Monsieur Sarcey himself (if Mr. Wilde will forgive my saying so) would "chortle in his joy" over John Worthing's entrance in deep mourning even down to his cane to announce the death of his brother Ernest, when we know that Ernest in the flesh— a false but undeniable Ernest—is at that moment in the house making love to Cecily. The audience does not instantly awaken to the meaning of his inky suit, but even as he marches solemnly down the stage, and before a word is spoken, you can feel the idea kindling from row to row, until a "sudden glory" of laughter fills the theatre.
>
> (Signed review in *The World*, 20 February 1895)

G. B. Shaw was almost a sole voice in dissenting from the general chorus of praise, writing that he found it old-fashioned in style and structure and heartless in content, adding that 'unless comedy touches me as well as amuses me, it leaves me with a sense of having wasted my evening' (*Our Theatres in the Nineties*, repr. 1954, vol. I, p. 42). Yet, it must be admitted, Shaw borrowed several of Wilde's comic devices and much of his comic style for his own heartless comedies and one would have expected him to have welcomed the underlying structure of social criticism in the play. Perhaps the most idiosyncratic comments were those of Arnold Bennett who true to his own major preoccupation stated that the notion that Wilde had received large sums of money for his plays was erroneous, that he made a few thousand pounds out of *The Importance of Being Earnest*, but that the 'other plays, very inferior, did not do much'. He found these other plays less powerful, less original and less veracious than those of Lonsdale and Maugham. When he saw the revival of *The Importance of Being Earnest* at the Haymarket—'what a mournful disillusion! What a perturbation of conscience for my critical blindness.' After this elegant piece of English which appears to indicate that Bennett had been a pupil of Miss Prism at some stage in his early life he goes on to attack Wilde's style for lack of 'the elements of permanence' ('Books and Persons', *Evening Standard*, 30 June 1927). A more recent piece of criticism by Mary McCarthy, entitled 'The Unimportance of Being Oscar', and frequently reprinted, consists of reflections on a performance of the play. Although there are some odd observations, notably that Ernest is the 'tamest' name in English (neither Gwendolen nor Cecily thought or felt so), that Lady Bracknell is a dowager, that Miss Prism is spectacled, that the rector is in clerical dress and has taken a vow of celibacy, and that Lady Bracknell is 'genuinely well-born', for which we have no proof at all, she sees the themes of the play from an American point of view which means her comments are comparatively original. She writes:

> Depravity is the hero and the only character, the people on the stage embodying various shades of it. It is deepest dyed in the pastoral region of respectability and innocence. The London roué is artless simplicity itself beside the dreadnought society dowager, and she, in her turn, is out-brazened by her debutante

daughter, and she by the country miss, and she by her spectacled governess, till finally the village rector with his clerical
clothes, his vow of celibacy, and his sermon on the manna
adjustable to all occasions, slithers noiselessly into the rose
garden, specious as the Serpent Himself.

'The Unimportance of Being Oscar', *Mary McCarthy's Theatre
Chronicle* N.Y., 1963, 106–110)

The Importance of Being Earnest is Wilde's masterpiece in which
his wit, his invention, his sense of social reality, his deep-seated
and radical love of justice and the fundamental benevolence of his
character are most perfectly mingled. He is able to laugh confi-
dently at the beauty and the grotesqueness of life which he sees
as the same thing, just as Miss Prism is 'a female of repellent
aspect, remotely connected with education' and at the same time,
'the most cultivated of ladies, and the very picture of respectability', and the Canon's sermon on the meaning of the manna in
the wilderness 'can be adapted to almost any occasion', while retaining, presumably, its basic form unchanged. Wilde touches on
money, property, marriage, social class, philanthropy, education
and aristocracy among other matters, all with the lightest but
sharpest flashes of humour, and leaves little doubt as to his own
sympathies. In fact, he made fun of everything the English held—
and hold—sacred, not least money, baptism, birth, religion, food,
and property—and in so nonsensical, light-hearted and fantastic
a way that the comedy never fails to amuse in even the poorest
of revivals. *The Importance of Being Earnest* is the only work that
Wilde wrote which is worthy of his genius; and the time has surely
come for a recognition of the great underlying strengths mentioned here which are the basis of its enduring life in the
theatre.

NOTES

1. Wilde's dilatoriness often created difficulties: see above, p. 62.
2. Alexander's casting also calls for consideration: the part of Lady Bracknell, for example, was played by Rose Leclercq who had a minor rôle in

A Woman of No Importance and was so nervous as to be almost inarticulate.

3. George Alexander's rehearsal copy (Harvard Theatre Collection) shows how he arranged the movements and stage groupings to emphasise the formal, operatic nature of the text.

8

Projects and Promises

In mid-January 1894 Wilde wrote to Lewis Waller offering to write for him an evening of three plays:

> What would you give me for a Triple Bill? I would require a certain sum of money down, and a certain sum on completion; the money down to be returned if you don't like the plays. Royalties on a triple bill which would be played at most two nights a week would not be anything important. I would sell you the plays right out—for Great Britain.
>
> *(Letters, 349)*

Nothing more can be gleaned about the plays he had in mind but although it is known that he played with ideas for a number of short dramas and even began a few it does not come as a surprise to readers acquainted with his temperament to learn that none was ever finished. However, there are drafts in existence to prove some seriousness of intention. When his home in Tite Street was despoiled at the time of his bankruptcy it is known that manuscripts were purloined and have never since come to light so that other works may exist.

We have incomplete scripts of two short plays, *La Sainte Courtisane* and *A Florentine Tragedy*, and from anecdotes jotted down by his friends we can conjecture how he would have finished them. From these friends we also learn of several projects which never took shape. One of these, which was to carry the title of *Mr. and Mrs. Daventry*, was taken over by Frank Harris[1] and eventually reached the stage, but in a controversial form, and in circumstances which were equally controversial.

Unfortunately we do not know the exact dates when he mentioned the various projects he had in mind. The letter to Lewis Waller seems to indicate he had some fairly definite ideas for a varied group of short plays but he may have thought of other subjects as Vincent O'Sullivan[2] who knew him well in the years after his release from imprisonment indicates:

> It was while reading the Bible in prison, at a time, as he explained, when no other book was allowed, that the ideas came to him for his two plays. He read the account of Jezebel and Jehu and said to himself: 'There is something wrong here—things left out. That is not the full account of the matter.' He made some connexion between Jezebel and Isabel which I did not grasp. I remember thinking at the time that from a philological point of view it was impossible; but took care not to say this to Wilde who no doubt perceived himself that his notion was fantastic. His aim was to bring out that Queen Jezebel was not the "bedizzened hussy', termagant and shrew, which her name connoted in the popular estimation.
>
> (*op. cit.*, 220)

> He told me very elaborately the plans of two plays which he thought of writing. They were both taken from the Bible—the story of Pharaoh and the captive Jews, and the story of Queen Jezebel. They were both impressive as he related them, and would doubtless have had great success if he had written them. But they were both in his old manner—the manner of *Salome*.
>
> (*ibid.*, 24)

However, since as we shall see O'Sullivan says that these plays were written with Sarah Bernhardt in mind, it is possible that Wilde had really thought of them much earlier in his career. Generous and forgiving as Wilde was by nature it seems extraordinary that he should still have been thinking of writing plays for Bernhardt after the actress had shown herself so callous with regard to his suffering. Here is O'Sullivan's story:

> . . . when he related to me his projected drama *Isabel* based on the story of Jezebel in the Bible (2 Kings, 14), he said that he meant it for the French actress; and I understood from him that one or two of his familiars were negotiating with her about it.
>
> (*ibid.*, 200–201)

Philippe Jullian tells us of another idea for a play intended for Bernhardt: it reveals that Wilde had divined that one of the reasons for Bernhardt's success, at any rate in her early career, was an androgynous quality which she was to exploit when she played Hamlet and l'Aiglon:

> Wilde had already wanted to write a play about Queen Elizabeth for the great actress in which during the whole of one act, she would be disguised as a page, having gone to ascertain the beauty of her rival, Mary Stuart.
>
> (*op. cit.*, 252)

O'Sullivan heard also of a play which was 'to deal with the captivity of Israel in Egypt, and the legend of Joseph' (*op. cit.*, 220). Robert Ross writes of two plays Wilde invented in prison, '*Ahab and Isabel* and *Pharaoh*; he would never write them down, though often importuned to do so. *Pharaoh* was intensely dramatic and perhaps more original than any of the group' (Preface to *Salome and Other Plays*, 1909, xvi). Curiously enough, we know that in Paris in 1898 Wilde met a young Russian called Serge de Diaghilev[3] who was to found a magnificent ballet company, among whose presentations was *La Légende de Joseph*, with music by Richard Strauss, first danced in Paris on 14 May 1914. Did Wilde's project for a drama on the biblical story of Joseph, possibly to be called *Pharaoh*, thus reach its fruition?

Arthur Ransome confirms these titles, adds yet another unfinished play to the list, and speculates on why they were never completed:

> He had imagined, while in Reading Gaol, two other such plays as *Salomé*—*Ahab and Isabel*, and *Pharaoh*. These, unfortunately, like *The Cardinal of Arragon*, portions of which Wilde was accustomed to recite, were never written. The non-existence and the incompleteness of these plays are explicable on other grounds than those of inclination. I think that if *Salomé* had been produced with success as soon as it was written, Wilde would very likely not have written his plays about good women and conscience-stricken men of State, or, having written one, would have written no more. It is possible that we owe *The Importance of Being Earnest* to the fact that the Censor prevented Sarah Bernhardt from playing *Salomé* at the Palace Theatre. For though Wilde had the secret of a wonderful laughter, he preferred to think of himself as a person with magnificent dreams. He would rather have been a magician than a jester.
>
> (*op. cit.*, 153–154)

From Sir Bernard Partridge, the artist and book-illustrator, comes an amusing story of Wilde as a possible writer of pantomime scripts:

> In the late eighties Oscar Barrett produced at the Lyceum a pantomime which broke away from tradition and reverted to the fanciful style of the old Planché extravaganzas, reducing the low comedy element to a minimum. Oscar Wilde, who was rather hard-up then, seemed to me the very man to make a success of this sort of thing, and I suggested to him that he ought to write a pantomime on these lines. He thought a moment, and then said, "Well, I'd write a pantomime tomorrow . . . if only they'd let me dramatise the Book of Revelations!"

(Pearson, 220)

Of the two short and unfinished plays previously mentioned the earliest was *La Sainte Courtisane* (the title is itself a typical Wildean paradox), of which we have the plot as told by Beerbohm Tree to whom it was related several times by Wilde:

> It is true: when you convert someone else to your own faith, you cease to believe in it yourself. Have you not heard the story of Honorius the Hermit? He was a very good man who lived alone in a cave . . . perhaps it was necessary to live alone in a cave in order to be a very good man . . . and the daughter of a king came to seek him out. She had heard that he was pleasant to look upon, and that he had forsworn the world. But she did not believe that he would remain true to his oath if he beheld herself, for no man had been able to resist her. So she left the city and went forth into the desert to find this holy man; and being directed to his cave by some peasants who brought him food, she stood without and called him by his name. And after she had called him many times he came forth and demanded the reason for her summons. And she told him that she was the daughter of a great king, and would make him a prince if he would come with her to Alexandria. But he did not regard her, and made answer that there was only one King, who had died upon the cross; and that there was only one love, the love of God; and he spoke with scorn of the body, and of earthly beauty, and of human passions and of the things of this world. And then he told her the story of the Son of God, who had lived and suffered as a man so that other men could be made to understand God, and so to love God. And as he spoke, his voice grew tender, and pity took possession

of him, and his eyes rested on the king's daughter, and he saw that she was very beautiful; and he had compassion on her; and said that she must unburden her soul, which was heavy with sin, and live henceforth as a servant of Him who had died for her.

So the king's daughter told him of her life in the great city, of the kings and princes who had been her lovers, of the slaves who did her bidding, of the men who had died for her, and of those whose deaths she had contrived; of the magnificence of her palace, the costliness of her apparel, and the splendour of her jewels. Nothing had been denied her, and she had denied herself nothing. But now, after listening to Honorius the Hermit, she had decided to abandon her life of luxury and lust, and to dedicate herself to God.

But while she was speaking, Honorius the Hermit began to yearn for the joys that had not been his, and to perceive that without experience of the pleasures one sacrifices there is no sacrifice. And he lusted after the body of the king's daughter. Then he said: 'I will come with you to Alexandria, and together we shall taste of the Seven Sins.' 'Nay,' she answered, 'for I know that what you told me of God and His Son was true. I know that my life has been evil; and I will not go with you to Alexandria.' 'Then I shall go alone,' said he. 'Farewell.' And he would not be persuaded.

So the king's daughter, who had come to tempt the holy man and by him had been converted, remained in the desert while the holy man, who had renounced this world until the king's daughter had revealed its delights, journeyed to Alexandria.

(Pearson, 238–239)

The aptest comment on this farrago would then come from Wilde himself who after its relation would pause for a while and then add: 'She, I regret to say, died of starvation. He, I fear, of debauchery. That is what comes of trying to convert people' (Pearson, 239).

In February 1893, when staying in Lady Mount-Temple's house at Babbacombe, just before starting rehearsals of *A Woman of No Importance* at the Haymarket Theatre, Wilde began thinking about a play in his *Salome* vein to be called *La Sainte Courtisane*. Later in the year, enjoying some moments of peace during Lord Alfred Douglas's visit to Egypt, he wrote down part of the play. Early in 1895 Charles Ricketts asked how it was progressing to which Wilde replied that the Sainte Courtisane herself continued to say wonderful things but that the Anchorite remained obstinately mute. He added, 'I think I shall have to indicate his replies by stars and asterisks!' As for La Sainte Courtisane, he said, 'Alas! she no longer says marvellous things; the robbers have buried her white body and carried away her jewels.'

From H.M. Prison, Holloway, awaiting trial, Wilde wrote to his friends More Adey and Robert Ross asking the latter to go to Tite Street and collect 'a type-written manuscript, part of my blank-verse tragedy, also a black book containing *La Sainte Courtisane* in bedroom' (*Letters*, 390). Ada Leverson kept possession of the manuscript during his imprisonment and returned it to him on his release, even going to Paris for the purpose. Wilde promptly left it in a cab, laughingly telling Ross that 'a cab was a very proper place for it'. However, he must have found it again or sat down and rewritten parts of it because Ross was able to include it in a collection of Wilde's miscellaneous works in 1908.

The fragment printed by Ross in vol. XIV (*Miscellanies*) of the *Collected Edition*, 1908, begins with the advent of the Emperor's daughter (actually called Myrrhina) to the cave inhabited by the hermit Honorius. The setting is particularly effective:

> A corner of a valley in the Thebaid. On the right hand of the stage is a cavern. In front of the cavern stands a great crucifix.
> On the left sand dunes.
> The sky is blue like the inside of a cup of lapis lazuli. The hills are of red sand. Here and there on the hills there are clumps of thorns.

Two men announce the coming of a beautiful woman with hair 'like threads of gold', and a purple robe. They tell her they worship the seven gods which they claim to have seen from a hiding place in a bush. She wishes to learn about the hermit:

> *Myrrhina*: Where does he dwell, the beautiful young hermit who will not look on the face of woman? Has he a house of reeds or a house of burnt clay or does he lie on the hillside? Or does he make his bed in the rushes?
> *First Man*: He dwells in that cavern yonder.
> *Myrrhina*: What a curious place to dwell in.
> *First Man*: Of old a centaur lived there. When the hermit came the centaur gave a shrill cry, wept and lamented, and galloped away.

Second Man: No. It was a white unicorn who lived in the cave. When it saw the hermit coming the unicorn knelt down and worshipped him. Many people saw it worshipping him.
First Man: I have talked with people who saw it.

Myrrhina's contribution to this symbolist dialogue is to remark that once as she was passing through the market place she heard a sophist from Galicia say that there was only one God. She soon returns to the subject of the Hermit, asking how he eats if he does not fish or raise crops or plough, weave or work at some profitable occupation. She eventually proceeds to the cave's mouth and loudly describes her charms and desirability in all men's eyes. She had had some extravagant loves: emperors, Caesar's minion, a Thracian gladiator, gymnasts and a Tyrian slave. She tells Honorius:

> The dust of the desert lies on your hair and your feet are scratched with thorns and your body is scorched by the sun. Come with me, Honorius, and I will clothe you in a tunic of silk. I will smear your body with myrrh and pour spikenard on your hair. I will clothe you in hyacinths and put honey in your mouth . . .

Honorius is not tempted:

> Thy body is vile, Myrrhina. God will raise thee up with a new body which will not know corruption, and thou wilt dwell in the Courts of the Lord and see Him whose hair is like fine wool and whose feet are of brass.

He sternly rebukes her, telling her there is but one love, that of the Son of God who died on the Cross and Whose Coming was prophesied by the groves and the oracles, by David and the prophets.

There now occurs a break in the manuscript which may represent a transitional point in the action which Wilde may never have written or where pages of the manuscript were lost.

When the dialogue resumes Honorius has emerged from the cave and seen Myrrhina who 'has birds' wings upon her sandals' and whose tunic is the colour of green corn, like 'young corn troubled by the shadow of hawks when she moves'. He has been overwhelmed by her charms:

> Myrrhina, the scales have fallen from my eyes and I see now
> clearly what I did not see before. Take me to Alexandria and let
> me taste of the seven sins.

Myrrhina is horrified that her beauty has had such an effect on
the hermit since she had intended by her coming to show Sin in
its painted mask and Death in its robe of Shame:

> Do not mock me, Honorius, nor speak to me with such bitter
> words. For I have repented of my sins and I am seeking a cavern
> in this desert where I too may dwell so that my soul may be-
> come worthy to see God.

On this inconclusive note the fragment ends.

The paradox of the sinner converting the righteous is an old
and much exploited one, rarely failing, however, to hold the attention of a theatrical audience. It was to be used with notable success
by Somerset Maugham in his short story 'Rain', later dramatised
and filmed as *Sadie Thompson*. Fond as he was of paradox, the plot
of *La Sainte Courtisane* was probably too silly for Wilde to have
taken seriously, although it must be admitted that it had some of
the religiosity of, for instance, *La Samaritaine* in which Bernhardt
triumphed, and he may have intended to offer it to one of the
distinguished actresses of the day.

The unusual title seems to indicate that Wilde had the French
theatre in mind and the long, complicated sentences encrusted with
Symbolist imagery point to sources of inspiration similar to those
of *Salome*. It could hardly have been made into anything more
than a short one-act play in the manner of Maeterlinck. It lacks
the dramatic and psychological conflicts of *Salome* and it is difficult to see how Wilde could have introduced much variety of
action or of character into his desert setting. Possibly he intended
it as an opera libretto (for which it would have done very well),
or as a prose poem not seriously intended for stage presentation.
Whatever the case, he never returned to it or made any serious
attempt at completion for which, in view of the passages printed
by Ross, we can only applaud his admirable commonsense.

After the unhappy failures of his *The Duchess of Padua* and
Salome—and, in the case of the former the interval of fourteen
years which he had to wait before it was produced in America—
Wilde's determination to continue writing dramas of a literary

and non-commercial nature is surprising. Moreover, he was working on these plays, in however desultory a fashion, at the time of his greatest popularity as a playwright when there must have been every inducement, not least financial, for him to produce commercial success after commercial success, whereas not one of the actor-managers of the day would have considered *La Sainte Courtisane* or *A Florentine Tragedy* for production in their theatres. Wilde's evident purpose in writing them must have been to satisfy a compulsive and deep urge to prove himself a serious man-of-letters, both versatile and profound, and the equal of his French contemporaries. Later, in self-imposed exile, when he had lost all self-esteem and surrendered all hopes of regaining a place in the society he most admired, despite his constant need of money he lost all interest in writing: for Wilde writing was a form of social behaviour. Another thought which presents itself is that he may have given expression to both his social sense and the open, sparkling wit for which he was famed in his social comedies while reserving the hidden, darker, violent, more fantastic sides of his nature for these unusual non-commercial dramas. In his career as a dramatist we can see him struggling gradually but surely to reconcile these disparate elements.

When we turn to *A Florentine Tragedy*, which is actually a dark comedy rather than a tragedy in any conventional sense, we are faced once again with textual problems, for in the autumn of 1897 Wilde wrote to Robert Ross that he must finish *A Florentine Tragedy* although, as we shall see, there is no documentary evidence that he ever wrote a beginning to it. We know its plot from Ross who frequently related it to Hesketh Pearson:

> Most people love beauty because their neighbours love the same beauty. They admire strength because everyone does so. Very few among us have the courage openly to set up our own standard of values and abide by it. You remember what happened to the Merchant of Florence? No? Then I will tell you.
>
> He had married a girl, who, it seemed to him, would fulfil all the requirements of a wife: she would mend his garments, attend to his house, and see that he was well fed. All of which she did. Their life together, like that of most married couples, was quite uneventful. Every day he went out to sell and to buy, and every evening he came home again, and ate his food, and talked of

what he had done, and went to bed. The neighbours called theirs an ideal married life, and it would have continued so to the end if one day a young prince of the ruling family had not stopped to make a purchase at their house when the merchant was away from home. This prince, you see, had not been told whether the merchant's wife was comely or otherwise, so he was able to make up his own mind on the subject, and he thought that she was comely. He came again and again; and as the good woman had never been encouraged to relate her experiences at home after her husband had finished speaking of his bargains abroad, she never mentioned her visitor. But the prince's tales of gallant exploits held her enthralled; she found them so much more interesting than her husband's stories of purchase and sale; and gradually she came to feel contempt for the merchant, who seemed so weak and unadventurous compared with her dashing carefree prince.

One day the merchant returned home earlier than usual and found the prince talking with his wife. He said that he was highly honoured that so distinguished a person should visit his humble dwelling; and thinking that the prince had come to buy his wares, he offered to display his best jewels and embroideries. But the prince showed no inclination to see them, and said that his steward would come in the morning and buy whatever the merchant wished to sell at his own terms. The merchant was astonished at such generous treatment, and said that in return he would give the prince whatever he asked. "What if I ask for your wife?" questioned the prince. "You joke, my lord," replied the merchant. "She is not worthy of your regard. She can cook and spin and keep the house; but that is all." "No, not at all," said the prince, "for she is good to look upon." Then the merchant spoke of his trade, but the prince did not heed him; of politics, but the prince did not hear. So he brought wine and asked the prince to drink with him. And now he surprised the secret of those two, for when the prince drank to his wife he caught the glance that passed between them, and he threw his cup to the ground. "That is a fine sword of yours," said he; "yet though my own is rusty, I dare swear its steel is better tempered. Good my lord, do me the honour to test them." The prince laughingly expressed his willingness, and they stood up to fight. At first it seemed they sparred in jest, but soon the swords flashed in earnest, and in a minute the prince was disarmed. "Now for our daggers," said the merchant, "for one of us must die." It was

G 193

even so. The merchant threw the prince to the ground and stabbed him in the throat. Then he arose and looked at his wife, who moved towards him with arms outstretched, half dazed with amazement and admiration. "I did not know that you were brave and strong," she said. "I did not know that you were beautiful," said he. And he took her in his arms.

(Pearson, 189–190)

Having dined out for some years on this tale of sexual prowess, Wilde decided, with his customary astuteness in such matters, to raise cash on it. We find him writing in February 1895 to George Alexander asking for the balance of some money owing to him, and adding that:

> On Sunday I hope to send you, or read you, the vital parts of my Florentine play. I think you will like it.

(Letters, 383)

One might have thought that with two plays running in London at the same time he could easily have persuaded a London manager to put on this piece which was, after all, the kind of vehicle in which Beerbohm Tree excelled and which he could have easily put on as a curtain-raiser. But Wilde may have occupied himself with the social comedies for which managers were clamouring and which produced the large sums of money of which he was increasingly in need. Whatever the case, he was soon to become involved with the law and to experience its lash.

In the misery of his prison cell he tried to complete the play in his mind if not actually on paper. But H.M. Prison, Reading, fulfilled its purpose in breaking his spirit. He wrote to his friend More Adey on 25 September 1896:

> I have tried to remember and write down the *Florentine Tragedy*: but only bits of it remain with me, and I find that I cannot invent: the silence, the utter solitude, the isolation from all humane and humanising influences, kills one's brain-power: the brain loses its life, becomes fettered to monotony of suffering.

(Letters, 410)

We may surmise that imprisonment and shame crowded out all thoughts in Wilde's mind save what perpetually beat there: the callousness and unconcern of Douglas and his own unheeding folly. On his release there came an opportunity to work further on his

194

many projects, including the 'Florentine' play, but his creative energy was then reserved for his 'The Ballad of Reading Gaol' which he was writing between July and August 1897. At the back of his mind was still the idea of the play and he told Robert Ross on 2 June 1897:

> I have determined to finish the Florentine Tragedy, and to get £500 for it—from somewhere. America perhaps.
>
> *(Letters, 591)*

Shortly afterwards he was telling him that he was shortly to 'rewrite my *Love and Death—Florentine Tragedy*', although he was more profitably writing the Ballad at the time. Hardly a month after the note just quoted he wrote again to Ross from the Villa Giudice at Posilippo, Naples, where he had taken up residence with Douglas:

> Tomorrow I begin the *Florentine Tragedy*. After that I must tackle *Pharaoh*.
>
> *(Letters, 649)*

During his years in prison he had written to Lord Alfred Douglas, regretting the time he had wasted with him when he should have been writing. Speaking from the bitterness of his heart and the humiliation of his prison sentence he addressed many harsh words to him, none of them more terrible than those in which he reproached him with having dispersed his energy during his days of creative productivity:

> My business as an artist was with Ariel. You set me to wrestle with Caliban. Instead of making beautiful coloured, musical things such as *Salome*, and the *Florentine Tragedy* and *La Sainte Courtisane*, I found myself forced to send long lawyers' letters to your father ...
>
> *(Letters, 492)*

The fact that he had welcomed Douglas and was living with him at Posilippo makes these words the more ironically comic. Inevitably he never finished the *Florentine Tragedy* or any other play: his creativity was dead.

There have been claims, notably by Hesketh Pearson, that Wilde had actually finished and written down *A Florentine Tragedy* before his trial and imprisonment and that the manuscript was among the papers and books stolen from Wilde's home during the forced sale of his effects on 24 April 1895 when he was under arrest in Holloway Prison awaiting his first trial. This does not seem substantiated by Wilde's own statements about finishing the play made either in prison or during his years abroad.

The narrative now passes to Robert Ross whose account may provide an incidental explanation of the missing manuscript:

> Some years after Wilde's death I was looking over the papers and letters rescued from Tite Street when I came across loose sheets of manuscript and typewriting, which I imagined were fragments of *The Duchess of Padua*; on putting them together in a coherent form I recognised that they belonged to the lost *Florentine Tragedy*. I assumed that the opening scene, though once extant, had disappeared. One day, however, Mr. Willard[4] wrote that he possessed a typewritten fragment of a play which Wilde had submitted to him, and this he kindly forwarded for my inspection. It agreed in nearly every particular with what I had taken so much trouble to put together. This suggests that the opening scene had never been written, as Mr. Willard's version began where mine did. It was characteristic of the author to finish what he never began.
>
> (*op. cit.*, xvii–xviii)

In other words, Wilde had written the most intriguing section of a one-act play in order to attract a commission (and hard cash)— a sprat to catch a mackerel! This is why he was able to tell Alexander in 1895 that he was sending him the 'vital' part of the play and why he was also able to talk of beginning it: presumably he had with him in Italy a typescript of the section he had completed.

When in 1906 the Literary Theatre Society presented *Salome* they asked Ross if he had some other play by Wilde which they might present at the same time. He offered them the fragment of *A Florentine Tragedy*. The Irish writer Thomas Sturge Moore who was on the committee accepted the task of writing an opening scene to complete the play which was presented in June 1906. It was first performed for the public by the New English Players at the Cripplegate Institute, Golden Lane, London, in 1907. There followed performances in translation in Germany, France and Hungary. In its completed form the play was published by Methuen in 1908 as part of the Collected Edition. A portion of the manuscript is owned by the American bibliophile Mary Hyde.

Wilde's typescript begins with the entrance of the husband Simone, although, as has been explained, this is prefaced in acting versions by some two hundred lines of blank verse written by Sturge Moore. The merchant is worn-out by the weight of his pack from which he has sold only one article all day:

> *Simone*: I have sold nothing:
> Save a furred robe unto the Cardinal's son,
> Who hopes to wear it when his father dies,
> And hopes that will be soon.

He finds his young wife, Bianca, entertaining a young man whom he at first thinks is a relative of hers. He seems flattered when the stranger introduces himself as Sir Guido Bardi, son of the ruler of Florence; and his business sense comes to the fore as he tries to interest him in some of his fine wares:

> . . . the collar all of pearls,
> As thick as moths in summer streets at night,
> And whiter than the moons that madmen see
> Through prison bars at morning. A male ruby
> Burns like a lightest coal within the clasp.
> The Holy Father has not such a stone,
> Nor could the Indies show a brother to it.
> The brooch itself is of most curious art,
> Cellini never made a fairer thing
> To please the great Lorenzo . . .

The Prince is interested only in Bianca and tries to ward off her husband's sales-talk by offering to send his servant round the next morning to buy the wares at double the price. Simone is already suspicious as he reveals when displaying a fine piece of weaving:

> I have a curious fancy
> To see you in this wonder of the loom
> Amidst the noble ladies of the court,
> A flower among flowers.
> They say, my lord,
> These highborn ladies do so affect Your Grace
> That where you go they throng like flies around you,
> Each seeking for your favour.

I have heard also
Of husbands that wear horns, and wear them brave,
A fashion most fantastical.

Guido does not heed these warning notes, asks jokingly for
Simone's wife, and is eventually persuaded to engage in sword
play with Simone. Bianca holds aloft a flaming torch as the two
men fight. As the men throw away the swords and begin fighting
with daggers Bianca calls on Guido to kill her husband. In return
he tells her to extinguish the torch. The men fight on in the darkness until Guido is vanquished and begs for his life, pleading that
he is an only son and that there will be no one left to carry on
the Bardi line. Even his request for a priest is refused. Relentlessly,
Simone kills him and then turns to revenge himself on Bianca. As
if in a dream she moves towards him with open arms:

> *Bianca*: Why
> Did you not tell me you were so strong?
> *Simone*: Why
> Did you not tell me you were so beautiful?
> *He kisses her on the mouth.*

There are Shakespearian echoes in this playlet; and, as *The
Duchess of Padua* had already demonstrated, Wilde had read
widely and well in Elizabethan and Jacobean tragedy:

> Let this mean room be as that mighty stage
> Whereon kings die, and our ignoble lives
> Become the stakes God plays for . . .

> Ravish my ears with some sweet melody;
> My soul is in a prison house, and needs
> Music to cure its madness . . .

At times we are treated to what seems like an extract from
Wilde's own poetry, possibly one of his 'impressions':

> the churlish moon
> Grows, like a miser, niggard of her beams,
> And hides her face behind a muslin mask
> As harlots do when they go forth to snare
> Some wretched soul in sin . . .

198

Wilde was fond of imagery connected with the moon as his *Salome* more than amply showed. Like that play, *A Florentine Tragedy,* about which there is a singularly 'decadent' air, ends violently and unexpectedly but not, in this case, with so unusual a death.

It is hard to see why Wilde did not finish this play (and make 'a quick £500' from it), for there were so few lines to write that he could easily have applied himself to its completion without undue strain. With three strong actors in the leading rôles it might have enjoyed a degree of success as a curtain-raiser, and more so if the scenic effects suggested by him had been realised on the stage. Short plays given before the main offering of the evening were popular; and Tennyson's *The Falcon,* slight in dramatic tension and feeble in plot, had served to display the polished art of the Bancrofts.[5] Henry Irving was fond of such pieces, the more particularly if they provided him with an interesting or showy part: and Bernard Shaw went so far as to write a short play *The Man of Destiny* with him and Ellen Terry in mind. It must have seemed an attractive idea to Wilde to be able to present an evening of his own drama in which a serious one-act preceded one of his three-act comedies thus proving his command of all literary forms, of verse as well as prose. What is remarkable is that a violent and murderous side of Wilde's literary character reveals itself in these plays, and a wilfulness of which no hint is given in his social comedies. Just as in *Salome* he tried to create a new poetic language, derived partly from blank verse but more strongly from biblical prose, so in this fragment he is pushing forward the movement of the verse from the rhythmical conservatism of the Elizabethans to a freer and lighter form in keeping with the impressionist nature of his own lyric verse. Slight as it is, *A Florentine Tragedy* represents a transition in Wilde's career as a dramatist, marking, perhaps, shadows which might increasingly have dominated his writing.

This is also true of his last thoughts for a full-length play. It frequently happened to Wilde that when he was working on one play the plot for another would come into his mind. Thus, in August 1894, while finishing *The Importance of Being Earnest* in its first draft, he thought of a plot about which he wrote to Alexander:

199

What do you think of this for a play for you? A man of rank and fashion marries a simple sweet country girl—a lady—but simple and ignorant of fashionable life. They live at his country place and after a time he gets bored with her, and invites down a lot of fashionable *fin-de-siècle* women and men; the play opens by his lecturing his wife how to behave—not to be prudish, etc. —and not to mind if anyone flirts with her—he says to her, "I have asked Gerald Lancing who used to admire you so much— flirt with him as much as you like."

The guests arrive, they are horrid to the wife—they think her dowdy and dull. The husband flirts with Lady X. Gerald is nice and sweet and friendly to the wife.

Act II. The same evening—after dinner—love scene between the husband and Lady X: they agree to meet in the drawing-room after everyone has retired. The guests bid good-night to the wife. The wife is tired and falls half-asleep on a sofa. Enter husband: he lowers the lamps: then Lady X arrives—he locks the door. Love scene between them—wife hears it all. Suddenly violent beating on the door. Voice of Lady X's husband outside—desiring admittance. Terror of Lady X! Wife rises, turns up the lamp and goes to the door and unlocks it—Lady X's husband enters! Wife says "I am afraid I have kept Lady X up too late; we were trying an absurd experiment in thought reading" (anything will do). Lady X retires with her husband. Wife then alone with her own husband. He comes towards her. She says "Don't touch me." He retires.

Then enter Gerald—says he had been alarmed by noises— thought there were robbers—wife tells him everything—he is full of indignation, it is evident he loves the wife. She goes to her room.

Act III.—Gerald's rooms—wife comes to see him—it is clear that they love each other. They settle to go away together— enter servant with card! The husband has called. The wife is frightened, but Gerald consents to see him. Wife retires into another room.

Husband is rather repentant. He implores Gerald to use his influence with the wife to make her forgive him. (Husband is a gross sentimental materialist.) Gerald promises he will do so—it is evident that it is a great act of self-sacrifice for him—exit husband with maudlin expressions of gratitude.

Enter wife: Gerald asks her to go back to her husband. She refuses with scorn—he says, "You know what it cost me to ask

you to do that. Do you not see that I am really sacrificing myself?" etc. She considers: "Why should you sacrifice me?—I love
you. You have made me love you—you have no right to hand
my life over to anyone else. All this sacrifice is wrong, we are
meant to live. That is the meaning of life." Etc. She forces him
by her appeals and her beauty and her love to take her away
with him.

Three months afterwards: Act IV.—Gerald and wife together—
she is reading Act IV of Frou-frou—they talk about it. A duel
between Gerald and the husband is fixed for the day on which
the scene takes place—she is confident he will not be killed—
he goes out. Husband enters. Wife proclaims her love for her
lover—nothing would induce her to go back to her husband—of
the two she wishes him to die. "Why?" said husband. "Because
the father of my child must live." Husband goes out—pistols are
heard—he has killed himself.

Enter Gerald, the husband not having appeared at the duel.
"What a coward," says Gerald. "No," she answers, "not at the
end—he is dead." "We must love one another devotedly now."
Curtain falls with Gerald and the wife clinging to each other as if
with a mad desire to make love eternal—Finis.

What do you think of this idea?

I think it extremely strong. I want the sheer passion of love to
dominate everything. No morbid self-sacrifice. No renunciation—
a sheer flame of love between a man and a woman. That is what
the play is to rise to—from the social chatter of Act I, through
the theatrical effectiveness of Act II, up to the psychology with
its great dénouement in Act III, till love dominates Act IV and
accepts the death of the husband as in a way its proper right—
leaving love its tragedy—and so making it a still greater passion.

Of course I have only scribbled this off—I only thought of the
plot this morning—but I send it to you—I see great things in it
—and, if you like it when done, you can have it for America.

(op. cit., 87)

On his arrival in France, after his release from Reading Gaol,
Wilde was contacted by the American actress Mrs. Cora Potter
who wanted a play starring herself and her stage partner Kyrle
Bellew.[6] An agreement was concluded once a suitable financial
advance had been made. Other people including Leonard Smithers,
the publisher who had issued the 'Ballad of Reading Gaol', advanced
money for the same purpose. During his stay at Posilippo, Wilde

thought of resuming work on a number of theatrical projects and wrote on 15 October 1897 to Reginald Turner:

> I now think of beginning my play for George Alexander, but I cannot see myself writing comedy. I suppose it is all in me somewhere, but I don't seem to feel it. My sense of humour is now concentrated on the grotesqueness of tragedy.
>
> (*Letters*, 659)

Three days later he wrote to More Adey on the subject: [7]

> As soon as I get rid of the *Ballad*, I am going to begin my comedy, but at present the *Ballad* still dominates.
>
> (*Letters*, 664)

Towards the end of the month he claimed to have begun work on it: 'I began my play the other day but the comedy troubles me.' (*Letters*, 670).

The comedy was to trouble a good many people both before and after Wilde's death. Its history is itself an improbable comedy. At first Wilde may have been serious in his intentions of beginning work on this play and on his other theatrical schemes but in the few years that remained to him he discovered to himself an extraordinarily novel idea—that if his literary productions were valuable then their creator should be even more valuable; and that as long as he promised a play he could expect occasional advances of a hundred pounds or so which might cease the moment he had, as it were, delivered the goods which might prove unsuitable and so yield no income at all. Thus a constant if irregular flow of money was forthcoming so long as he could deceive friends and strangers into thinking that some kind of literary production would eventually be forthcoming. Incidentally, the eagerness of such people to give him an advance is proof that his work was acceptable and that he had not lost his public.

By 1899 Wilde may have produced the bones of a play. His sister-in-law, Mrs. Willy Wilde, wrote that she had heard he had written 'a brilliant play', and wished to show it to the manager of the Globe Theatre. About the same time, Horace Sedger, yet another theatre manager, who had also paid an advance on the play, announced the production of a new comedy by Wilde. This was at once denied in a letter to Ross:

There is no truth at all in Sedger's advertisement, and I am
very angry about it. It is quite monstrous. My only chance is a
play produced anonymously. Otherwise the First Night would
be a horror and people would find meanings in every phrase.

(*Letters*, 783–784)

On 3 June 1899, Wilde wrote to Smithers:

You will be pleased to hear that I have written more than half
of the Fourth Act: it is a serious, a tragic act, so I began with it.
It is the comedy of Act I and II that frightens me a little. It is
difficult for *me* to laugh at life, as I used to.

(*Letters*, 799)

The name of the play varied from letter to letter: 'Love is Law',
and 'Her Second Choice' are among the titles proposed, none of
them sounding memorable. A curious circumstance should be mentioned in this connection: the typescript of *The Importance of
Being Earnest* submitted to the Lord Chamberlain carries the title,
'Lady Lancing. A Serious Comedy for Trivial People. By Oscar
Wilde.' There is no Lady Lancing in this last comedy, but in the
draft sent to Alexander in 1894 the young man with whom the
wife runs away is called Gerald Lancing which begs the question
whether it was *The Importance of Being Earnest* which was to
have been 'A Serious Comedy for Trivial People' or another play
that never progressed far beyond a draft. Having thought of this
amusing sub-title Wilde was unlikely to waste it, would, in fact,
use it even if not entirely appropriate for the comedy he had completed.

In the event circumstances connected with the play became
farcical. In his time Wilde had said some cutting things about the
editor and journalist Frank Harris—who in the account he wrote of
Wilde's life did not curb his pen—but it was he who befriended
Wilde in his last years. He, too, had heard about the play:

By the way, Smithers says that you have been working on your
play; you know the one I mean, the one with the great screen
scene in it.

Wilde objected that he had merely written out the plot and showed
no interest. But sometime later when Wilde asked Harris for money
and was refused, Harris brought up the subject, suggesting the play
might bring in money. Wilde burst out:

203

I shall never write again, Frank. I can't, I simply can't face my thoughts. Don't ask me.

And after a pause, he asked, 'Why don't you buy the scenario and write the play yourself?' Harris had never written for the stage and dismissed the idea but that very night he conveniently remembered that he had been thinking of writing a story similar to the plot which Wilde had by now so frequently outlined. Next morning he told Wilde:

> I have a story in my head, which would fit into that scenario of yours, so far as you have sketched it to me. I could write it as a play and do the second, third and fourth acts very quickly, as all the personages are alive to me. Could you do the first act?
> Of course I could, Frank.
> But will you?
> What would be the good? You could not sell it.
> I could try. But I would infinitely prefer you to write the whole play, if you would. Then it would sell fast enough.
> Oh, Frank, don't ask me.
> (See Frank Harris, *Mr. and Mrs. Daventry*, edited with an introduction by H. Montgomery Hyde, 1956.)

After some argument Wilde agreed to write the first act for which he accepted fifty pounds from Harris on the understanding that he would have another fifty pounds when he had completed it.

Harris returned to London convinced that he had bought the scenario of a play to be called *Mr. and Mrs. Daventry*, and set about writing the second, third, and fourth acts while waiting for Wilde to send him the first act. Meanwhile he called on Mrs. Patrick Campbell who was about to go into management, having taken over the lease of the Royalty Theatre. She listened to Harris reading his script and professed herself to be delighted. Wilde, on the other hand, was *not* delighted: he decried Harris's script, said he could not and would not write the first act, and wished to have the action changed in Act IV so that instead of Mr. Daventry killing himself he would be shot by the husband of the woman to whom he had made love in Act II. Harris went ahead and wrote a first Act (changed after the fifteenth performance), and announced the first public performance of the play on 25 October 1900.

By now the other people who had given or loaned money to

Wilde on the understanding that they had acquired the scenario wrote to Harris asking for an explanation, for permission to produce the play or for the return of their money. Among these unhappy claimants were Mrs. Brown Potter, Horace Sedger, Leonard Smithers, Beerbohm Tree, George Alexander, Ada Rehan, and Louis Nethersole.[8] Wilde was angry, complaining that Harris had deprived him of his only source of interest by using a scenario on which he could always have raised £100. Wilde died in Paris on 30 November 1900 during the successful run of the play from which he might have reaped considerable financial benefit.

Mr. and Mrs. Daventry had an excellent cast in Mrs. Campbell who played Mrs. Daventry, Frederick Kerr as Mr. Daventry, Gerald du Maurier as the lover (called Ashurst and not Lancing), and George Arliss as a servant. After a difficult opening night it ran for 121 performances, one of them attended by the Prince of Wales who showed great pleasure, being especially amused by a scene featuring Arliss.

The critics were less amused. Clement Scott described it in the *Daily Telegraph* as 'a drama of the dust-bin' (26 October 1900), while W. L. Courtney suggested it should be called 'The Adulterers'. On the other hand, Max Beerbohm whose one-act play *The Happy Hypocrite* was used as a curtain-raiser after Harris had re-written and abbreviated the first act wrote a favourable review. G. B. Shaw saw that there was an incongruity between what Harris had taken over from Wilde and his attempts at drawing characters in the style of the 'impossible drawing-room epigrammatists of the Wilde theatre', and the true style of Wilde. In effect, he was saying that Harris was playing at old-fashioned dramatics whereas 'Wilde's manner . . .' was 'immeasurably nearer akin to the new manner than the old comic relief was' (*Collected Letters of Bernard Shaw, 1898–1910*, ed. Dan H. Laurence, 1972, 194) and that he himself had begun by providing comic relief in the 'Robertson-to-Pinero' manner but had adopted a witty style basically following in the footsteps of Wilde who played with an idea and made 'people laugh by showing *its* absurdity' (*ibid.*, 193). Lively and striking as was Harris's play it lacked the intellectual quality of Wilde's social comedies of which wit was a prime ingredient.

Mr. and Mrs. Daventry remained unpublished until Mr. Montgomery Hyde found a complete acting version with other material in the Gabrielle Enthoven Collection in the Victoria and Albert Museum and published it, together with an illuminating introduction, in 1956. There is, however, another version of this plot called *Constance* and known only in a French publication. After his release from prison Wilde was approached by several people with theatrical interests asking him for new work or for his services as an experienced dramatist.[9] Among them was the American actress Mrs. Cora Brown Potter who advanced him money on the understanding that she was to have a play from him. It appears she did receive a scenario, probably entitled *Constance*, his wife's name, which he had intended to use in a drama about a good woman—as he absolutely correctly believed his wife to be. On her death in France, before the 1939–1945 war, Mrs. Potter left the Wilde manuscript to her friend, the writer Guillot de Saix. Apparently Wilde (or Mrs. Potter) had written sufficient dialogue for M. de Saix and the Comte Henri de Briel to produce a text which they published in French in 1954, the English original having been destroyed in mysterious circumstances. There are several similarities of characterisation and plot between *Mr. and Mrs. Daventry* and *Constance*, but the differences, notably those of the fourth Act which is set in an inn on the edge of Lake Constance (an ostentatiously ironic setting), where Mr. Daventry is killed by the Rev. George Preston, a mentally unbalanced clergyman, whose wife had been the subject of his amorous attentions in the second act. Although the dialogue as printed in the French version is so different from that of *Mrs. and Mrs. Daventry* there is one epigram common to them both which presents a problem (*Les Oeuvres Libres*, No. 101, Paris, October 1954, 201–302). In Act I, set in the Daventrys' country house, there is a conversation during which Mr. Daventry addresses Lady Hallingdon, one of his guests:

Mr. Daventry: Is there such a thing, Lady Hallingdon, as an English vice? What is the peculiarly English vice?
Lady Hallingdon: Oh, I thought everyone knew that, Mr. Daventry. The English vice is adultery with home comforts.

(*op. cit.*, 31)

After the drama critic Clement Scott had drawn attention to this passage which he considered offensive, the Lord Chamberlain insisted on its being cut from the text. However, the fact that it occurs in both versions seems to indicate that there was a common text, perhaps that which Wilde had asked Smithers to have typed out on good paper, and which Wilde may have amended as was his custom either before or after it had been promised to Mrs. Potter. He may have worked on it during his stay at Posilippo with Douglas in 1897, when he mentions a play called *Constance* in his letters, but the extent to which he worked on the original scenario which he had sent to Alexander in 1894 seems likely to remain unknown.

An account of Wilde's unfinished projects is by its nature a melancholy chapter in his career as a dramatist. Frequently and eagerly asked to write a play or to adapt translations he replied with promises and requests for more and more money, sometimes needlessly since he had a moderate income and could have greatly increased it by his writing. What he lacked was an audience—not necessarily that of the theatre but of listeners and viewers whose laughter and admiration encouraged him to greater and more amazing displays of wit. He told Frank Harris that he had the theatre in his blood: and this is true, there was no difference for him between the drawing-room and the theatre. As he exiled himself from London society so he exiled himself forever from the theatre and wrote no more. With his *The Ballad of Reading Gaol* he made his swan-song to the world of literature.

This study has traced Wilde's development as a dramatist, but a few last points must be made in support of the high claims made on his behalf.

The social territory covered by Wilde, limited in its confinement to the aristocratic classes, has been compared adversely with Ibsen's wider range, but each was writing of the social environment with which he was best acquainted, and if Wilde does not write of working people neither does Ibsen write of leisured aristocrats. As far as his social comedies are concerned Wilde's plots, which are possible within the society he was satirising, allowed full scope to the basic irony of his manner which would have been inappropriate and heartless in dealing with the poorer classes where loss of reputation or the discovery of secrets would not be cushioned by wealth or privileges of birth and social position.

In fact, Wilde's range of settings and societies, themes and styles, is greater than is generally supposed. He wrote for the commercial theatre of his day, drawing on its strengths—its sense of community so marked at the St. James's Theatre but also strong in other theatres, its sense of style strengthened by the continuity of the actor-manager tradition, the abundant resources available in terms of settings, furnishings, costumes and excellent actors—but he also wrote for a theatre which did not then exist, as he learnt slowly and painfully through experiences connected with his *Salome* and *The Duchess of Padua*. To the end of his life he had projects for dramas of an extraordinary variety, although, ironically, it was only his idea for yet another social drama, albeit on a darker, sombre theme, which actually reached the commercial theatre in the form of *Mr. and Mrs. Daventry*. No small part of his achievement lay in his ability to devise an effective style for each of the different kinds of dramas he wrote.

Wilde and G. B. Shaw had much in common: both were educated in the commercial theatre of the eighties and nineties; Wilde claimed he loved the theatre and never missed a first night, and as a drama critic Shaw never missed a first night either; both loved to attend rehearsals of their plays, frequently to the exasperation of directors and actors; both men were stage-struck. Bearing this in mind many students of Shaw have been puzzled by his harsh strictures on *The Importance of Being Earnest* which appear somewhat illogical; but they should remember that whereas throughout his life Shaw retained an affection for the strong plot, Wilde, from whom he had learned much and whose 'new manner' he adopted as the basis of his own argumentative style, never much cared for plot and for most of his career was easing his way towards a new kind of drama, anticipating the style of Pirandello and the developments of this century. When he wrote this review Shaw (who was also a pupil of Ibsen) was bewildered by the originality of *The Importance of Being Earnest* and, perhaps subconsciously, for he was not by nature a jealous man, may have anticipated that Wilde was growing in stature and would dominate the stage for years to come, not foreseeing that Wilde's career had come to an end. As it was, Wilde's downfall and later withdrawal from literary life left the way open for Shaw.

Wilde's dramatic work has an asset of tremendous value, that of appealing to the common man. Hesketh Pearson said disapprovingly that the sentimental speeches and scenes in his plays betrayed the stunted emotional growth of the dramatist, adding that they are adolescent and conventional. O'Sullivan on the other hand—and more perceptively—sees this as a strength:

> . . . it was just the coarse strain in Wilde which made the popularity of his plays. He was sentimental in his dramas—not at all aristocratic. Now the populace in all countries are sentimental. But the Wilde plays have more than the coarse sentiment which was the cause of their success. A work of art conveys a message which is valueless to the recipient unless it be understood by the sender, and the message he undertook to send to the public was perfectly clear to Wilde. Unlike English dramatists who were working at the same time, Pinero, Henry Arthur Jones, and some others, the accidents of the plot did not interest him so much as the sentiments and emotions of the characters.
>
> (*op. cit.*, 204–205)

Wilde himself, as we have seen, boasted that he had taken the plot of *A Woman of No Importance* from the *Family Herald*; Ibsen was in the habit of cutting paragraphs from newspapers which appeared likely to supply material for his plays, and Henry James continually jotted down anecdotes, pieces of gossip and similarly intriguing items from newspapers, the point being that it is what the writer does with the subject that ultimately counts rather than the intrinsic value of the material itself. In using a situation from a family newspaper of wide and popular appeal Wilde showed his grasp of popular sentiment; and without this basis in everyday life, sentimental or adolescent, Wilde would not have achieved his place in the history of drama. Had a sufficient amount of hard cash been offered, he could no doubt have dramatised the telephone directory, but his concern was never with technique but with ideas and emotions—the two rarely being so apart in life as some writers seem to believe. Wilde's critical sense shows itself in his awareness of the society about which he was writing, realising that its interest lay in its very superficiality. He saw that there was much more on the surface of society than is generally supposed to meet the eye, perceiving that other writers had strayed in trying to give their society characters a depth which such people did not possess in real life. His plots had the exact degree of sardonic flippancy for the balance of comic and dramatic effect, so that while they could not be described as cynical or criticised as blatantly unrealistic they were satirical to a point sensed if not openly recognised by his audiences.[10]

When Shaw wrote of Wilde and the 'new manner' he was indicating the substitution of verbal humour for the knock-about farcical antics of the old school of dramatists. He should have included Wilde's attitude to plot and, what is of even great importance, his sense of language, for Wilde's dramatic genius is almost exclusively verbal. Eric Bentley says of his dialogue, which is both the blood and skeleton of his plays, that it is 'an unbroken stream of comment on all the themes of life which the plot is so far from broaching' (*op. cit.*, 141). Unlike many dramatists he did not write a basic play which he later embellished with witticisms (although he did make additions at various stages) but from first to last engaged his creative intellect on the theme so that, in effect, every joke, every epigram, almost every line of dialogue adds to the accumulative and total drama. If his plays do not add up to a criticism of life they are certainly a criticism of the society of the day and of the continual preoccupations of the English social mind with class, prestige, and money. Max Beerbohm may have the last word:

> His work was distinct from that of most other playwrights in that he was a man who had achieved success outside the theatre. He was not a mere maker of plays. Taking up dramaturgy when he was no longer a young man, taking it up as a kind of afterthought, he brought to it a knowledge of the world which the life-long playwright seldom possesses.[11] But this was only one point in his advantage. He came as a thinker, a weaver of ideas, and as a wit, and as a master of literary style. It was, I think, in respect of literary style that his plays were most remarkable.
> (*Saturday Review*, 8 December 1902, xc, 720)

And this is why, in the last resort, his plays continue to delight audiences all over the world while the works of those dramatists from whom he is alleged to have borrowed plots and characters and themes are now unactable.

Early in his career Wilde, who could say monstrously stupid things as well as exceedingly wise ones, stated that he had put his genius not into his work but into his life—a statement on which he must have often reflected bitterly in the dreary and barren isolation of his life abroad. It is useless to speculate on his fate, self-willed or otherwise, but it is tragic that his career came to so premature an end. He willed exile for himself but there was no reason why he should have abandoned writing; for, after all it was in exile and prison that Dantë, Cervantes, Bunyan and Villon wrote their greatest work. But Wilde was not altogether wrong in saying that he had put his genius into his life in the sense that having conquered the drawing-rooms of London he went on to conquer its theatres, seeing no essential difference between the two. When he went before the curtain, cigarette in hand, to speak to the audience after a successful first night, he treated them as fellow-guests who had supped and dined of his wit and his humour. The anecdotes, the paradoxes, the epigrams, the jokes, and the social comment with which he regaled the dinner-tables of London were given with generous prodigality to the audiences who flocked to his plays. After his downfall he felt that the great houses of London were shut to him and that must be equally true of its theatres; and in Paris those French intellectuals and creative artists he had admired so inordinately shunned him like a leprous creature so that the will to write died in him and he laid down his pen as a writer. Thus it is we can only speak of Wilde as a dramatist whose early progress we can trace, whose achievements and successes we can record and discuss, but whose probable triumphs have been wrested from us by accidents of character and fate.

NOTES

1. Editor and writer, who showed continued kindness to Wilde in his last years.
2. Irish-American poet and novelist, who lived much of his adult life in France.
3. Diaghilev was also an impressario, art critic, and a leader of artistic taste in Western Europe.
4. Edward Smith Willard (1853–1915): English actor noted for his acting of melodramatic villains. Wilde had tried to interest him in commissioning a play previously.
5. Marie Effie Wilton (1839–1921): English actress, married Squire Bancroft (1841–1926): actor-manager. Their productions were noted for elegant speech, deportment, and costuming.

6. An American society woman who became a professional actress and manager in association with Kyrle Bellew.
7. William More Adey, translator of Ibsen and art critic.
8. Brother of the noted actress Olga Nethersole, and theatre manager.
9. There is a mistaken belief that after his release from imprisonment Wilde was unable to make a living as a writer. This is certainly not true as far as the theatre was concerned, for he was continually being offered commissions which he turned down. As early as July 1897 Charles Wyndham was asking Wilde to adapt Scribe's *Le Verre d'Eau*. See *Max Beerbohm: Letters to Reggie Turner*, ed. Rupert Hart-Davis (1964), 133.
10. The central situation of *Lady Windermere's Fan* is said to have been taken from the work of Haddon Chambers, a writer now lost in the mists of oblivion; Clement Scott claimed that much of the plot of *An Ideal Husband* came from Sardou's *Dora*: and when a distinguished actress remarked to Wilde that a scene in one of his social comedies reminded her of a play by Scribe he remarked airily, 'Taken bodily from it, dear lady. Why not? Nobody reads nowadays.'
11. Beerbohm is mistaken in thinking that Wilde took up drama when he was no longer a young man: *Vera* was written when he was twenty-two.

Bibliography

Bax, Sir Arnold, *Farewell My Youth* (1943)

Beecham, Sir Thomas, *A Mingled Chime* (1944)

Bentley, Eric, *The Playwright as a Thinker*, N.Y. (1957 edn.)

Cottin, Madame, *Elizabeth or the Exiles of Siberia* (1880)

Croft-Cooke, Rupert, *The Unrecorded Life of Oscar Wilde* (1972)

Douglas, Lord Alfred, *Oscar Wilde: A Summing Up* (1950)

—— (ed.) *The Spirit Lamp* (1893)

Ellmann, Richard, *Oscar Wilde: Twentieth-Century Views* (1969)

Gielgud, Sir John, *Stage Directions* (1963 edn.)

Gilbert, W. S., *Engaged* (1877; 1881)

Glover, James H., *Jimmy Glover His Book* (1911)

Hart-Davis, Rupert (ed.), *The Letters of Oscar Wilde* (1962)

—— (ed.) *Max Beerbohm: Letters to Reggie Turner* (1964)

Harris, Frank, *Oscar Wilde* (1938 edn.)

Hingley, Ronald, *Nihilists* (1967)

Holland, Vyvyan, *Explanatory Foreword: The original Four-Act Version of The Importance of Being Earnest* (1957)

—— (ed.) *The Complete Works of Oscar Wilde* (1966)

Hyde, H. Montgomery (ed.), *Frank Harris: Mr. and Mrs. Daventry* (1956)

—— *Oscar Wilde* (1976)

Jackson, Holbrook, *Introduction to the Limited Editions Club issue of Salome*, N.Y. (1938)

Jullian, Philippe, *Oscar Wilde*, translated by Violet Wyndham (1969)

Laurence, Dan H., *Collected Letters of Bernard Shaw* (1972)

Mason, A. E. W., *Sir George Alexander and the St. James's Theatre* (1935)

Mason, Stuart, *Bibliography of Oscar Wilde* (1914); reprinted with an introduction by Timothy d'Arch Smith (1967)

McCarthy, Mary, *Mary McCarthy's Theatre Chronicle*, N.Y. (1963)

Notes and Queries (February 1959)

O'Sullivan, Vincent, *Aspects of Wilde* (1936)

Pearson, Hesketh, *The Life of Oscar Wilde* (1946)
—— *The Last Actor-Managers* (1950)
—— *Beerbohm Tree* (1956)
Praz, Mario, *The Romantic Agony* (rpr. 1966)
Pullar, Philippa, *Frank Harris* (1975)
Ransome, Arthur, *Oscar Wilde: A Critical Study* (1912)
Richards, Kenneth & Thomson, Peter, *Nineteenth Century British Theatre* (1971)
Richardson, Joanna, *Sarah Bernhardt* (1951)
Robertson, Graham, *Time Was* (1931)
Ross, Margery (ed.), *Robert Ross: Friend of Friends* (1952)
Rothenstein, William, *Men and Memories* (1931)
Shaw, Bernard, *Our Theatres in the Nineties* (rpr. 1954)
Sherard, Robert Harborough, *Bernard Shaw, Frank Harris and Oscar Wilde* (1937)
Taylor, John Russell, *The Rise and Fall of the Well-Made Play* (1967)
Twain, Mark, *The Gilded Age* (1903 edn.)
Weintraub, Stanley, *Beardsley, A Biography* (1967)
—— *Shaw, An Autobiography* (1969)
Wyndham, Horace, *Speranza* (1951)

Index

215

Sarcey, Francisque, 180
Sardou, Victorien: *Fédora*, 21, 104; *Dora*, 144, 156, 157; *Madame Sans-Gêne*, 159, 212
Savoy Hotel, 115
Savoy Theatre, 12
Schuster, Adela, 52
Schwob, Marcel, 74, 90
Scott, Clement, 103, 113, 116, 155, 205–6, 212
Scribe, Eugène, 37, 104, 157; *Le Verre d'Eau*, 212
Seagull (Chekhov), 133
Sedger, Horace, 202–3, 205
Shakespeare, 37; *Julius Caesar, Hamlet*, and *Antony and Cleopatra*, 38
Shannon, Charles Hazlewood, 90, 94, 156
Shaw, George Bernard: *Widowers' Houses*, 22; *Apple Cart*, 23, 63, 74, 90, 104, 106; *Devil's Disciple*, 113, 149–150, 156–8, 170, 181; *Man of Destiny*, 199, 205, 208, 210
Sherard, Robert Harborough, 65–6
Sheridan, Richard Brinsley: *School for Scandal*, 94, 108
Shone, R. V., 165
Smith, Sydney, 23
Smithers, Leonard, 169, 172, 201, 203, 205, 207
Soul of Man under Socialism, 22, 125
Speaker, 104, 113, 144, 156
Spirit Lamp, 81
St. James's Gazette, 104, 164
St. James's Place Hotel, 135
St. James's Theatre, 52, 92, 94, 102, 110–12, 152, 160, 164–5, 170, 208
Standard Theatre, New York, 14
Sterling Library, University of London, 90
Strachey, Lytton, 179
Strauss, Richard: *Salome*, 55, 73, 77, 78–9, 82; *La Légende de Joseph*, 186
Stuart, Mary, Queen of Scotland, 186
Sunday Special, 66
Sunday Sun, 104
Swinburne, A. C., 41, 76

Taylor, John Russell, 26, 158
Tchernyshevsky, Nicholas, 20–1
Tennyson, Alfred Lord: *Promise of May*, 165; *The Falcon*, 199

Terry, Ellen, 11, 53, 106, 199
Terry, Fred, 115
Terry, Marion, 94, 101, 106, 109
Texas, University of (Manuscript Collection), 56, 99
Théâtre d'Art, 59
Théâtre de la Porte St. Martin, 65
Théâtre de l'Oeuvre, 65
Théodora, 60
Tite Street, 189, 196
Tree, Lady Beerbohm, 115
Tree, Sir Herbert Beerbohm, 63, 73, 90, 114–16, 120–1, 130, 137, 159, 187, 194, 205
Trepov, General, 20
Trovatore, Il (Azucena), 173
Turner, Reggie, 132, 202, 212
Twain, Mark & C. D. Warner: *The Gilded Age*, 145–7

Union Square Theatre, New York, 15, 24

Vanbrugh, Irene, 164
Venice Preserved, 31
Vera, or the Nihilists, 11–28, 32, 39, 41, 50, 52, 57, 87, 106, 116, 133, 147
Vera, 37, 124
Victoria, Queen of England, 178–9
Victoria and Albert Museum (Gabrielle Enthoven Collection), 206
Vigilante, 67
Villon, 211
Vincent, R. H., 94

Wagner, Richard, 78, 80, 88
Walkley, A. B., 104, 113, 132, 144, 156
Wallack's Theatre, New York, 28
Waller, Lewis, 137, 153, 159, 184
Watson, William: *Lachrymae Musarum*, 40, 65
Wellington, Duke of, 148
Wells, H. G., 155
Weintraub, Stanley, 90, 107
West, Florence, 137
Whitman, Walt, 12
Whistler, Rex, 152
Widowers' Houses, 22
Wilde, Mrs. Constance, 110